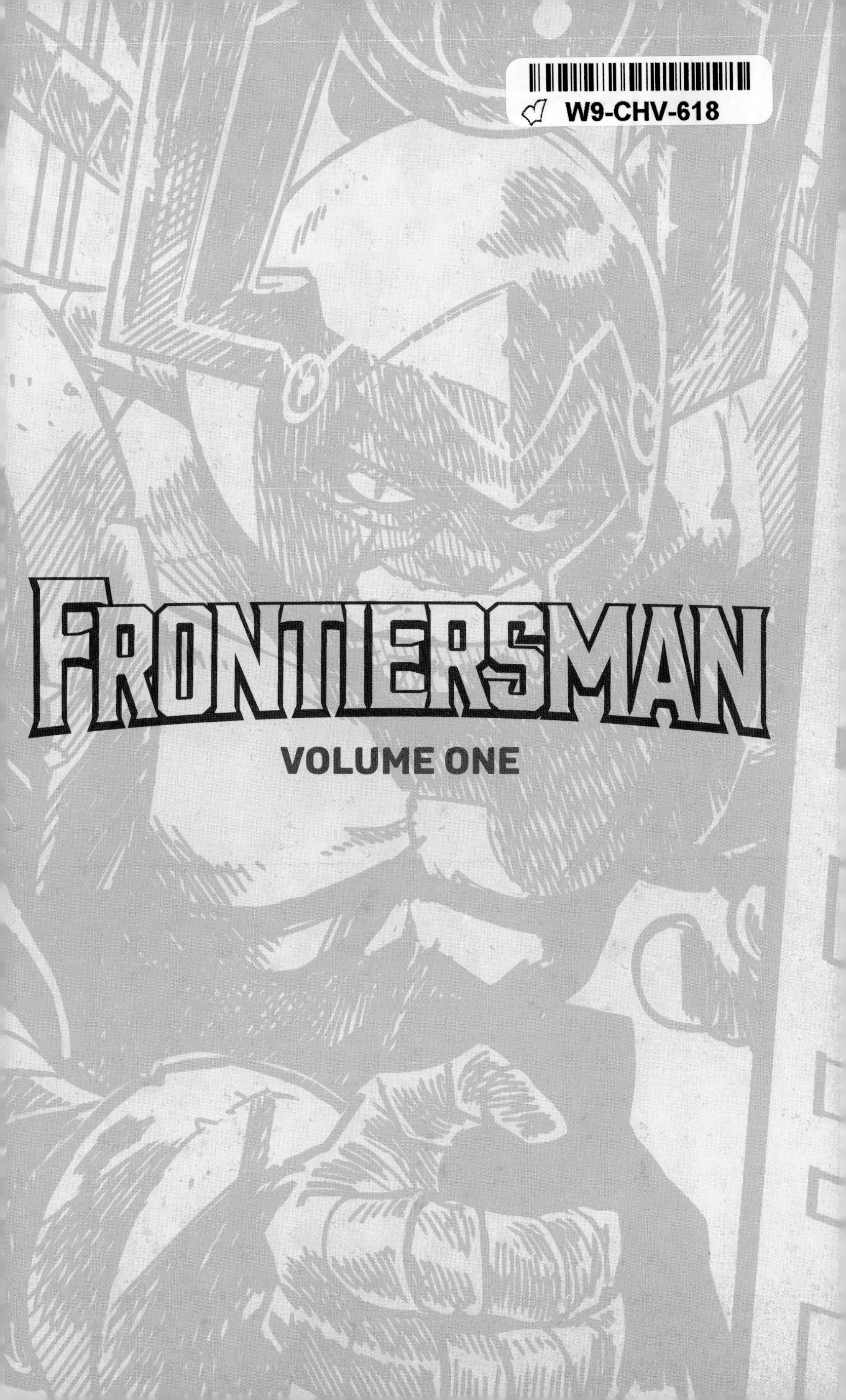

# FRONTIERSMAN

## VOLUME ONE

FRONTIERSMAN, VOL. 1. First printing. March 2022. Published by Image Comics, Inc. Office of publication: PO BOX 14457, Portland, OR 97293. Copyright © 2022 Patrick Kindlon & Marco Ferrari. All rights reserved. Contains material originally published in single magazine form as FRONTIERSMAN #1-5. "Frontiersman," its logos, and the likenesses of all characters herein are trademarks of Patrick Kindlon & Marco Ferrari, unless otherwise noted. "Image" and the Image Comics logos are registered trademarks of Image Comics, Inc. No part of this publication may be reproduced or transmitted, in any form or by any means (except for short excerpts for journalistic or review purposes), without the express written permission of Patrick Kindlon & Marco Ferrari, or Image Comics, Inc. All names, characters, events, and locales in this publication are entirely fictional. Any resemblance to actual persons (living or dead), events, or places, without satirical intent, is coincidental. Printed in Canada. For international rights, contact: foreignlicensing@imagecomics.com. ISBN: 978-1-5343-2111-3.

# FRONTIERSMAN

WORDS BY
**PATRICK KINDLON**

ART BY
**MARCO FERRARI**

LETTERS BY
**JIM CAMPBELL**

COVER BY
**MARCO FERRARI**

EDITED BY
**JAMES HEPPLEWHITE**

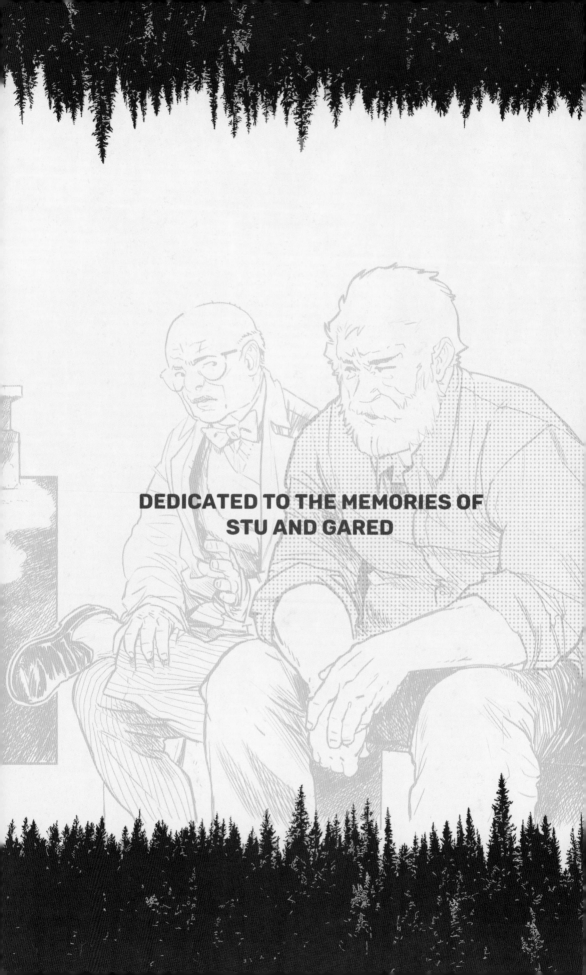

DEDICATED TO THE MEMORIES OF
STU AND GARED

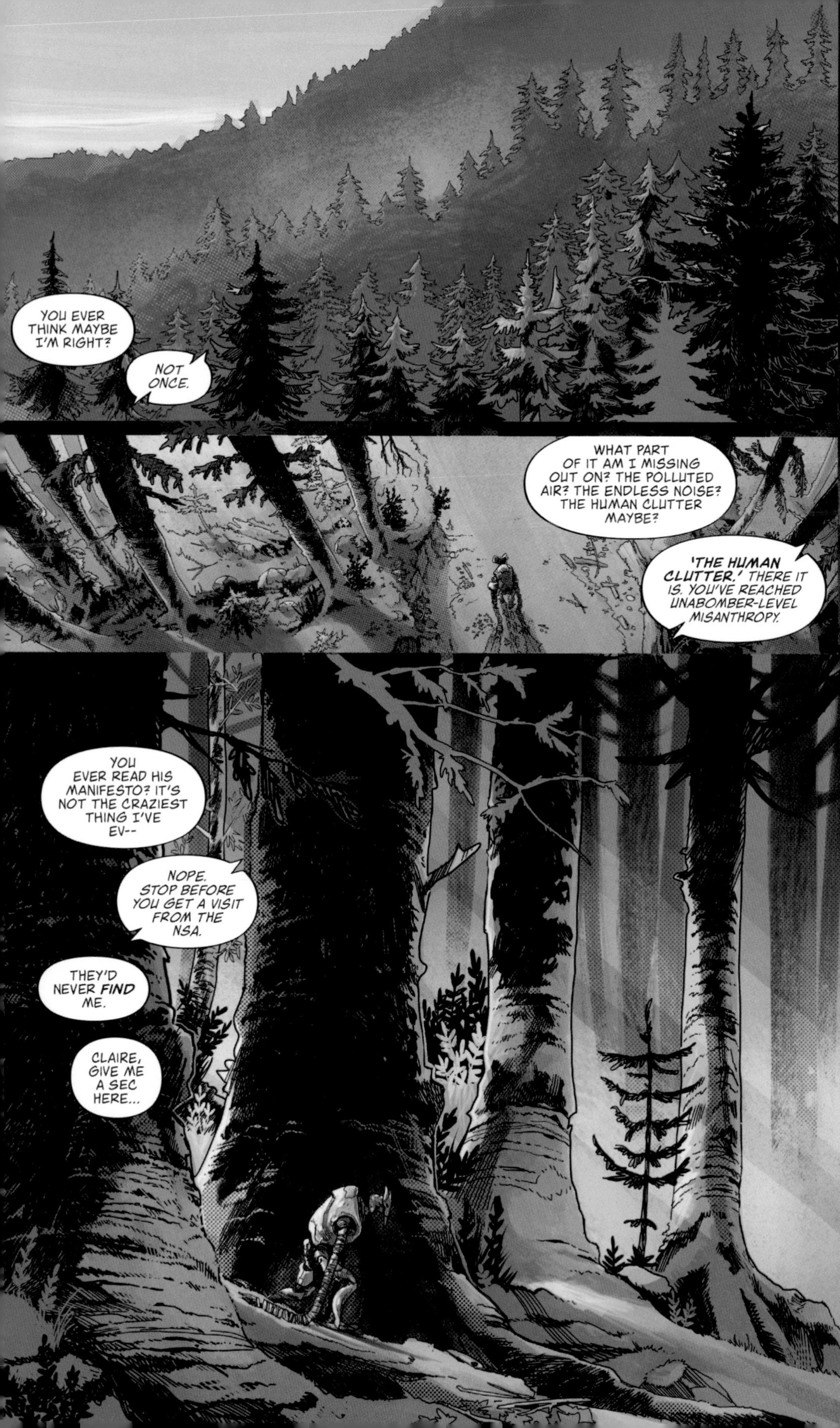
YOU EVER THINK MAYBE I'M RIGHT?
NOT ONCE.
WHAT PART OF IT AM I MISSING OUT ON? THE POLLUTED AIR? THE ENDLESS NOISE? THE HUMAN CLUTTER MAYBE?
'THE HUMAN CLUTTER.' THERE IT IS. YOU'VE REACHED UNABOMBER-LEVEL MISANTHROPY.
YOU EVER READ HIS MANIFESTO? IT'S NOT THE CRAZIEST THING I'VE EV--
NOPE. STOP BEFORE YOU GET A VISIT FROM THE NSA.
THEY'D NEVER FIND ME.
CLAIRE, GIVE ME A SEC HERE...

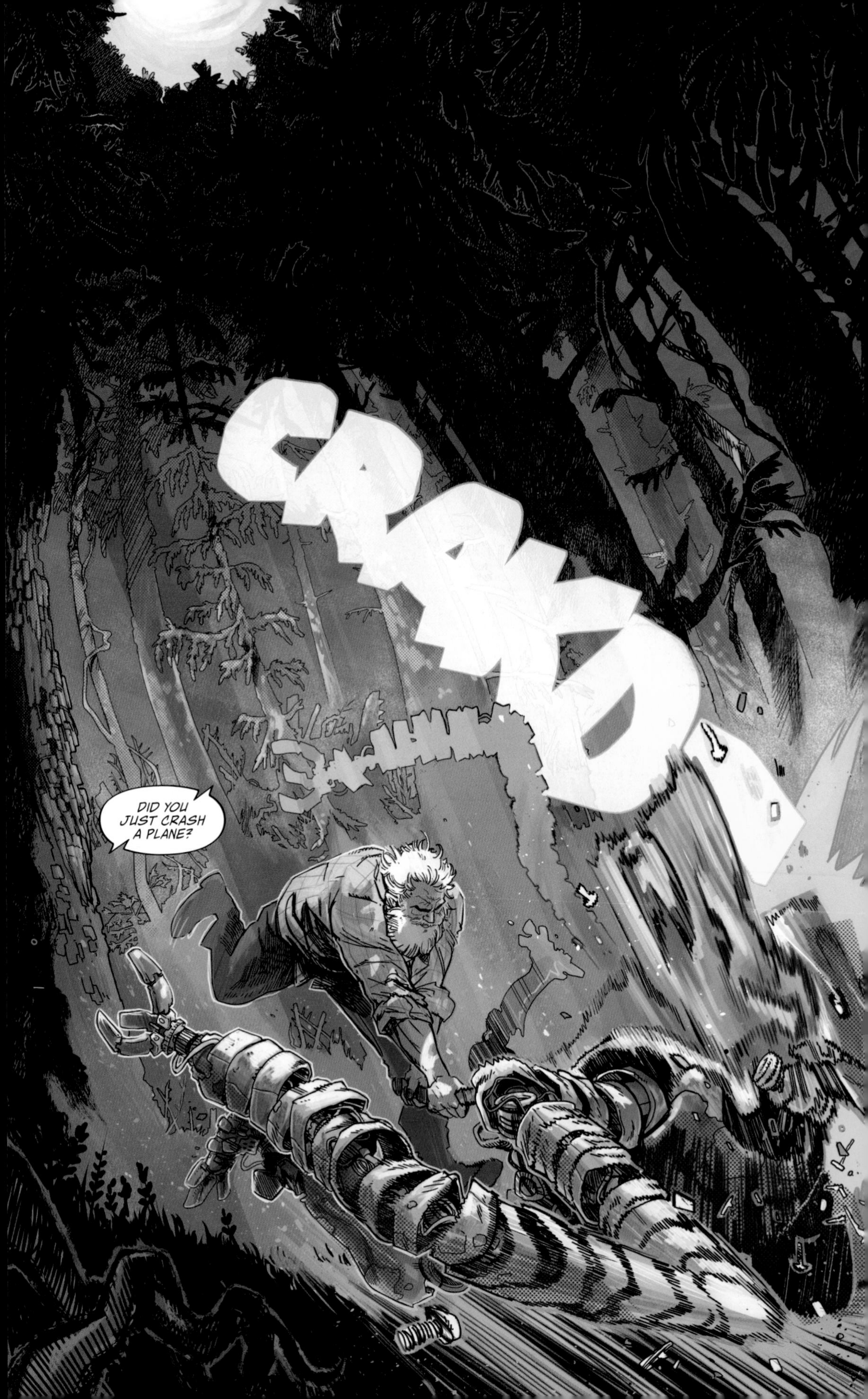
CRAKD
DID YOU JUST CRASH A PLANE?

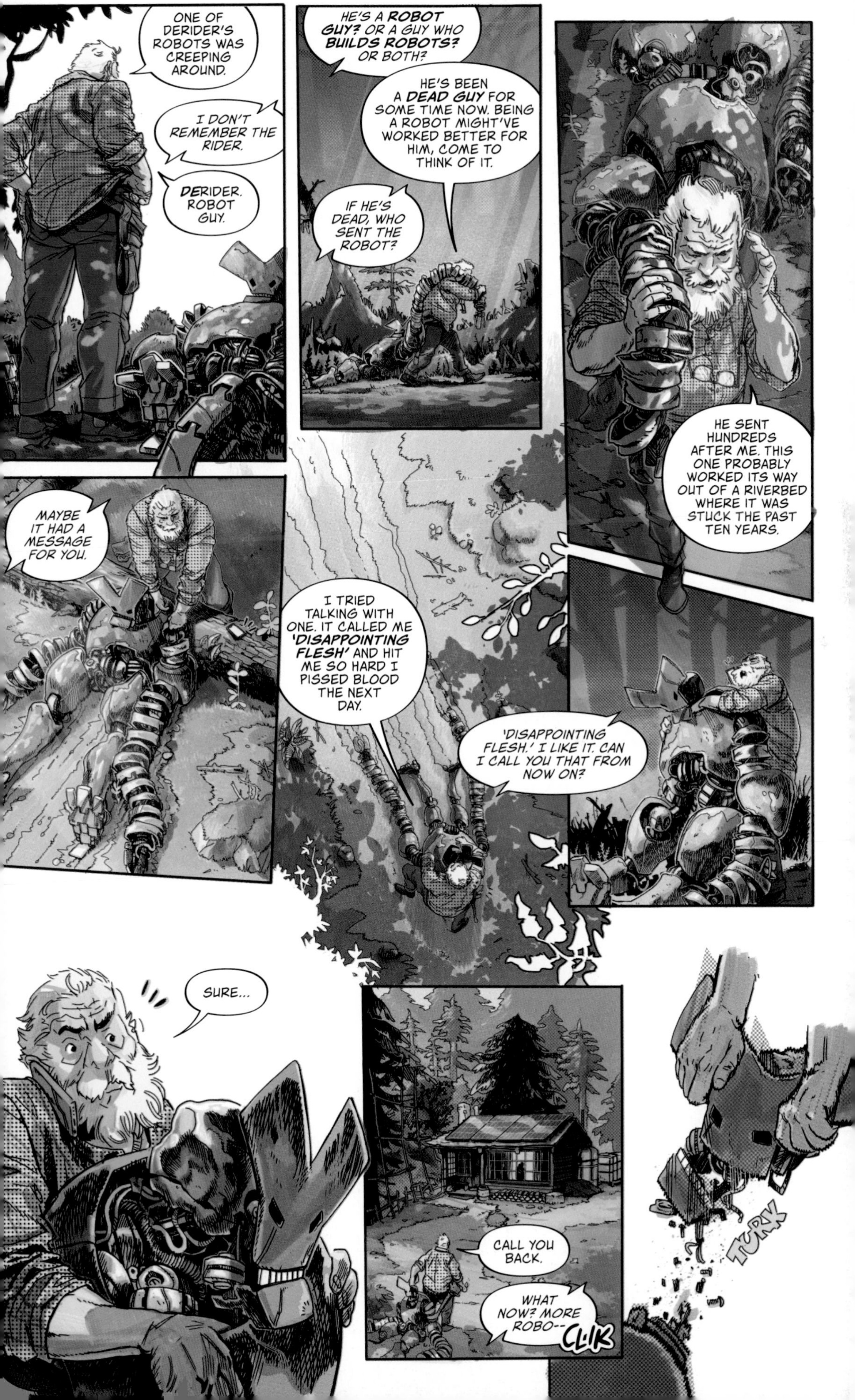

ONE OF DERIDER'S ROBOTS WAS CREEPING AROUND.
I DON'T REMEMBER THE RIDER.
DERIDER. ROBOT GUY.
HE'S A ROBOT GUY? OR A GUY WHO BUILDS ROBOTS? OR BOTH?
HE'S BEEN A DEAD GUY FOR SOME TIME NOW. BEING A ROBOT MIGHT'VE WORKED BETTER FOR HIM, COME TO THINK OF IT.
IF HE'S DEAD, WHO SENT THE ROBOT?
HE SENT HUNDREDS AFTER ME. THIS ONE PROBABLY WORKED ITS WAY OUT OF A RIVERBED WHERE IT WAS STUCK THE PAST TEN YEARS.
MAYBE IT HAD A MESSAGE FOR YOU.
I TRIED TALKING WITH ONE. IT CALLED ME 'DISAPPOINTING FLESH' AND HIT ME SO HARD I PISSED BLOOD THE NEXT DAY.
'DISAPPOINTING FLESH.' I LIKE IT. CAN I CALL YOU THAT FROM NOW ON?
SURE...
CALL YOU BACK.
WHAT NOW? MORE ROBO--
CLIK
TURK

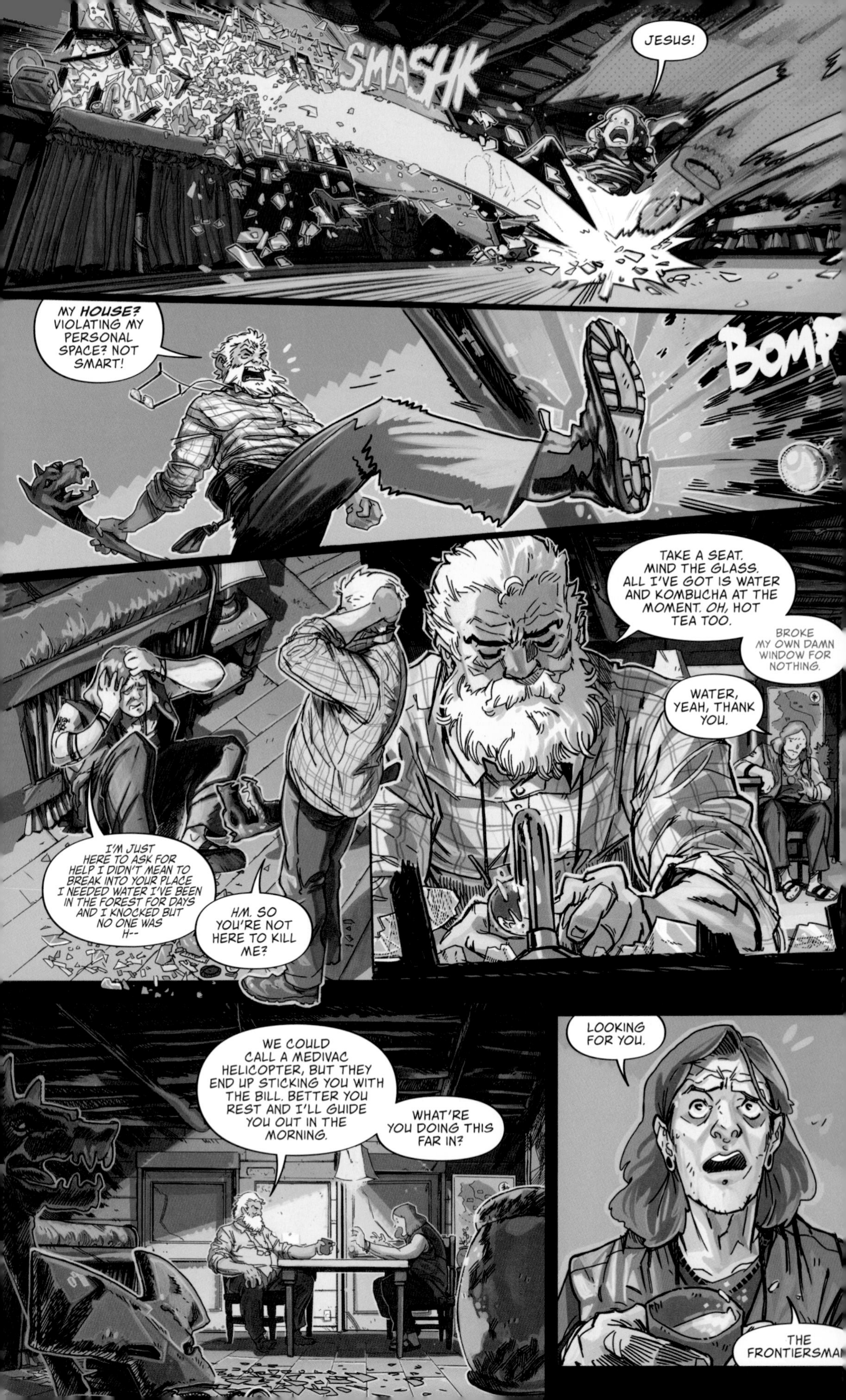
SMASHK
JESUS!
MY HOUSE? VIOLATING MY PERSONAL SPACE? NOT SMART!
BOMP
TAKE A SEAT. MIND THE GLASS. ALL I'VE GOT IS WATER AND KOMBUCHA AT THE MOMENT. OH, HOT TEA TOO.
BROKE MY OWN DAMN WINDOW FOR NOTHING.
WATER, YEAH, THANK YOU.
I'M JUST HERE TO ASK FOR HELP I DIDN'T MEAN TO BREAK INTO YOUR PLACE I NEEDED WATER I'VE BEEN IN THE FOREST FOR DAYS AND I KNOCKED BUT NO ONE WAS H--
HM. SO YOU'RE NOT HERE TO KILL ME?
WE COULD CALL A MEDIVAC HELICOPTER, BUT THEY END UP STICKING YOU WITH THE BILL. BETTER YOU REST AND I'LL GUIDE YOU OUT IN THE MORNING.
WHAT'RE YOU DOING THIS FAR IN?
LOOKING FOR YOU.
THE FRONTIERSMA

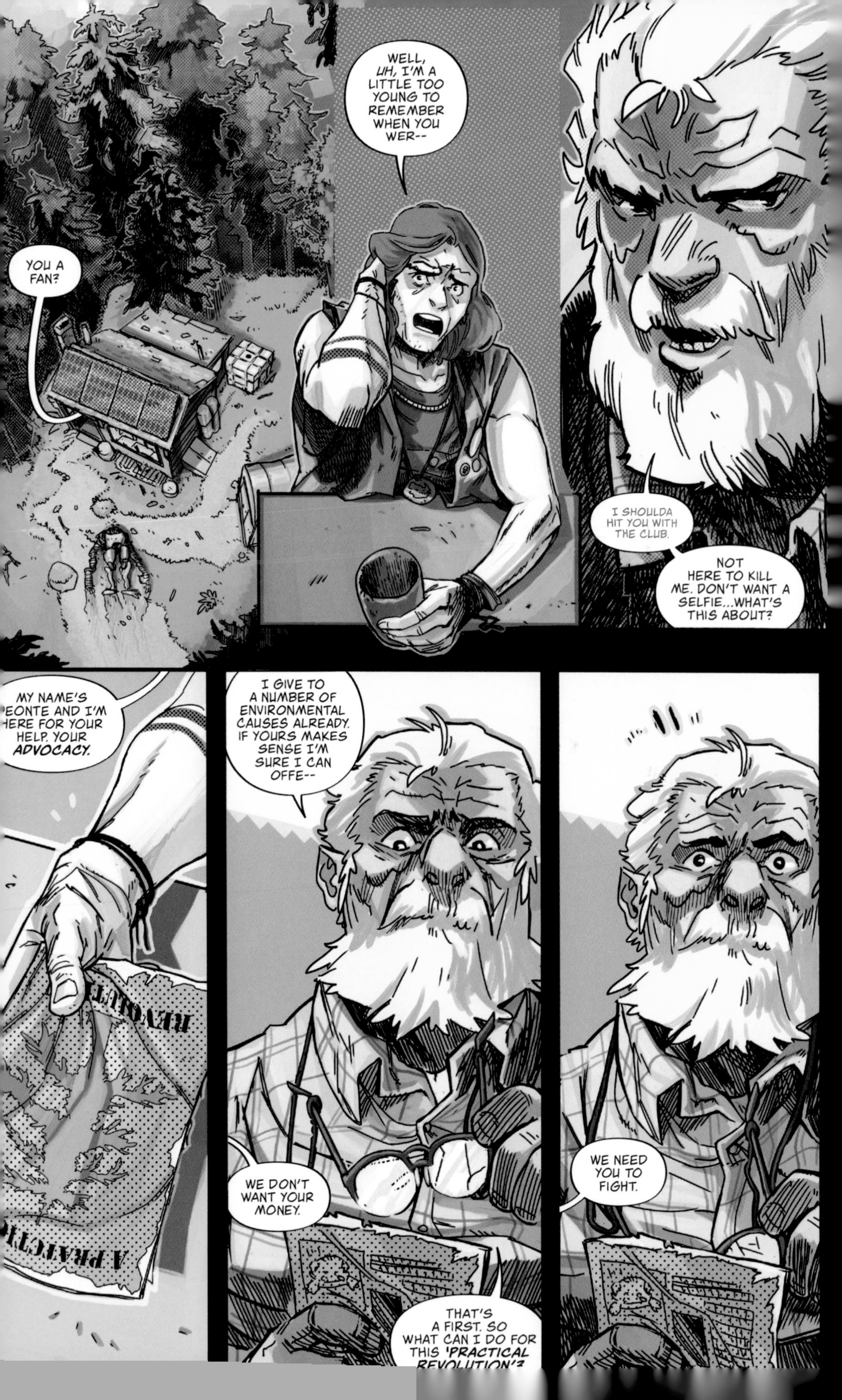

YOU A FAN?
WELL, UH, I'M A LITTLE TOO YOUNG TO REMEMBER WHEN YOU WER--
I SHOULDA HIT YOU WITH THE CLUB.
NOT HERE TO KILL ME. DON'T WANT A SELFIE...WHAT'S THIS ABOUT?
MY NAME'S EONTE AND I'M HERE FOR YOUR HELP. YOUR ADVOCACY.
I GIVE TO A NUMBER OF ENVIRONMENTAL CAUSES ALREADY. IF YOURS MAKES SENSE I'M SURE I CAN OFFE--
WE DON'T WANT YOUR MONEY.
THAT'S A FIRST. SO WHAT CAN I DO FOR THIS 'PRACTICAL REVOLUTION'?
WE NEED YOU TO FIGHT.

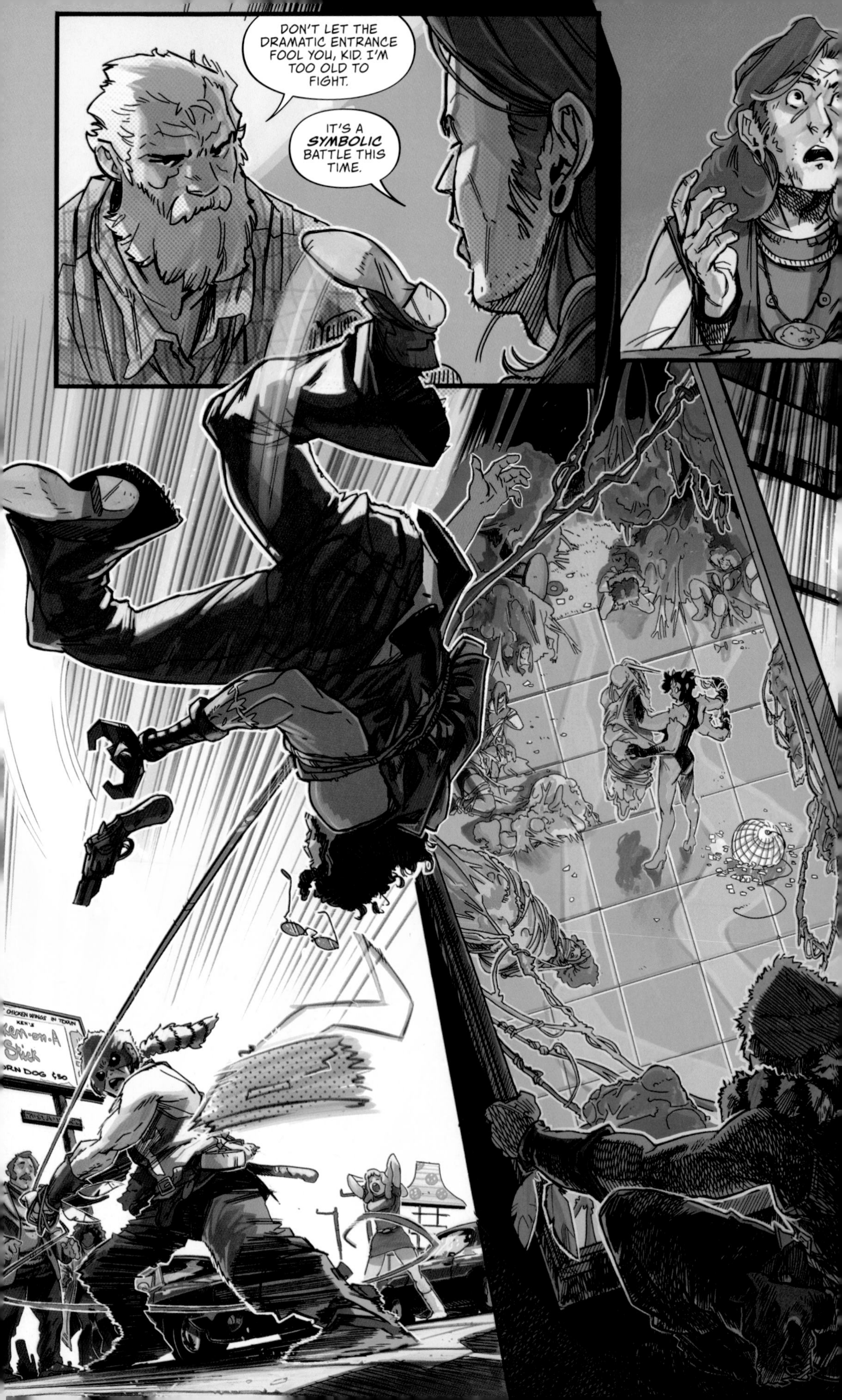
DON'T LET THE DRAMATIC ENTRANCE FOOL YOU, KID. I'M TOO OLD TO FIGHT.
IT'S A ***SYMBOLIC*** BATTLE THIS TIME.
CHICKEN WINGS IN TOWN
KEN'S

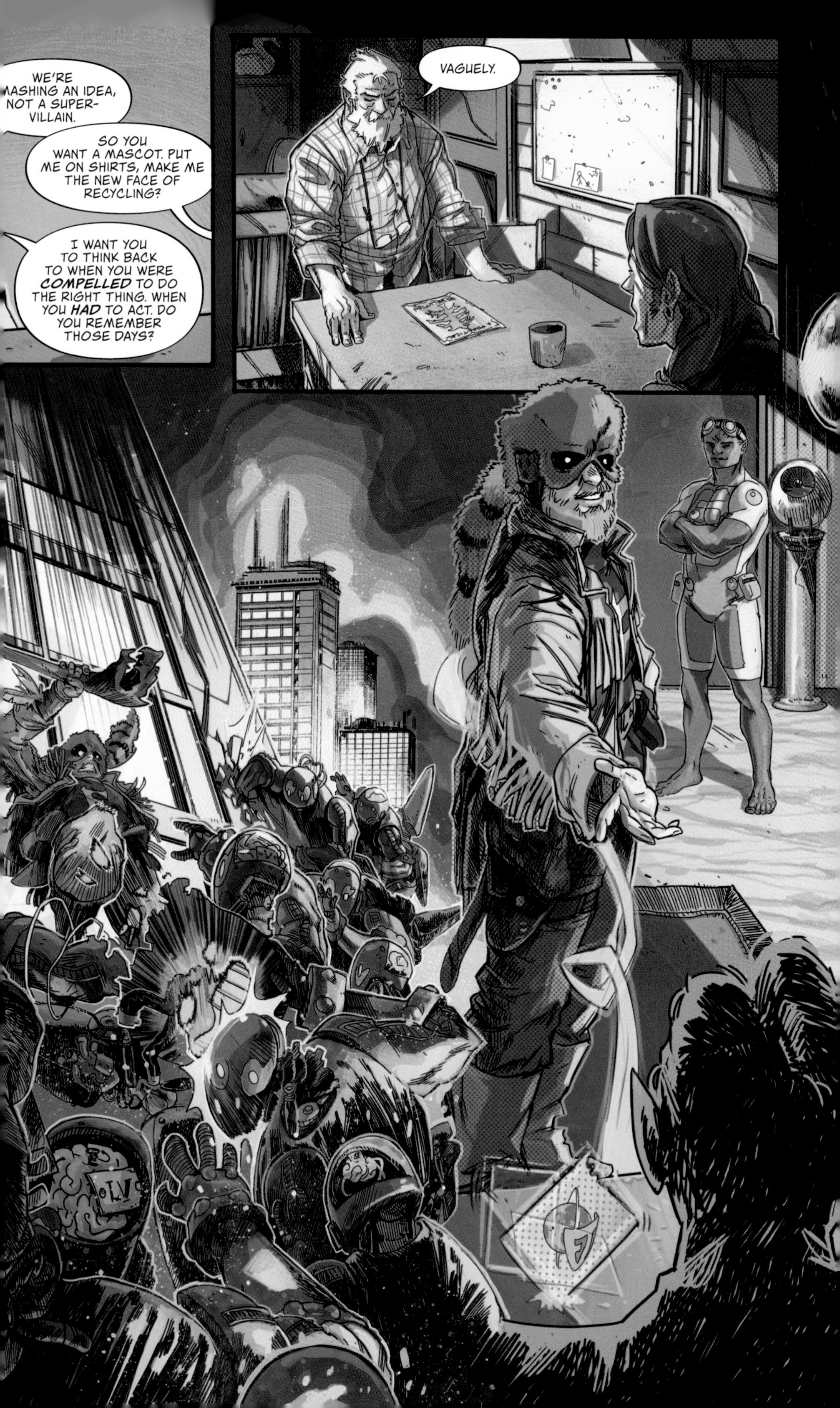
WE'RE
MASHING AN IDEA,
NOT A SUPER-
VILLAIN.
VAGUELY.
SO YOU WANT A MASCOT. PUT ME ON SHIRTS, MAKE ME THE NEW FACE OF RECYCLING?
I WANT YOU TO THINK BACK TO WHEN YOU WERE COMPELLED TO DO THE RIGHT THING. WHEN YOU HAD TO ACT. DO YOU REMEMBER THOSE DAYS?

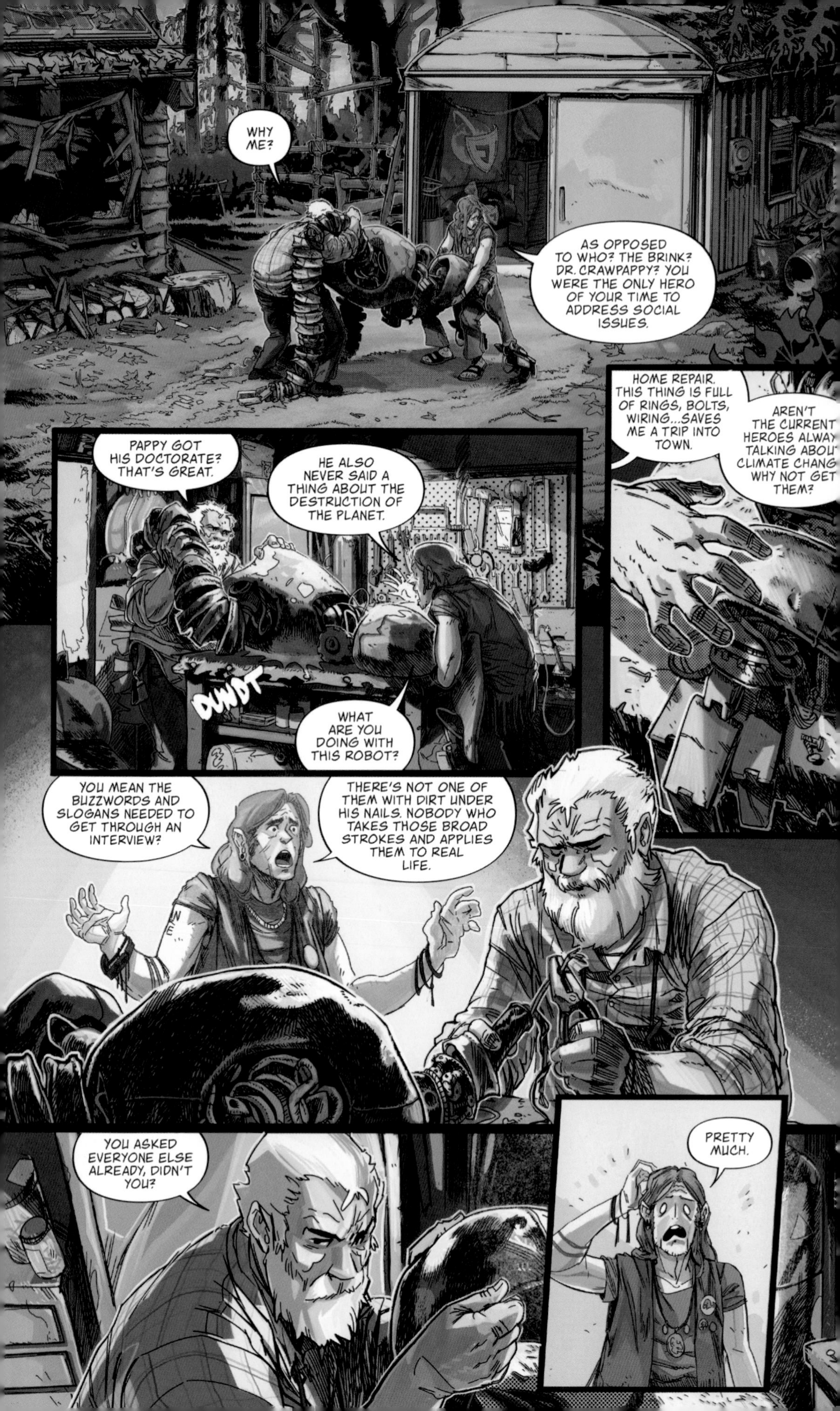
WHY ME?
AS OPPOSED TO WHO? THE BRINK? DR. CRAWPAPPY? YOU WERE THE ONLY HERO OF YOUR TIME TO ADDRESS SOCIAL ISSUES.
PAPPY GOT HIS DOCTORATE? THAT'S GREAT.
HE ALSO NEVER SAID A THING ABOUT THE DESTRUCTION OF THE PLANET.
DWDT
WHAT ARE YOU DOING WITH THIS ROBOT?
HOME REPAIR. THIS THING IS FULL OF RINGS, BOLTS, WIRING...SAVES ME A TRIP INTO TOWN.
AREN'T THE CURRENT HEROES ALWAY TALKING ABOU CLIMATE CHANG WHY NOT GET THEM?
YOU MEAN THE BUZZWORDS AND SLOGANS NEEDED TO GET THROUGH AN INTERVIEW?
THERE'S NOT ONE OF THEM WITH DIRT UNDER HIS NAILS. NOBODY WHO TAKES THOSE BROAD STROKES AND APPLIES THEM TO REAL LIFE.
YOU ASKED EVERYONE ELSE ALREADY, DIDN'T YOU?
PRETTY MUCH.

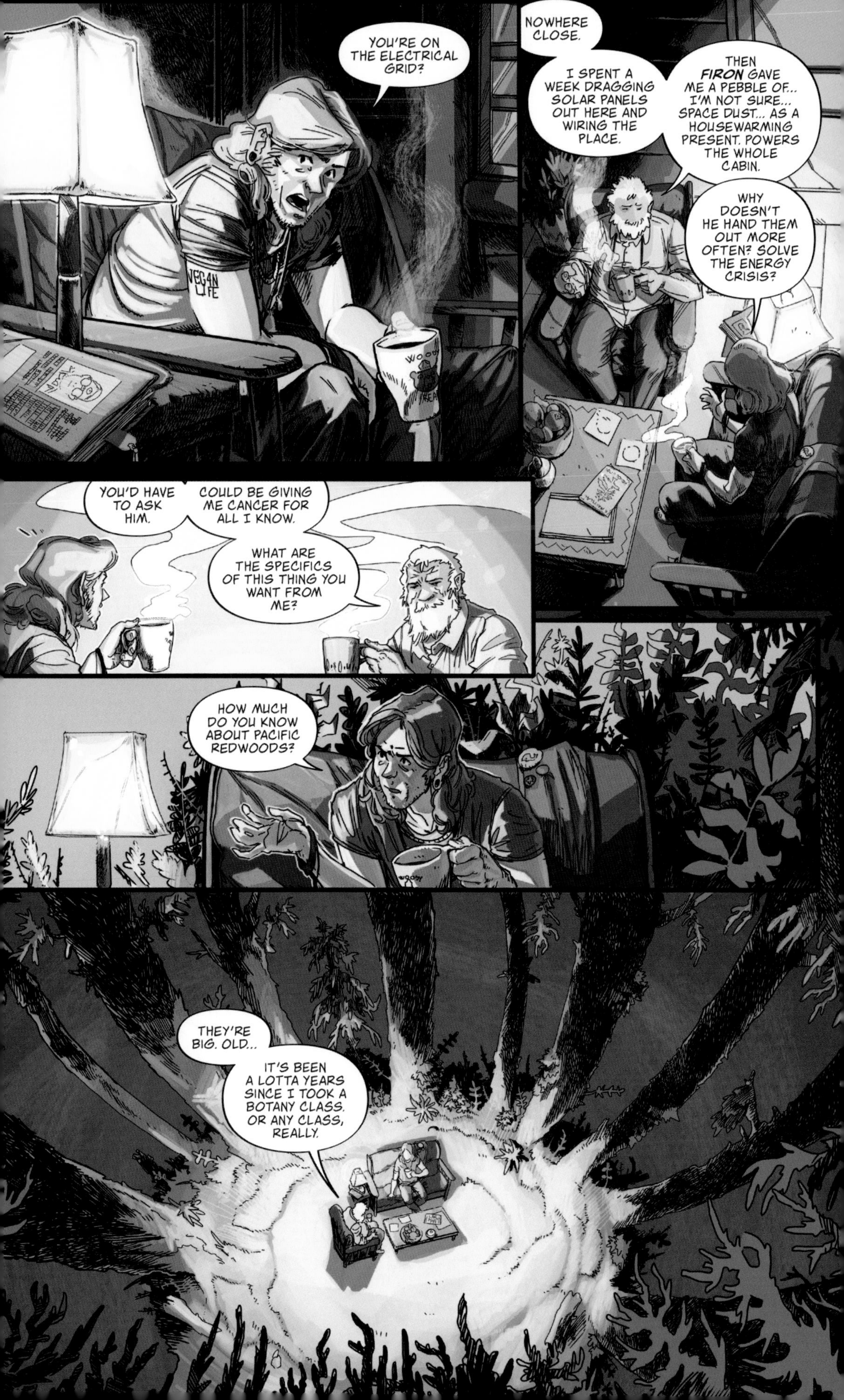
YOU'RE ON THE ELECTRICAL GRID?
NOWHERE CLOSE.
I SPENT A WEEK DRAGGING SOLAR PANELS OUT HERE AND WIRING THE PLACE.
THEN **FIRON** GAVE ME A PEBBLE OF... I'M NOT SURE... SPACE DUST... AS A HOUSEWARMING PRESENT. POWERS THE WHOLE CABIN.
WHY DOESN'T HE HAND THEM OUT MORE OFTEN? SOLVE THE ENERGY CRISIS?
YOU'D HAVE TO ASK HIM.
COULD BE GIVING ME CANCER FOR ALL I KNOW.
WHAT ARE THE SPECIFICS OF THIS THING YOU WANT FROM ME?
HOW MUCH DO YOU KNOW ABOUT PACIFIC REDWOODS?
THEY'RE BIG. OLD...
IT'S BEEN A LOTTA YEARS SINCE I TOOK A BOTANY CLASS. OR ANY CLASS, REALLY.

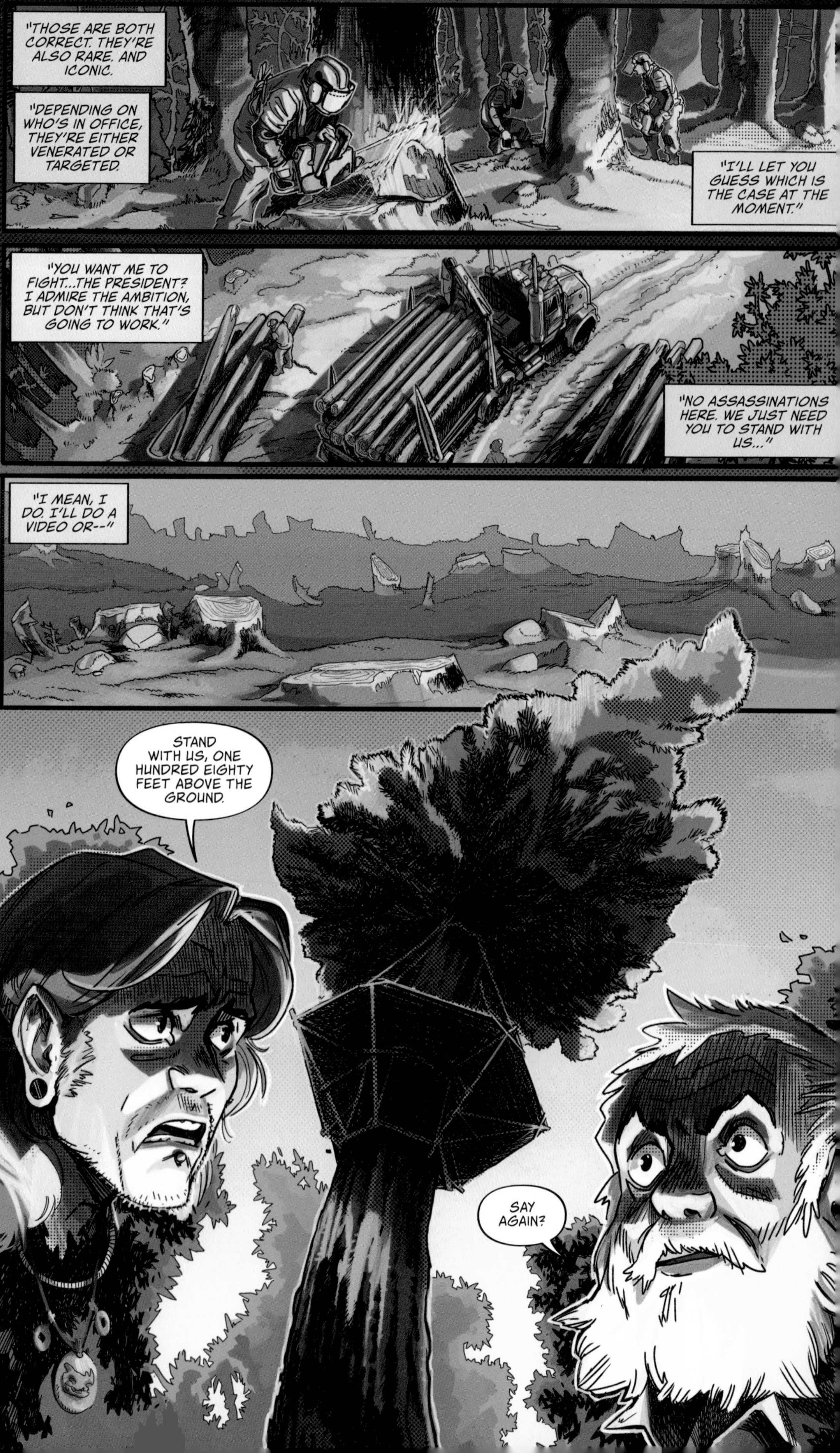
"THOSE ARE BOTH CORRECT. THEY'RE ALSO RARE. AND ICONIC.
"DEPENDING ON WHO'S IN OFFICE, THEY'RE EITHER VENERATED OR TARGETED.
"I'LL LET YOU GUESS WHICH IS THE CASE AT THE MOMENT."
"YOU WANT ME TO FIGHT...THE PRESIDENT? I ADMIRE THE AMBITION, BUT DON'T THINK THAT'S GOING TO WORK."
"NO ASSASSINATIONS HERE. WE JUST NEED YOU TO STAND WITH US..."
"I MEAN, I DO. I'LL DO A VIDEO OR--"
STAND WITH US, ONE HUNDRED EIGHTY FEET ABOVE THE GROUND.
SAY AGAIN?

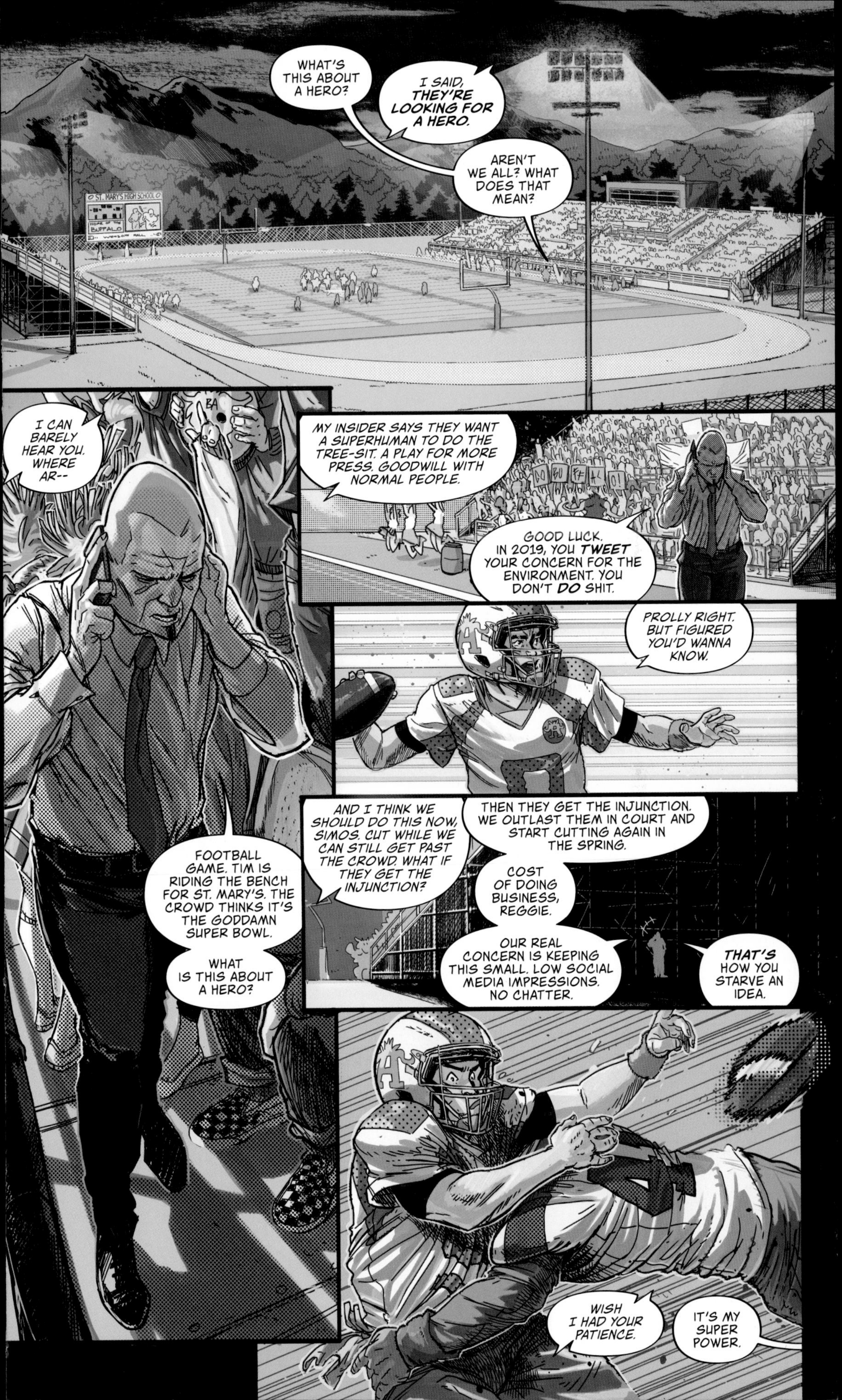
WHAT'S THIS ABOUT A HERO?
I SAID, THEY'RE LOOKING FOR A HERO.
AREN'T WE ALL? WHAT DOES THAT MEAN?
ST. MARY'S HIGH SCHOOL
BUFFALO
I CAN BARELY HEAR YOU. WHERE AR--
MY INSIDER SAYS THEY WANT A SUPERHUMAN TO DO THE TREE-SIT. A PLAY FOR MORE PRESS. GOODWILL WITH NORMAL PEOPLE.
GOOD LUCK. IN 2019, YOU TWEET YOUR CONCERN FOR THE ENVIRONMENT. YOU DON'T DO SHIT.
PROLLY RIGHT. BUT FIGURED YOU'D WANNA KNOW.
FOOTBALL GAME. TIM IS RIDING THE BENCH FOR ST. MARY'S. THE CROWD THINKS IT'S THE GODDAMN SUPER BOWL.
WHAT IS THIS ABOUT A HERO?
AND I THINK WE SHOULD DO THIS NOW, SIMOS. CUT WHILE WE CAN STILL GET PAST THE CROWD. WHAT IF THEY GET THE INJUNCTION?
THEN THEY GET THE INJUNCTION. WE OUTLAST THEM IN COURT AND START CUTTING AGAIN IN THE SPRING.
COST OF DOING BUSINESS, REGGIE.
OUR REAL CONCERN IS KEEPING THIS SMALL. LOW SOCIAL MEDIA IMPRESSIONS. NO CHATTER.
THAT'S HOW YOU STARVE AN IDEA.
WISH I HAD YOUR PATIENCE.
IT'S MY SUPER POWER.

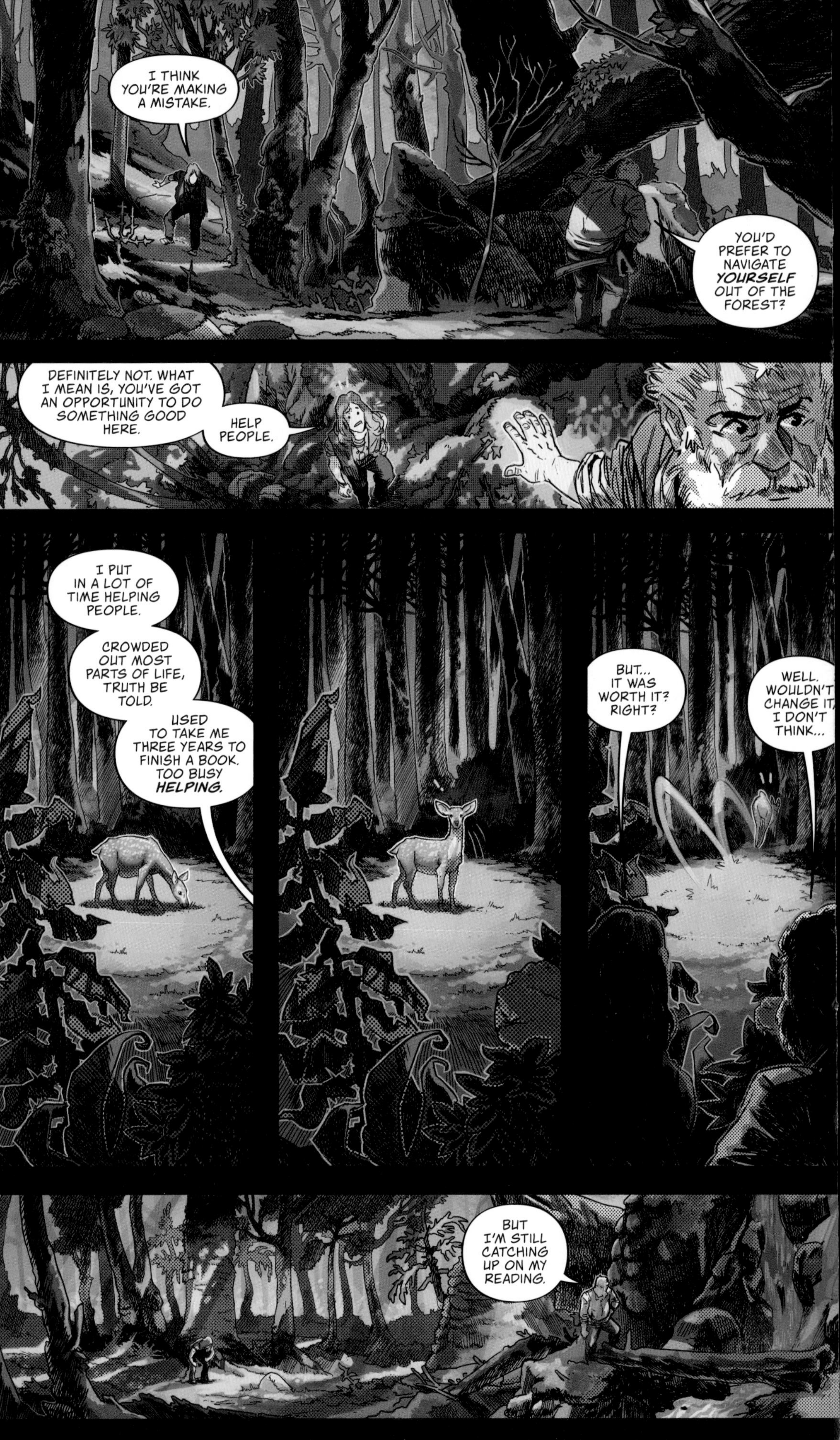
I THINK YOU'RE MAKING A MISTAKE.
YOU'D PREFER TO NAVIGATE YOURSELF OUT OF THE FOREST?
DEFINITELY NOT. WHAT I MEAN IS, YOU'VE GOT AN OPPORTUNITY TO DO SOMETHING GOOD HERE.
HELP PEOPLE.
I PUT IN A LOT OF TIME HELPING PEOPLE.
CROWDED OUT MOST PARTS OF LIFE, TRUTH BE TOLD.
USED TO TAKE ME THREE YEARS TO FINISH A BOOK. TOO BUSY HELPING.
BUT... IT WAS WORTH IT? RIGHT?
WELL. WOULDN'T CHANGE IT, I DON'T THINK...
BUT I'M STILL CATCHING UP ON MY READING.

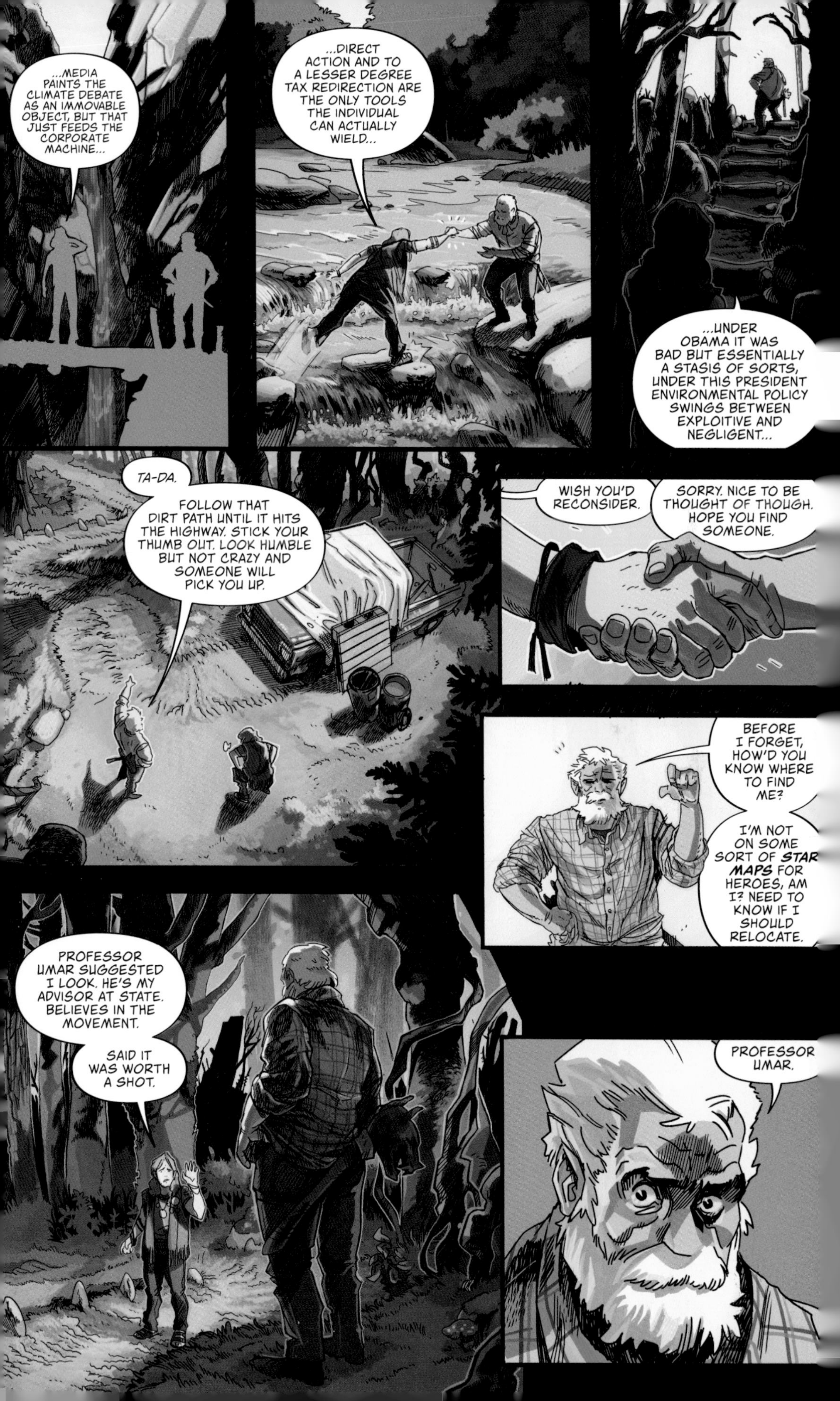
...MEDIA PAINTS THE CLIMATE DEBATE AS AN IMMOVABLE OBJECT, BUT THAT JUST FEEDS THE CORPORATE MACHINE...
...DIRECT ACTION AND TO A LESSER DEGREE TAX REDIRECTION ARE THE ONLY TOOLS THE INDIVIDUAL CAN ACTUALLY WIELD...
...UNDER OBAMA IT WAS BAD BUT ESSENTIALLY A STASIS OF SORTS, UNDER THIS PRESIDENT ENVIRONMENTAL POLICY SWINGS BETWEEN EXPLOITIVE AND NEGLIGENT...
TA-DA.
FOLLOW THAT DIRT PATH UNTIL IT HITS THE HIGHWAY. STICK YOUR THUMB OUT. LOOK HUMBLE BUT NOT CRAZY AND SOMEONE WILL PICK YOU UP.
WISH YOU'D RECONSIDER.
SORRY. NICE TO BE THOUGHT OF THOUGH. HOPE YOU FIND SOMEONE.
BEFORE I FORGET, HOW'D YOU KNOW WHERE TO FIND ME?
I'M NOT ON SOME SORT OF STAR MAPS FOR HEROES, AM I? NEED TO KNOW IF I SHOULD RELOCATE.
PROFESSOR UMAR SUGGESTED I LOOK. HE'S MY ADVISOR AT STATE. BELIEVES IN THE MOVEMENT.
SAID IT WAS WORTH A SHOT.
PROFESSOR UMAR.

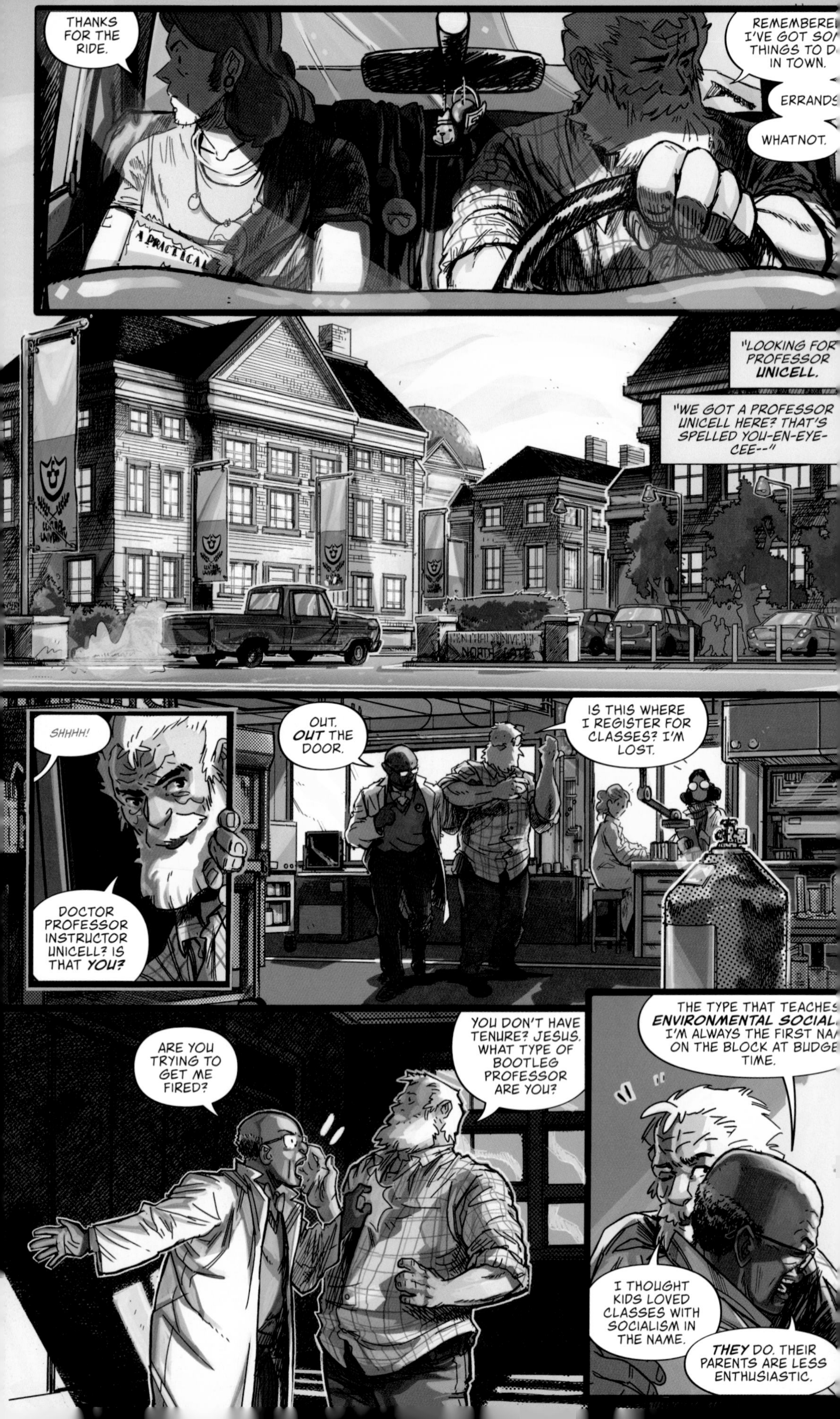

THANKS FOR THE RIDE.
REMEMBERED I'VE GOT SO THINGS TO D IN TOWN.
ERRANDS
WHATNOT.
A PRACTICAL
"LOOKING FOR PROFESSOR UNICELL.
"WE GOT A PROFESSOR UNICELL HERE? THAT'S SPELLED YOU-EN-EYE-CEE--"
SHHHH!
DOCTOR PROFESSOR INSTRUCTOR UNICELL? IS THAT YOU?
OUT. OUT THE DOOR.
IS THIS WHERE I REGISTER FOR CLASSES? I'M LOST.
ARE YOU TRYING TO GET ME FIRED?
YOU DON'T HAVE TENURE? JESUS. WHAT TYPE OF BOOTLEG PROFESSOR ARE YOU?
THE TYPE THAT TEACHES ENVIRONMENTAL SOCIAL I'M ALWAYS THE FIRST NA ON THE BLOCK AT BUDGE TIME.
I THOUGHT KIDS LOVED CLASSES WITH SOCIALISM IN THE NAME.
THEY DO. THEIR PARENTS ARE LESS ENTHUSIASTIC.

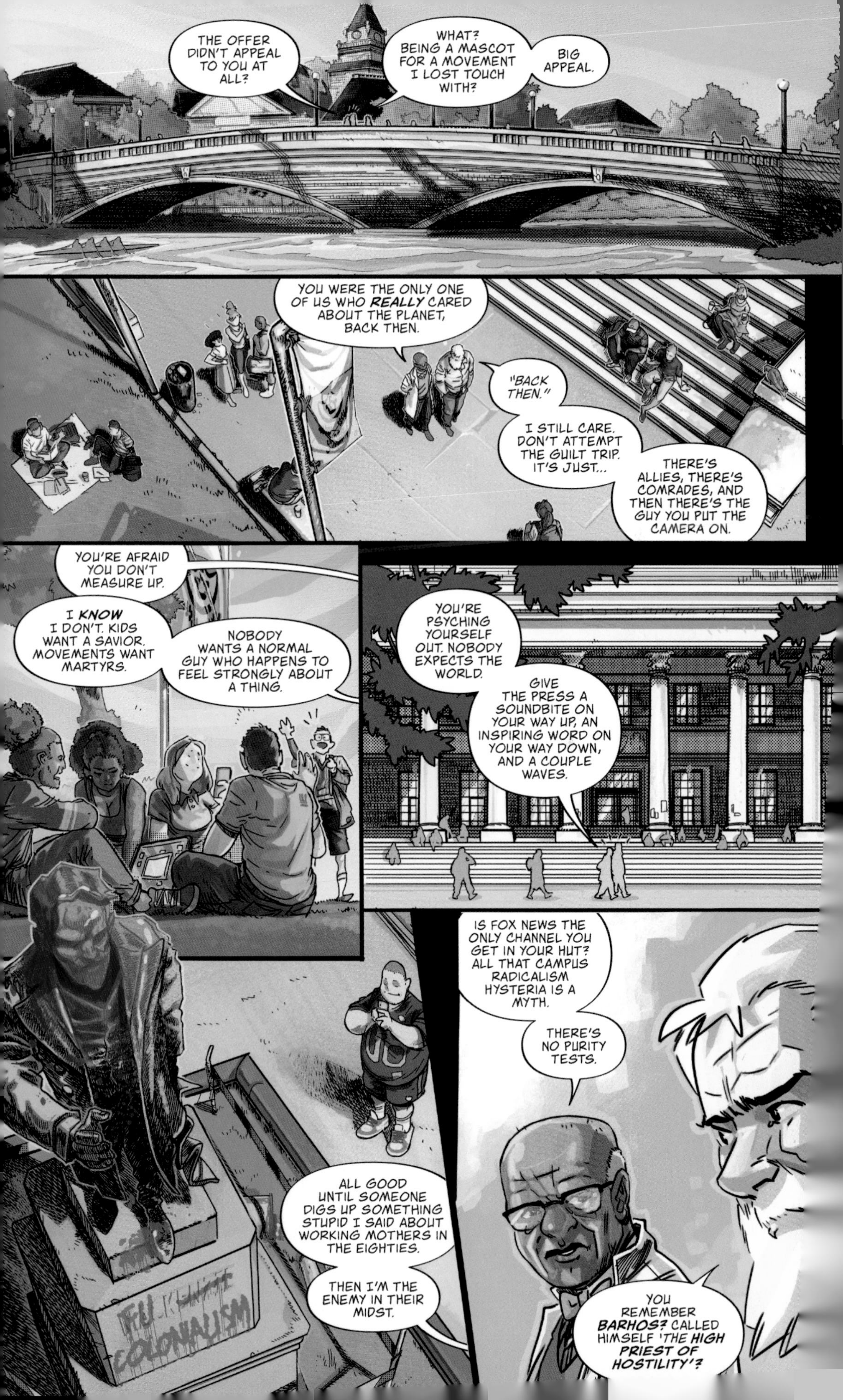

THE OFFER DIDN'T APPEAL TO YOU AT ALL?
WHAT? BEING A MASCOT FOR A MOVEMENT I LOST TOUCH WITH?
BIG APPEAL.
YOU WERE THE ONLY ONE OF US WHO **REALLY** CARED ABOUT THE PLANET, BACK THEN.
"BACK THEN."
I STILL CARE. DON'T ATTEMPT THE GUILT TRIP. IT'S JUST...
THERE'S ALLIES, THERE'S COMRADES, AND THEN THERE'S THE GUY YOU PUT THE CAMERA ON.
YOU'RE AFRAID YOU DON'T MEASURE UP.
I **KNOW** I DON'T. KIDS WANT A SAVIOR. MOVEMENTS WANT MARTYRS.
NOBODY WANTS A NORMAL GUY WHO HAPPENS TO FEEL STRONGLY ABOUT A THING.
YOU'RE PSYCHING YOURSELF OUT. NOBODY EXPECTS THE WORLD.
GIVE THE PRESS A SOUNDBITE ON YOUR WAY UP, AN INSPIRING WORD ON YOUR WAY DOWN, AND A COUPLE WAVES.
IS FOX NEWS THE ONLY CHANNEL YOU GET IN YOUR HUT? ALL THAT CAMPUS RADICALISM HYSTERIA IS A MYTH.
THERE'S NO PURITY TESTS.
ALL GOOD UNTIL SOMEONE DIGS UP SOMETHING STUPID I SAID ABOUT WORKING MOTHERS IN THE EIGHTIES.
THEN I'M THE ENEMY IN THEIR MIDST.
COLONIALISM
YOU REMEMBER **BARHOS?** CALLED HIMSELF **'THE HIGH PRIEST OF HOSTILITY'?**

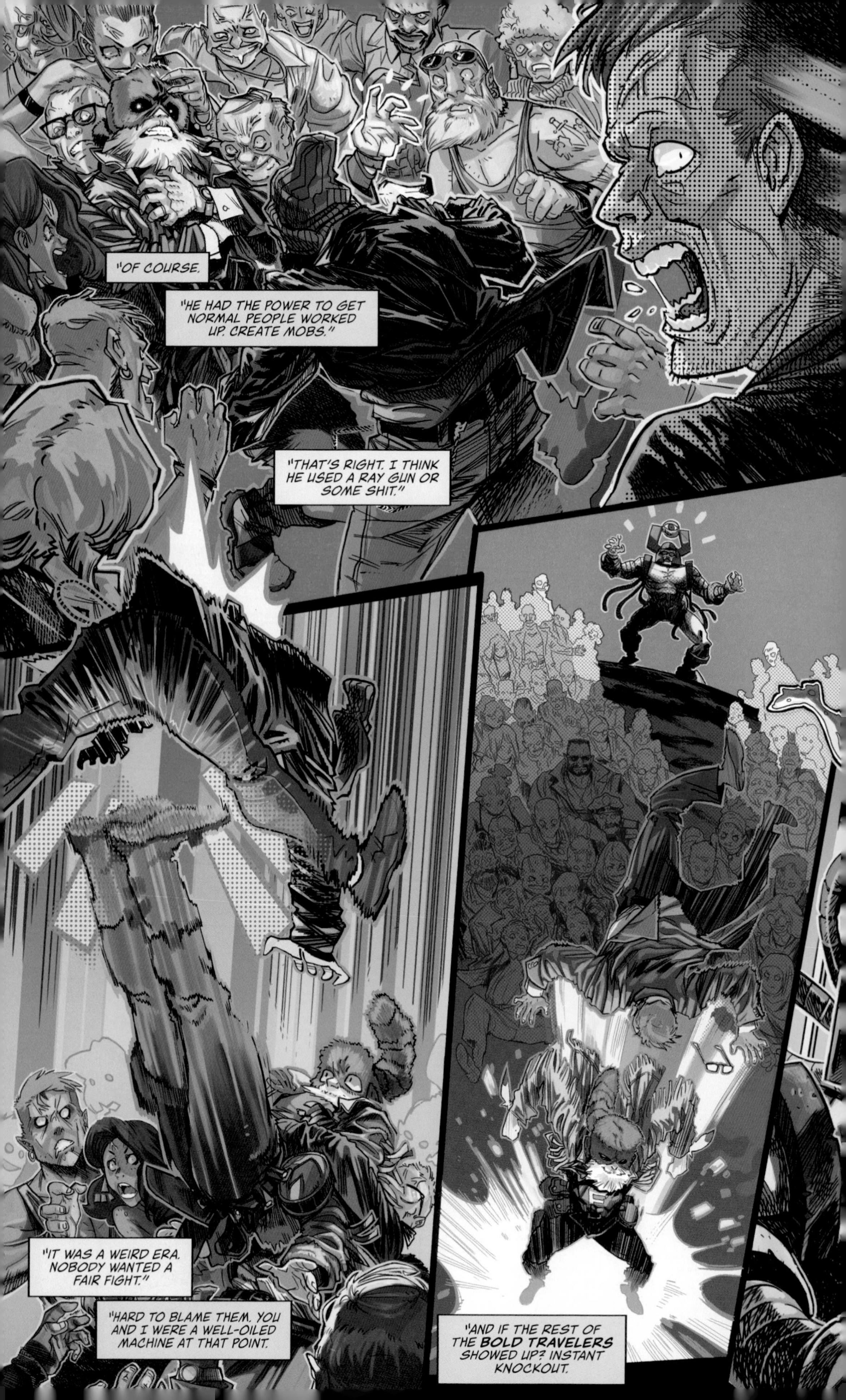
"OF COURSE.
"HE HAD THE POWER TO GET NORMAL PEOPLE WORKED UP. CREATE MOBS."
"THAT'S RIGHT. I THINK HE USED A RAY GUN OR SOME SHIT."
"IT WAS A WEIRD ERA. NOBODY WANTED A FAIR FIGHT."
"HARD TO BLAME THEM. YOU AND I WERE A WELL-OILED MACHINE AT THAT POINT.
"AND IF THE REST OF THE **BOLD TRAVELERS** SHOWED UP? INSTANT KNOCKOUT.

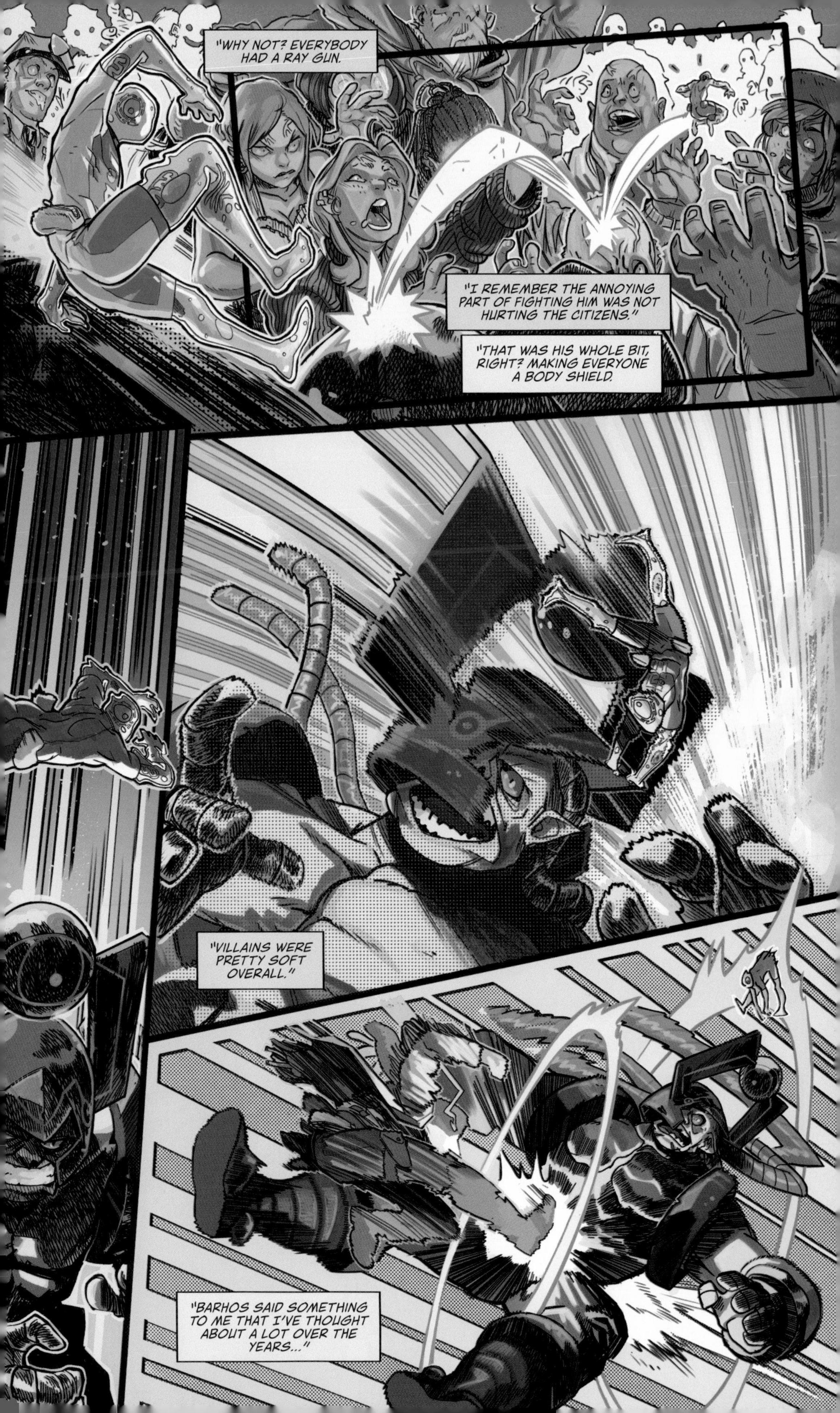
"WHY NOT? EVERYBODY HAD A RAY GUN.
"I REMEMBER THE ANNOYING PART OF FIGHTING HIM WAS NOT HURTING THE CITIZENS."
"THAT WAS HIS WHOLE BIT, RIGHT? MAKING EVERYONE A BODY SHIELD.
"VILLAINS WERE PRETTY SOFT OVERALL."
"BARHOS SAID SOMETHING TO ME THAT I'VE THOUGHT ABOUT A LOT OVER THE YEARS..."

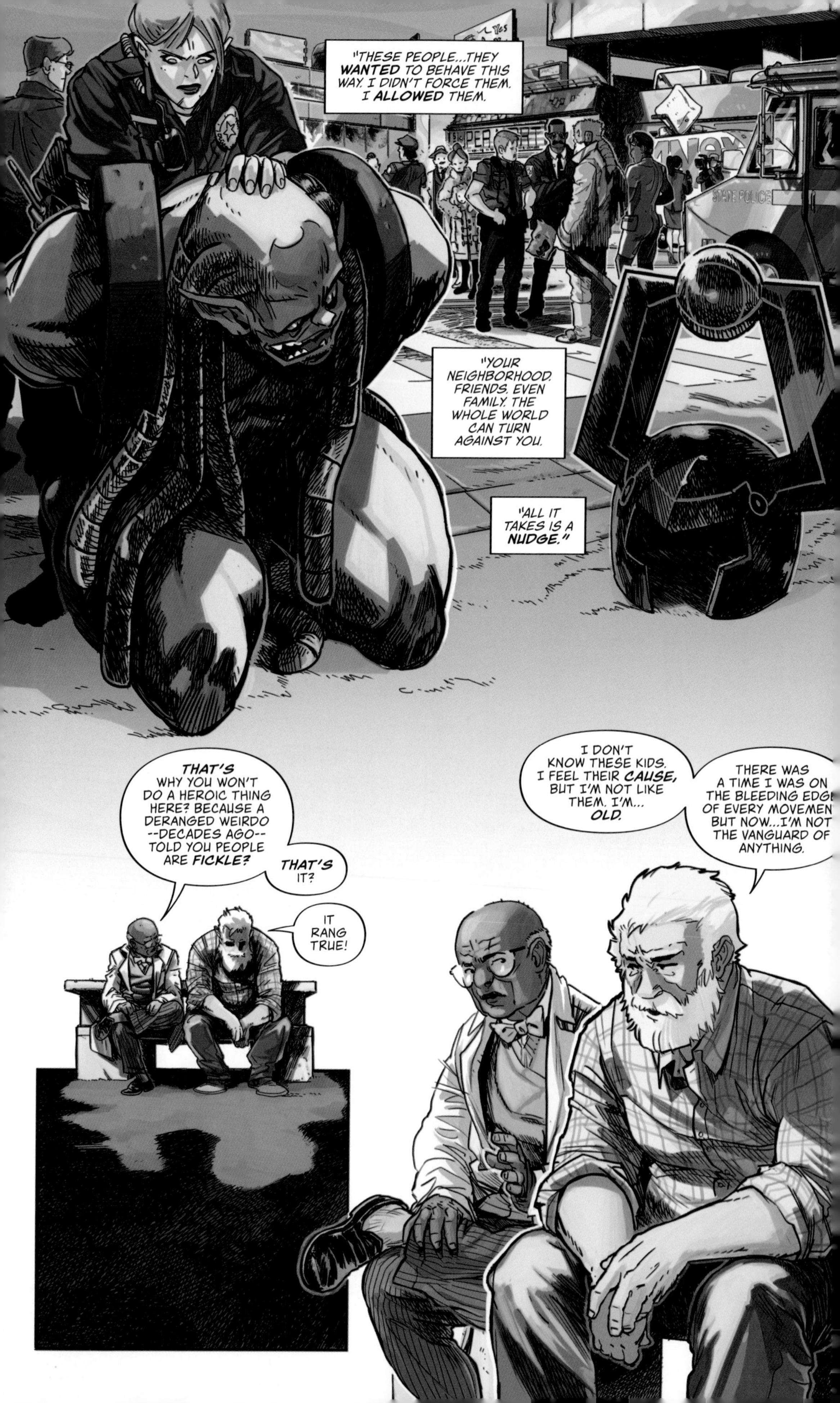

"THESE PEOPLE...THEY WANTED TO BEHAVE THIS WAY. I DIDN'T FORCE THEM. I ALLOWED THEM.
"YOUR NEIGHBORHOOD. FRIENDS. EVEN FAMILY. THE WHOLE WORLD CAN TURN AGAINST YOU.
"ALL IT TAKES IS A NUDGE."
STATE POLICE
THAT'S WHY YOU WON'T DO A HEROIC THING HERE? BECAUSE A DERANGED WEIRDO --DECADES AGO-- TOLD YOU PEOPLE ARE FICKLE?
THAT'S IT?
IT RANG TRUE!
I DON'T KNOW THESE KIDS. I FEEL THEIR CAUSE, BUT I'M NOT LIKE THEM. I'M... OLD.
THERE WAS A TIME I WAS ON THE BLEEDING EDG OF EVERY MOVEMEN BUT NOW...I'M NOT THE VANGUARD OF ANYTHING.

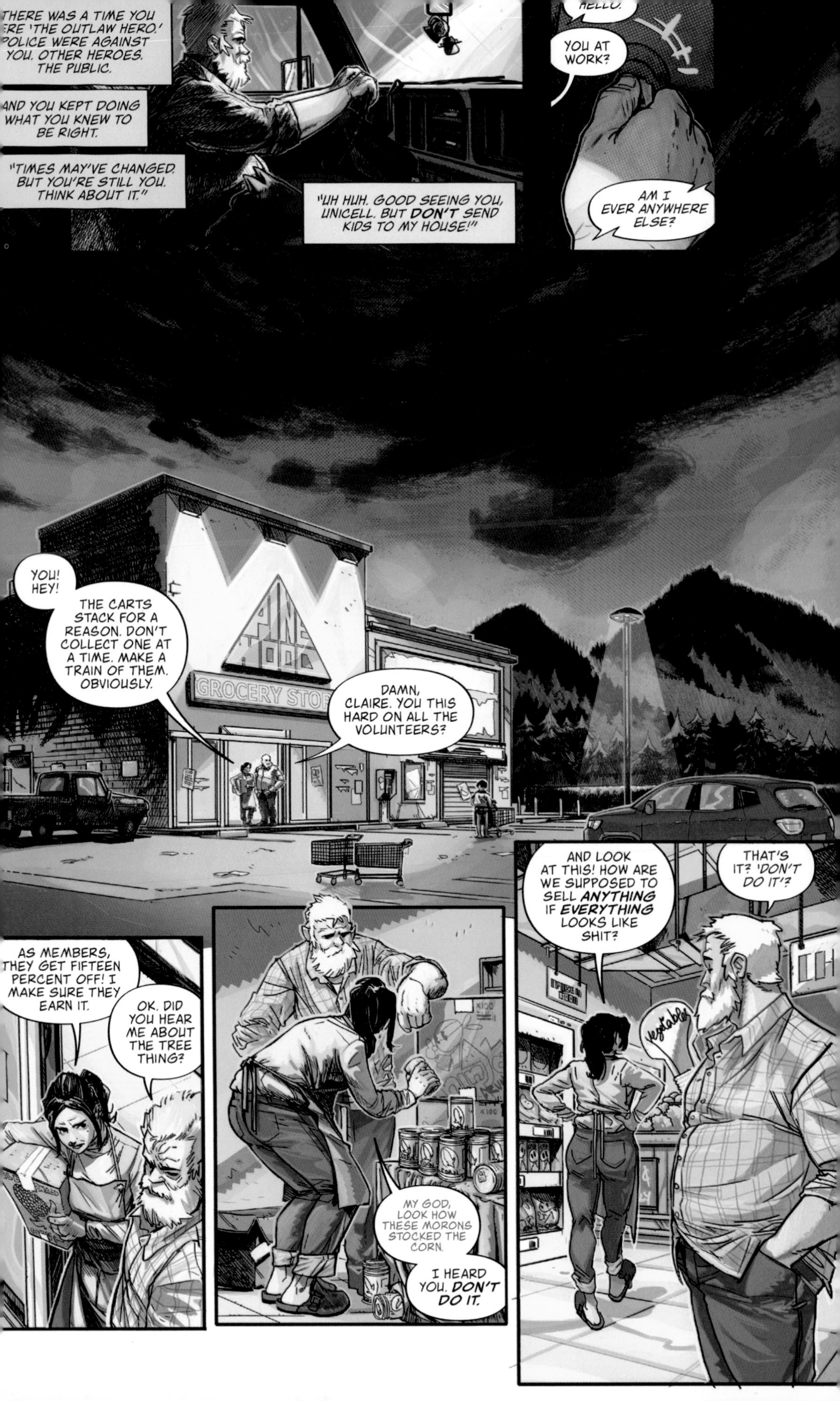
THERE WAS A TIME YOU
ERE 'THE OUTLAW HERO.' POLICE WERE AGAINST YOU. OTHER HEROES. THE PUBLIC.
AND YOU KEPT DOING WHAT YOU KNEW TO BE RIGHT.
"TIMES MAY'VE CHANGED. BUT YOU'RE STILL YOU. THINK ABOUT IT."
"UH HUH. GOOD SEEING YOU, UNICELL. BUT DON'T SEND KIDS TO MY HOUSE!"
HELLO.
YOU AT WORK?
AM I EVER ANYWHERE ELSE?
YOU! HEY!
THE CARTS STACK FOR A REASON. DON'T COLLECT ONE AT A TIME. MAKE A TRAIN OF THEM. OBVIOUSLY.
GROCERY STO
DAMN, CLAIRE. YOU THIS HARD ON ALL THE VOLUNTEERS?
AS MEMBERS, THEY GET FIFTEEN PERCENT OFF! I MAKE SURE THEY EARN IT.
OK. DID YOU HEAR ME ABOUT THE TREE THING?
MY GOD, LOOK HOW THESE MORONS STOCKED THE CORN.
I HEARD YOU. DON'T DO IT.
AND LOOK AT THIS! HOW ARE WE SUPPOSED TO SELL ANYTHING IF EVERYTHING LOOKS LIKE SHIT?
THAT'S IT? 'DON'T DO IT'?
vegetables

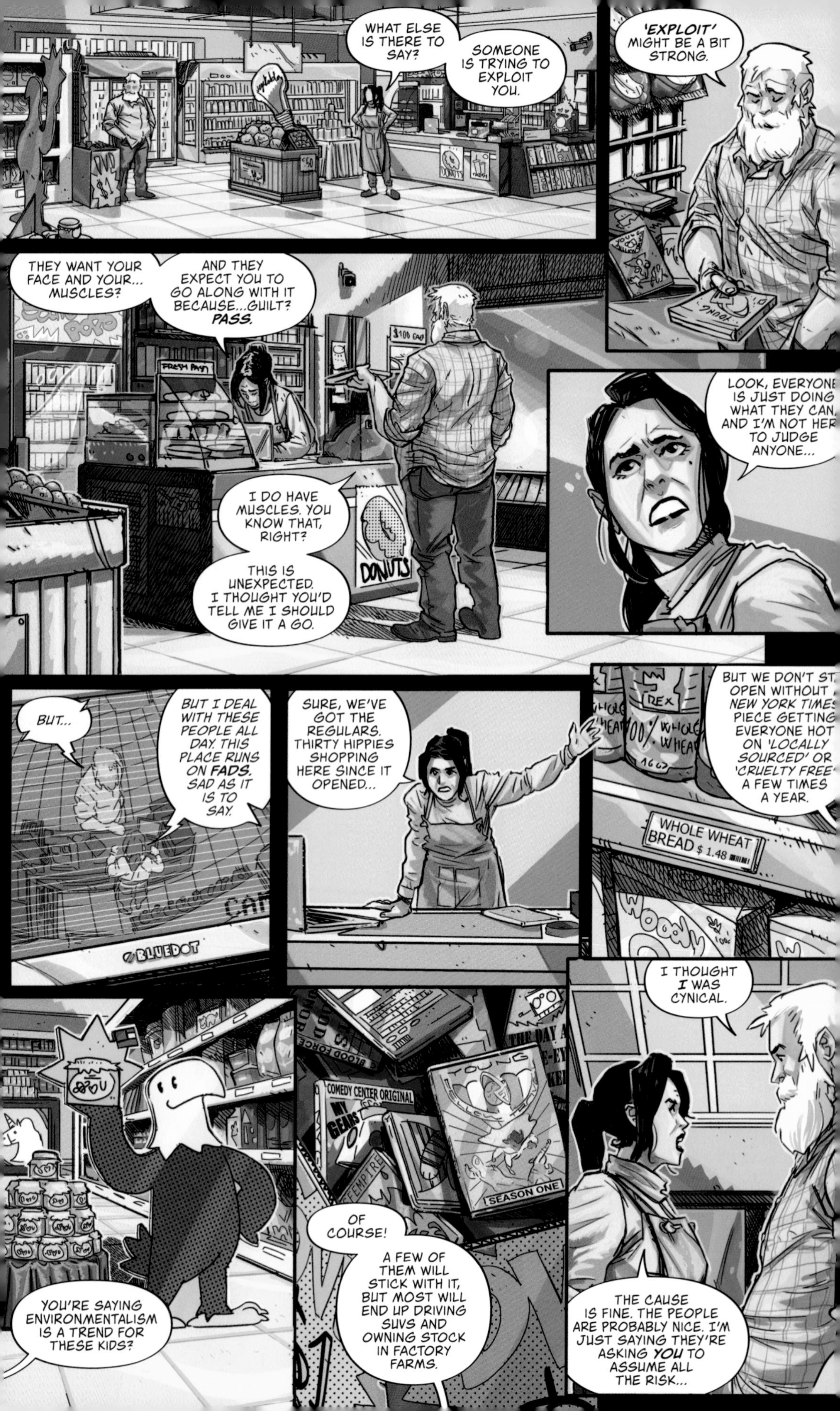
WHAT ELSE IS THERE TO SAY?
SOMEONE IS TRYING TO EXPLOIT YOU.
'EXPLOIT' MIGHT BE A BIT STRONG.
THEY WANT YOUR FACE AND YOUR... MUSCLES?
AND THEY EXPECT YOU TO GO ALONG WITH IT BECAUSE...GUILT? PASS.
I DO HAVE MUSCLES. YOU KNOW THAT, RIGHT?
THIS IS UNEXPECTED. I THOUGHT YOU'D TELL ME I SHOULD GIVE IT A GO.
DONUTS
LOOK, EVERYONE IS JUST DOING WHAT THEY CAN. AND I'M NOT HER TO JUDGE ANYONE...
BUT...
BUT I DEAL WITH THESE PEOPLE ALL DAY. THIS PLACE RUNS ON FADS. SAD AS IT IS TO SAY.
BLUEDOT
SURE, WE'VE GOT THE REGULARS. THIRTY HIPPIES SHOPPING HERE SINCE IT OPENED...
BUT WE DON'T ST OPEN WITHOUT NEW YORK TIMES PIECE GETTING EVERYONE HOT ON 'LOCALLY SOURCED' OR 'CRUELTY FREE' A FEW TIMES A YEAR.
WHOLE WHEAT BREAD $ 1.48
YOU'RE SAYING ENVIRONMENTALISM IS A TREND FOR THESE KIDS?
COMEDY CENTER ORIGINAL
SEASON ONE
OF COURSE!
A FEW OF THEM WILL STICK WITH IT, BUT MOST WILL END UP DRIVING SUVS AND OWNING STOCK IN FACTORY FARMS.
I THOUGHT I WAS CYNICAL.
THE CAUSE IS FINE. THE PEOPLE ARE PROBABLY NICE. I'M JUST SAYING THEY'RE ASKING YOU TO ASSUME ALL THE RISK...

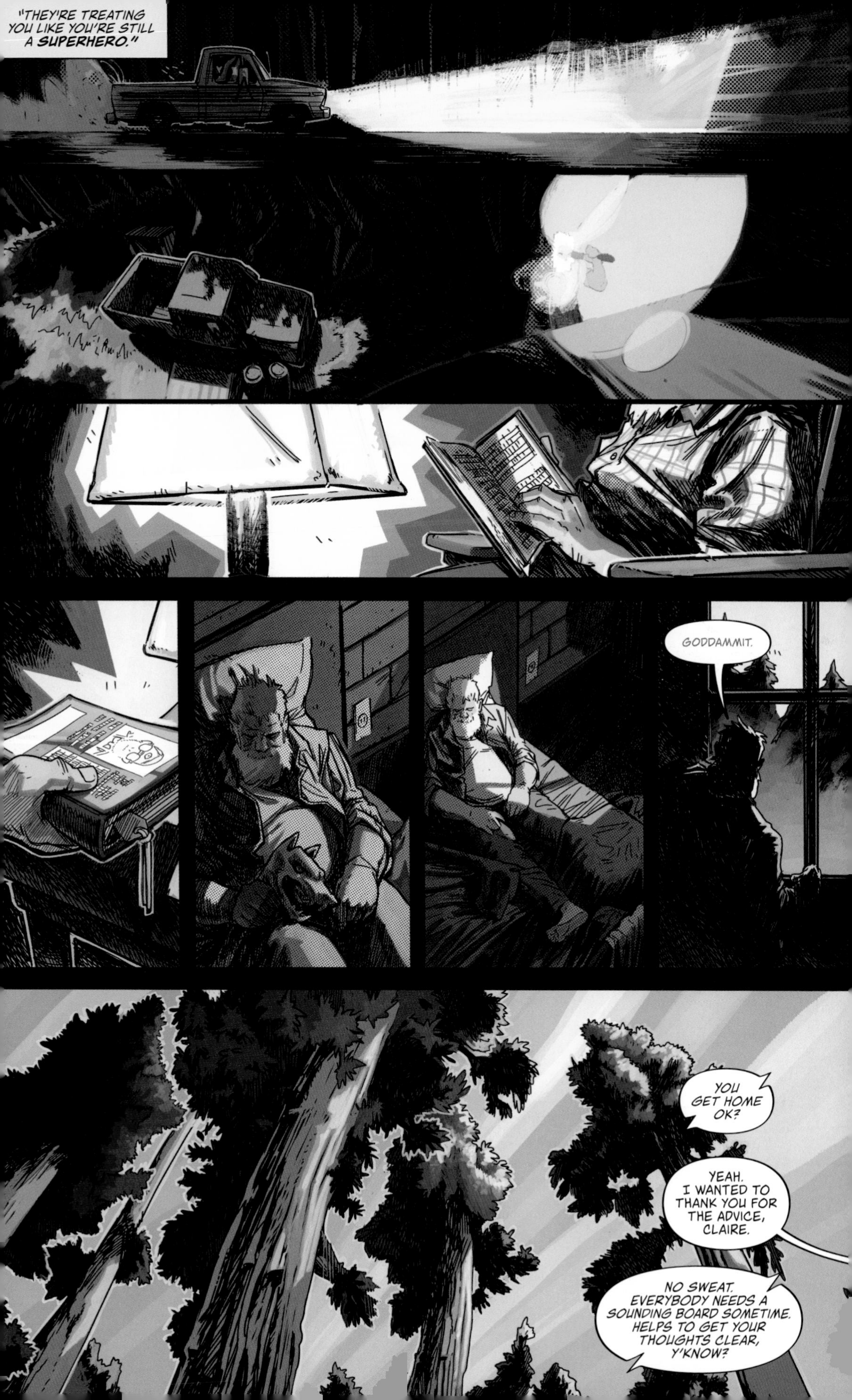
"THEY'RE TREATING YOU LIKE YOU'RE STILL A SUPERHERO."
GODDAMMIT.
YOU GET HOME OK?
YEAH. I WANTED TO THANK YOU FOR THE ADVICE, CLAIRE.
NO SWEAT. EVERYBODY NEEDS A SOUNDING BOARD SOMETIME. HELPS TO GET YOUR THOUGHTS CLEAR, Y'KNOW?

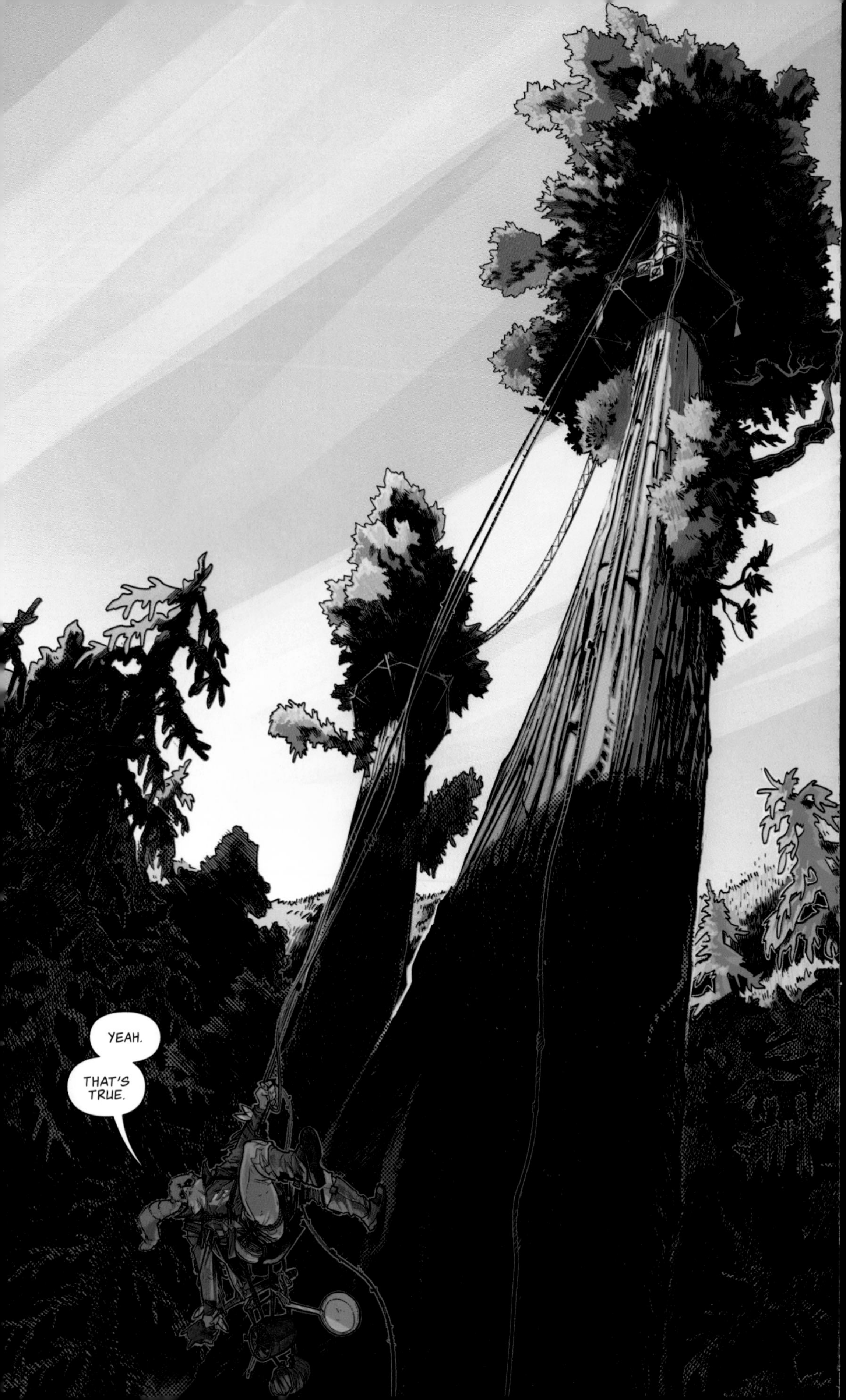
YEAH.
THAT'S TRUE.

# PROFESSOR UNICELL

**Real name**: Khalid Umar

**Occupation**: University professor

**Identity**: Secret to his students and coworkers, known to a few in government

**Legal status**: Citizen of the United States with no criminal record

**Former aliases**: Unicellular Man

**Known relatives**: Marie (wife; deceased), Mohammad (son)

**Group affiliation**: Bold Travelers (former); Yellow Travelers (inactive)

**History**: Khalid Umar was born with a gifted intellect, but rarely had a place to hone it. Coming from an impoverished public school system, and having no family resources to attend a top tier university, Umar took the long road to a diploma. He worked in a machine shop during the day and attended night classes at a local community college. The owner of the machine shop, Thad Burlo, saw something in the young man and asked him to come by after hours. It was there Umar learned his boss was none other than the super-villain Neutron Real. His power to increase or decrease the atom density of inanimate objects made him among the most powerful rogues of this day.

Burlo's time as a villain had passed but he still possessed his unique ability over matter. And, as an effort at redemption, he wanted to pass it on to someone who would do "something good" with it. The ambitious and intelligent Umar was his first pick. Burlo planned on using a particle accelerator excavated from a former base of the Devious Three, but Umar refused when he learned it would cause Burlo to disintegrate. Burlo had been diagnosed with an inoperable brain tumor and, after months of trying, realized he could not use his power to save himself. He was resigned to the knowledge he would die during the power handoff with Umar.

The two men fought and Umar was shoved into the particle accelerator's outer chamber. As he punched and kicked against the glass, the device began to spin. Burlo's power was being siphoned into the chamber while Burlo himself was stripped of his own atom density. Still struggling, Umar punched through the glass and exposed himself to untreated air. This caused a change in the power set transfer by Burlo. Instead of changing the density of an object, Umar could reduce his own cell count.

Emerging from the chamber with this new power, Umar adopted the name The Unicellular Man. After an embarrassing first attempt at crime-stopping, Umar sought out the scientist/adventurer Danny Universal. The two formed a bond over their love of inquiry and Universal became a mentor to Umar, teaching him how to get the most from his power and from the hero experience. When Universal was kidnapped to the Interrealm by the mad ruler Carsor, Umar teamed with an early incarnation of the Bold Travelers to rescue him. The group identified Umar's worthy qualities and offered him a membership when they returned to Earth.

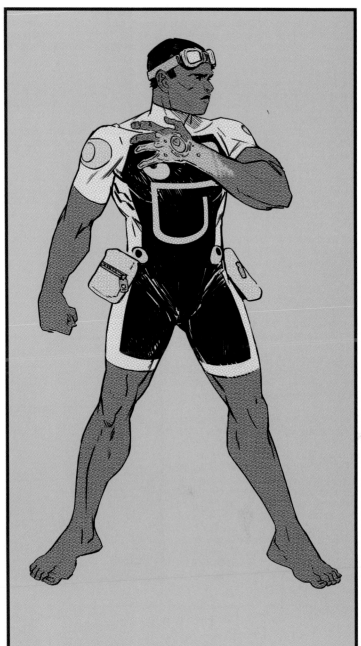

Umar's science acumen served the group in the field. It was The Unicellular man who solved the 'Glubman's Cube' puzzle that Nero Shrine used to trap humanity in a circular-time stasis. Later, Umar was responsible for stopping the Exterminator Seeds causing unchecked, cancerous, growth on farms across the United States.

But his time with the Bold Travelers wasn't without controversy. Umar clashed with Kroon politically, leading to a rift in the BT. The two later reconciled and became friends, even teaming up on several adventures without the BT, though they never saw eye-to-eye on climate change and reproductive rights. Umar left the Travelers for the first time over his perception that the team wasn't doing enough to educate. Arguing that everything they do is in reaction to atrocities in already in motion, Umar lobbied the BT to take clear and science-first public stances on issues of the day. The idea was to lead by example, but many Travelers saw it as against their mandate. Umar rejoined the BT after the Big Link event caused the 'classic' lineup to fight back-to-back for the fate of Jersey City. But Umar left again during the reformations the BT undertook in the fallout of the Schenectady Incident. He rejected the need for government oversight and eventually turned in his membership card. As Umar has joined the BT in several adventures since, it's unclear if he's a member-in-reserve or acting fully independent of the group.

As the Chief Science Officer of the Bold Travelers, Umar saw it as his responsibility to set an example for young people. To that end, he pursued higher education throughout his time with the BT and earned two doctorates. Believing he could do more good as a spokesperson than a crimefighter, he changed his superhero name to Professor Unicell and became an outspoken advocate for STEM education.

**Height:** 5'8" (as Umar) as small as 1μ (as Unicell)
**Weight:** 170lbs (as Umar) nearly weightless (as Unicell)
**Eyes:** Brown
**Hair:** Black
**Strength level:** As Professor Unicell, he can lift several times his human body weight.
**Known superhuman powers:** Professor Unicell can reduce his mass to that of a unicellular organism. As he shrinks in size his features become similar to a protozoa. Through concentration he's able to maintain a humanoid shape, though his skin becomes transparent and his features nondescript. He's able to stop shrinking at any point before 1μ and typically stays at roughly 1" while crimefighting. His strength is increased as he shrinks, however it never reaches true superhuman levels. He has, on rare occasion, broken the 1μ barrier and gone subatomic once.

While in his protozoa form, Professor U cell has an increased invulnerabi though he can still be burnt and elect cuted. With the help of Danny Univers Unicell has increased his size above t of a normal human but the effects were timately life-threatening.

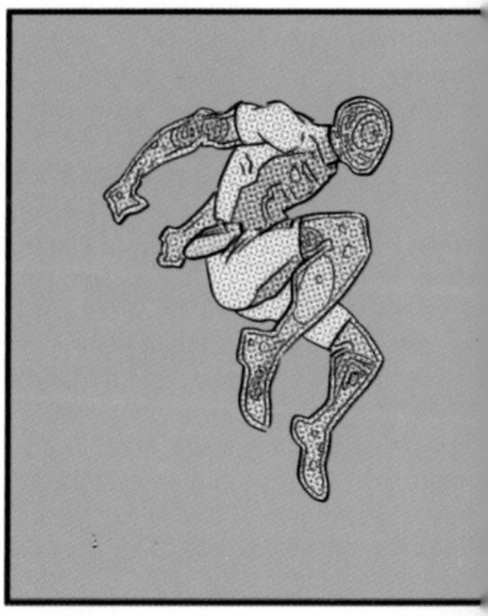

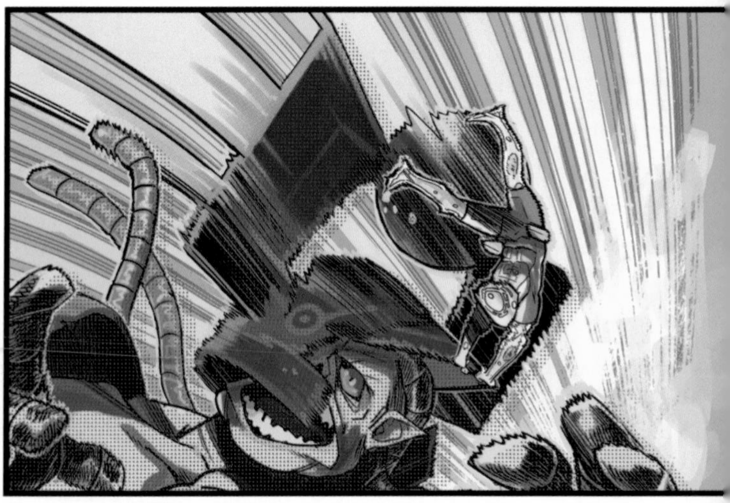

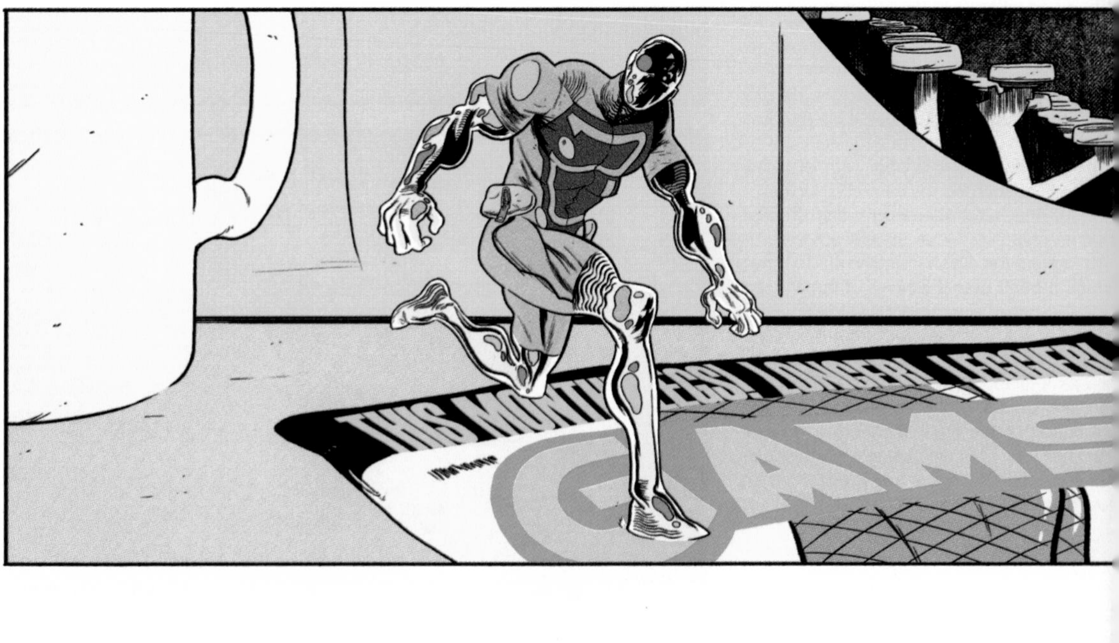

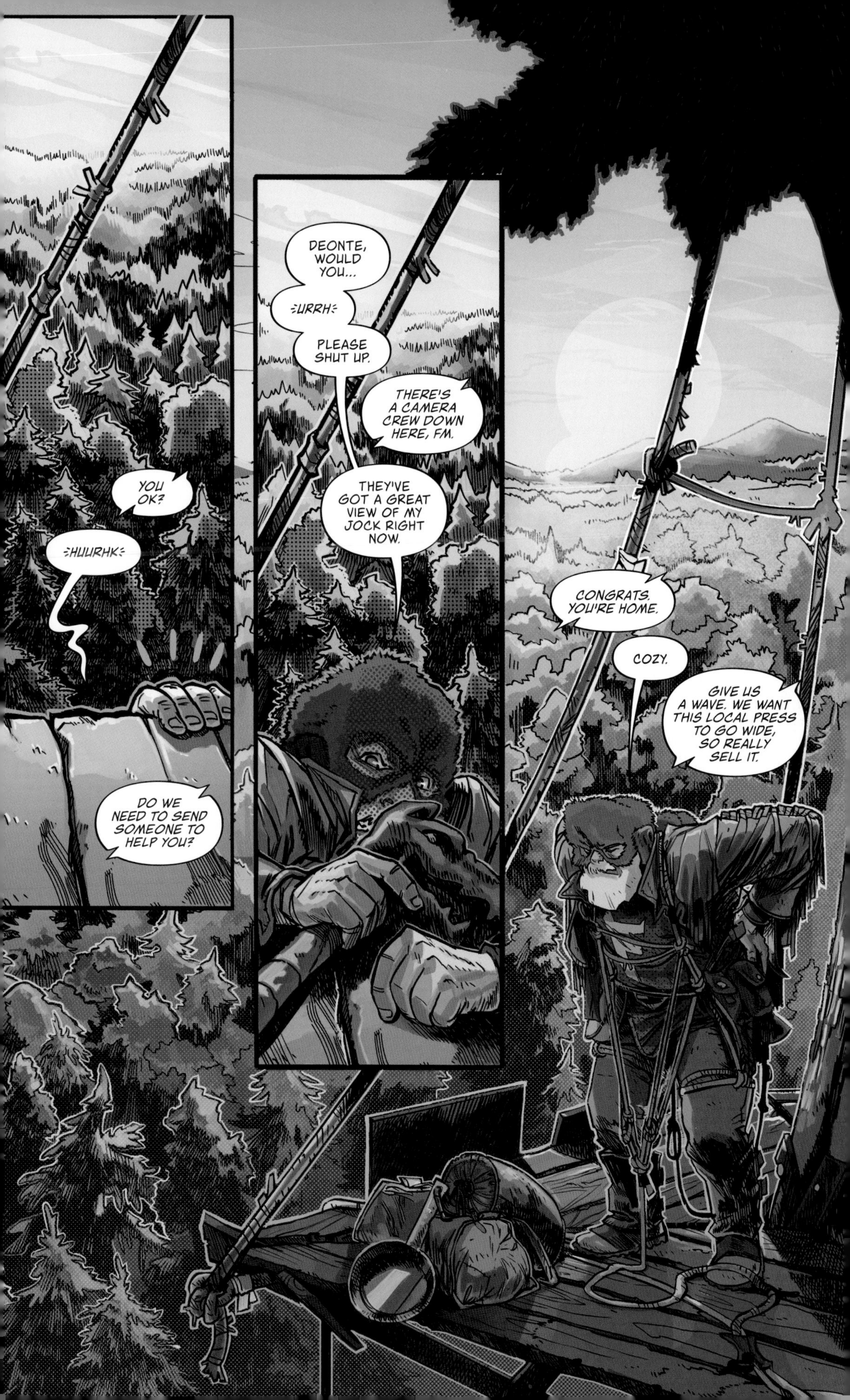
YOU OK?
HUURHK
DO WE NEED TO SEND SOMEONE TO HELP YOU?
DEONTE, WOULD YOU...
URRH
PLEASE SHUT UP.
THERE'S A CAMERA CREW DOWN HERE, FM.
THEY'VE GOT A GREAT VIEW OF MY JOCK RIGHT NOW.
CONGRATS. YOU'RE HOME.
COZY.
GIVE US A WAVE. WE WANT THIS LOCAL PRESS TO GO WIDE, SO REALLY SELL IT.

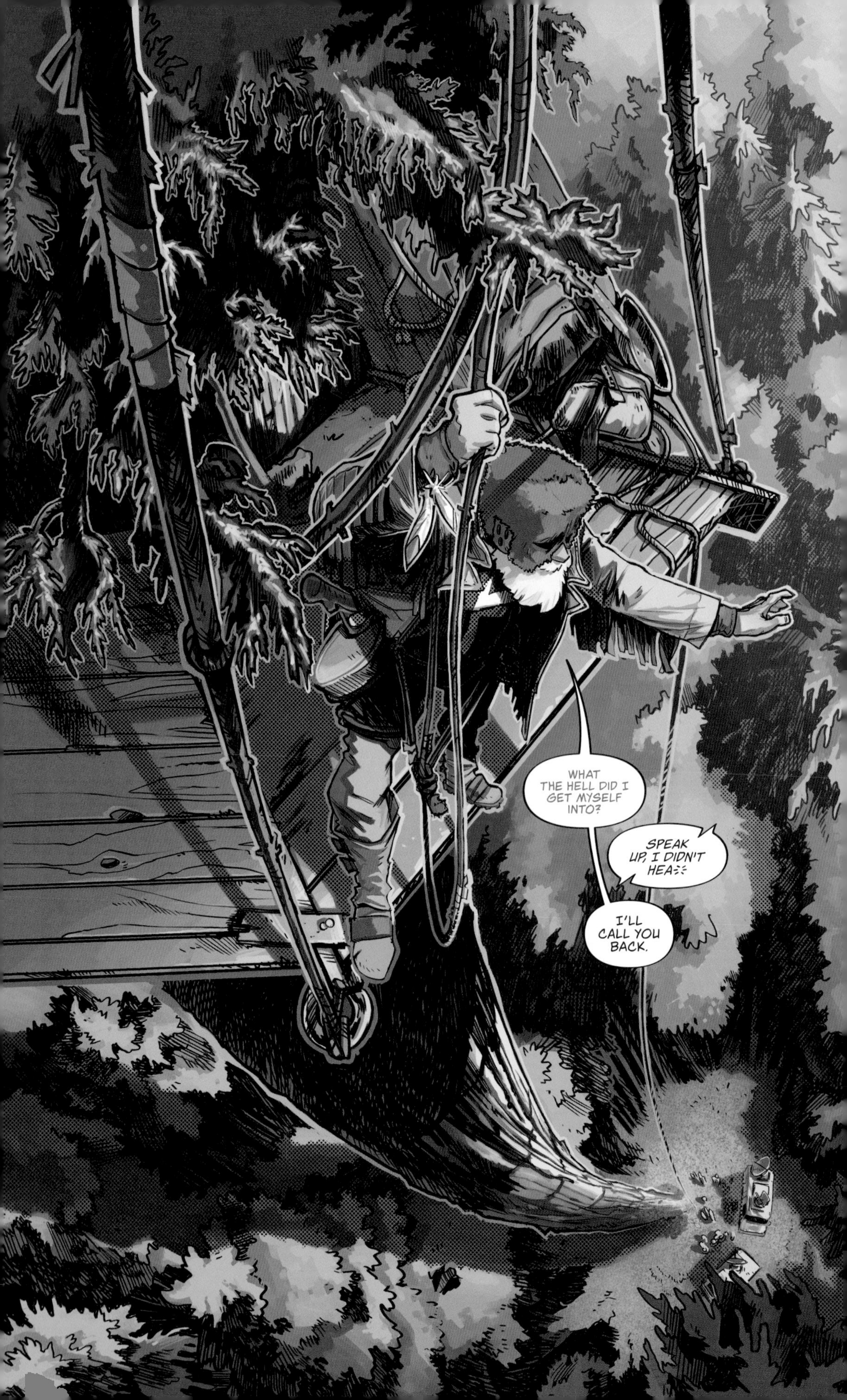
WHAT THE HELL DID I GET MYSELF INTO?
SPEAK UP, I DIDN'T HEA--
I'LL CALL YOU BACK.

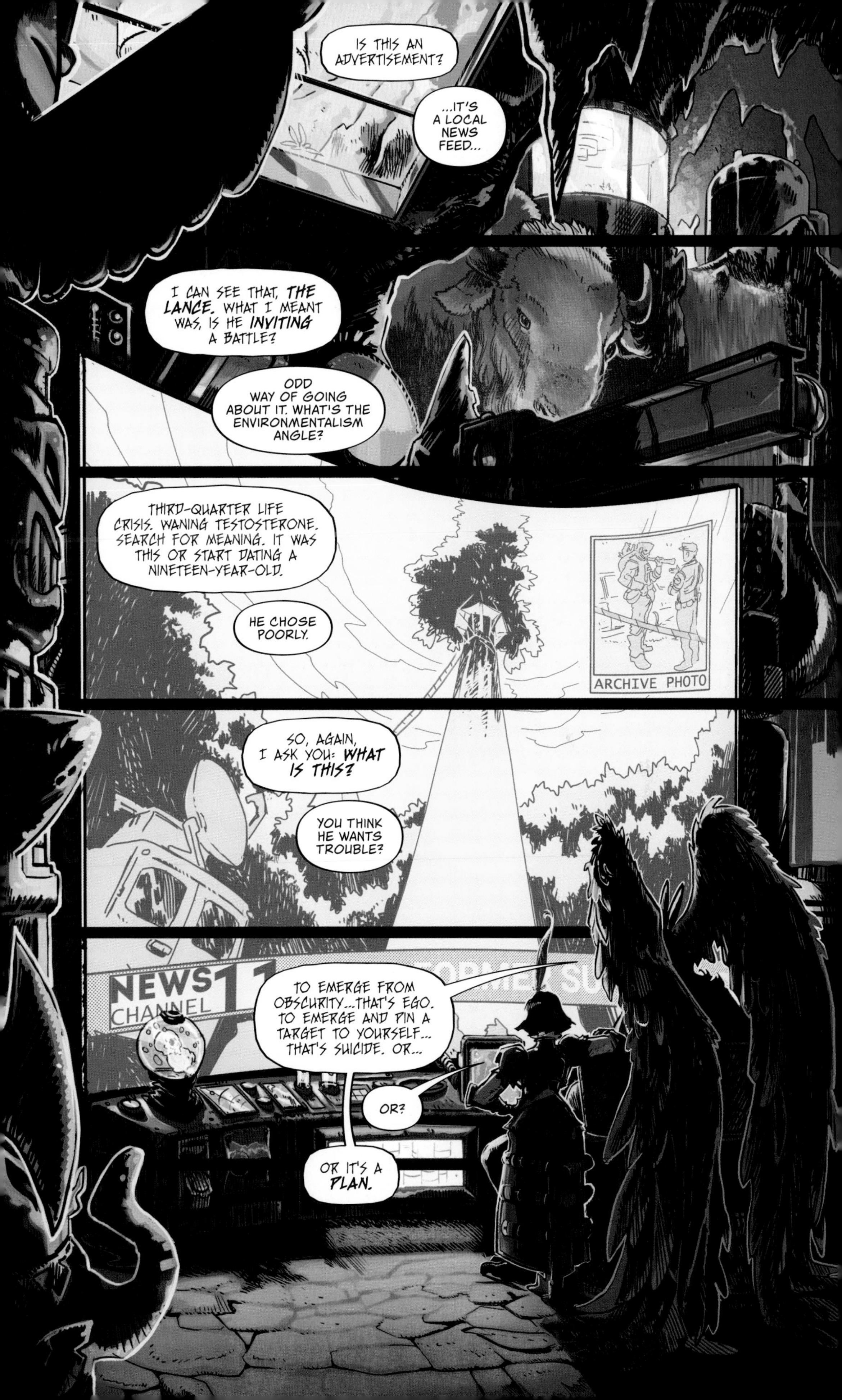
IS THIS AN ADVERTISEMENT?
...IT'S A LOCAL NEWS FEED...
I CAN SEE THAT, THE LANCE. WHAT I MEANT WAS, IS HE INVITING A BATTLE?
ODD WAY OF GOING ABOUT IT. WHAT'S THE ENVIRONMENTALISM ANGLE?
THIRD-QUARTER LIFE CRISIS. WANING TESTOSTERONE. SEARCH FOR MEANING. IT WAS THIS OR START DATING A NINETEEN-YEAR-OLD.
HE CHOSE POORLY.
ARCHIVE PHOTO
SO, AGAIN, I ASK YOU: WHAT IS THIS?
YOU THINK HE WANTS TROUBLE?
NEWS CHANNEL 11
TO EMERGE FROM OBSCURITY...THAT'S EGO. TO EMERGE AND PIN A TARGET TO YOURSELF... THAT'S SUICIDE. OR...
OR?
OR IT'S A PLAN.

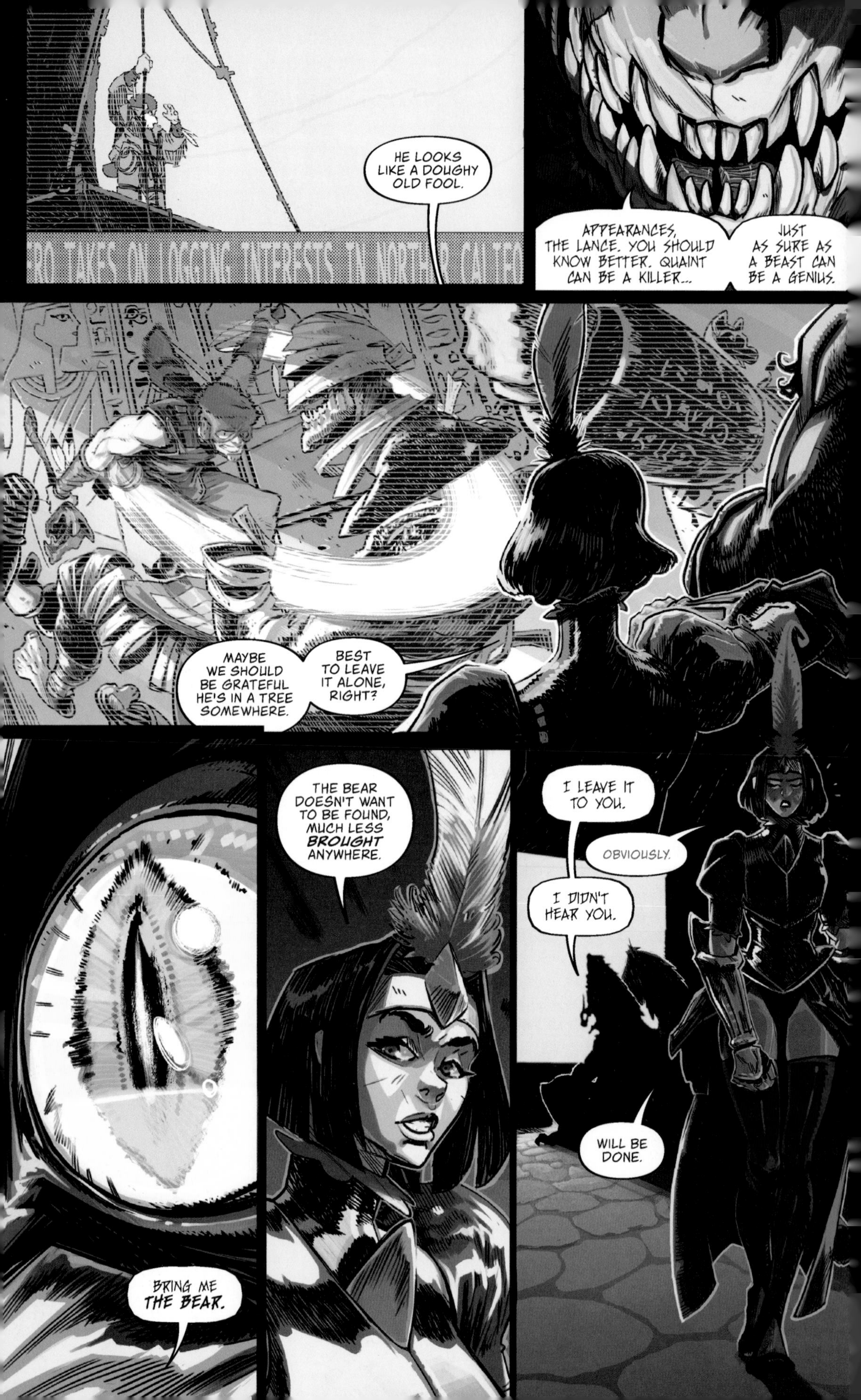

HE LOOKS LIKE A DOUGHY OLD FOOL.
APPEARANCES, THE LANCE. YOU SHOULD KNOW BETTER. QUAINT CAN BE A KILLER...
JUST AS SURE AS A BEAST CAN BE A GENIUS.
MAYBE WE SHOULD BE GRATEFUL HE'S IN A TREE SOMEWHERE.
BEST TO LEAVE IT ALONE, RIGHT?
BRING ME *THE BEAR.*
THE BEAR DOESN'T WANT TO BE FOUND, MUCH LESS ***BROUGHT*** ANYWHERE.
I LEAVE IT TO YOU.
OBVIOUSLY.
I DIDN'T HEAR YOU.
WILL BE DONE.

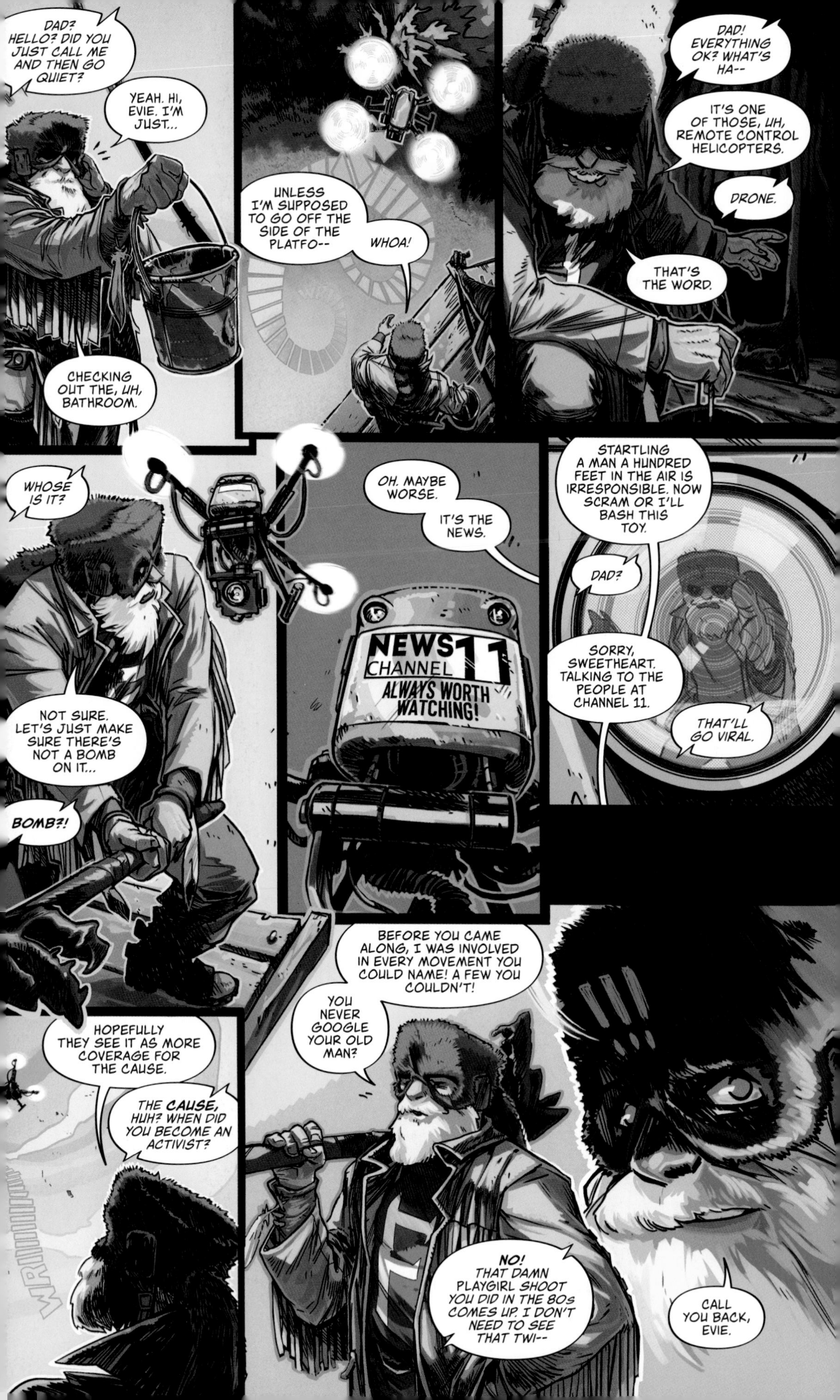
DAD? HELLO? DID YOU JUST CALL ME AND THEN GO QUIET?
YEAH. HI, EVIE. I'M JUST...
CHECKING OUT THE, UH, BATHROOM.
UNLESS I'M SUPPOSED TO GO OFF THE SIDE OF THE PLATFO--
WHOA!
DAD! EVERYTHING OK? WHAT'S HA--
IT'S ONE OF THOSE, UH, REMOTE CONTROL HELICOPTERS.
DRONE.
THAT'S THE WORD.
WHOSE IS IT?
NOT SURE. LET'S JUST MAKE SURE THERE'S NOT A BOMB ON IT...
BOMB?!
OH. MAYBE WORSE.
IT'S THE NEWS.
NEWS CHANNEL 11
ALWAYS WORTH WATCHING!
STARTLING A MAN A HUNDRED FEET IN THE AIR IS IRRESPONSIBLE. NOW SCRAM OR I'LL BASH THIS TOY.
DAD?
SORRY, SWEETHEART. TALKING TO THE PEOPLE AT CHANNEL 11.
THAT'LL GO VIRAL.
HOPEFULLY THEY SEE IT AS MORE COVERAGE FOR THE CAUSE.
THE CAUSE, HUH? WHEN DID YOU BECOME AN ACTIVIST?
WRRRRRRR
BEFORE YOU CAME ALONG, I WAS INVOLVED IN EVERY MOVEMENT YOU COULD NAME! A FEW YOU COULDN'T!
YOU NEVER GOOGLE YOUR OLD MAN?
NO! THAT DAMN PLAYGIRL SHOOT YOU DID IN THE 80s COMES UP. I DON'T NEED TO SEE THAT TWI--
CALL YOU BACK, EVIE.

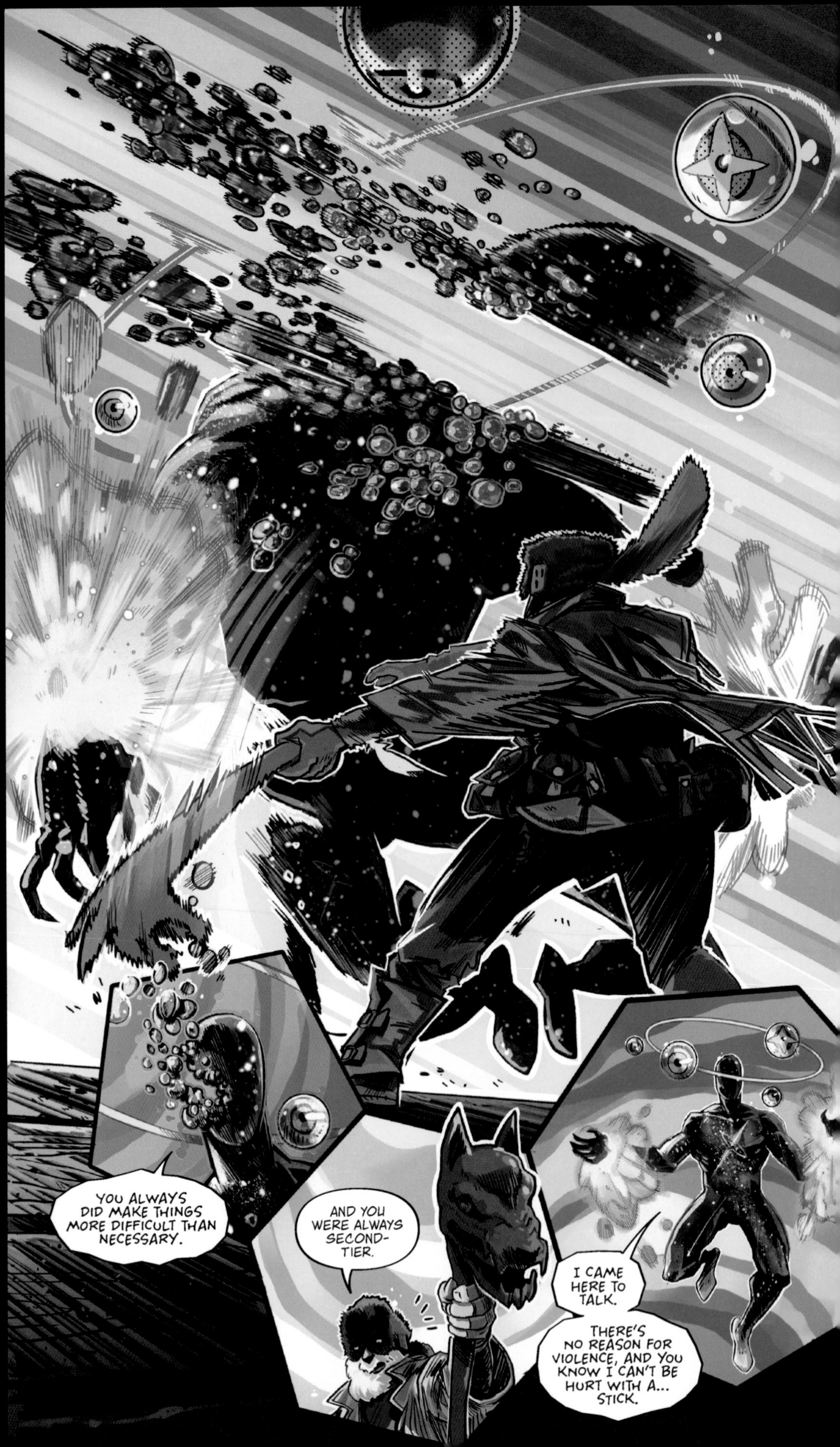
YOU ALWAYS DID MAKE THINGS MORE DIFFICULT THAN NECESSARY.
AND YOU WERE ALWAYS SECOND-TIER.
I CAME HERE TO TALK.
THERE'S NO REASON FOR VIOLENCE, AND YOU KNOW I CAN'T BE HURT WITH A... STICK.

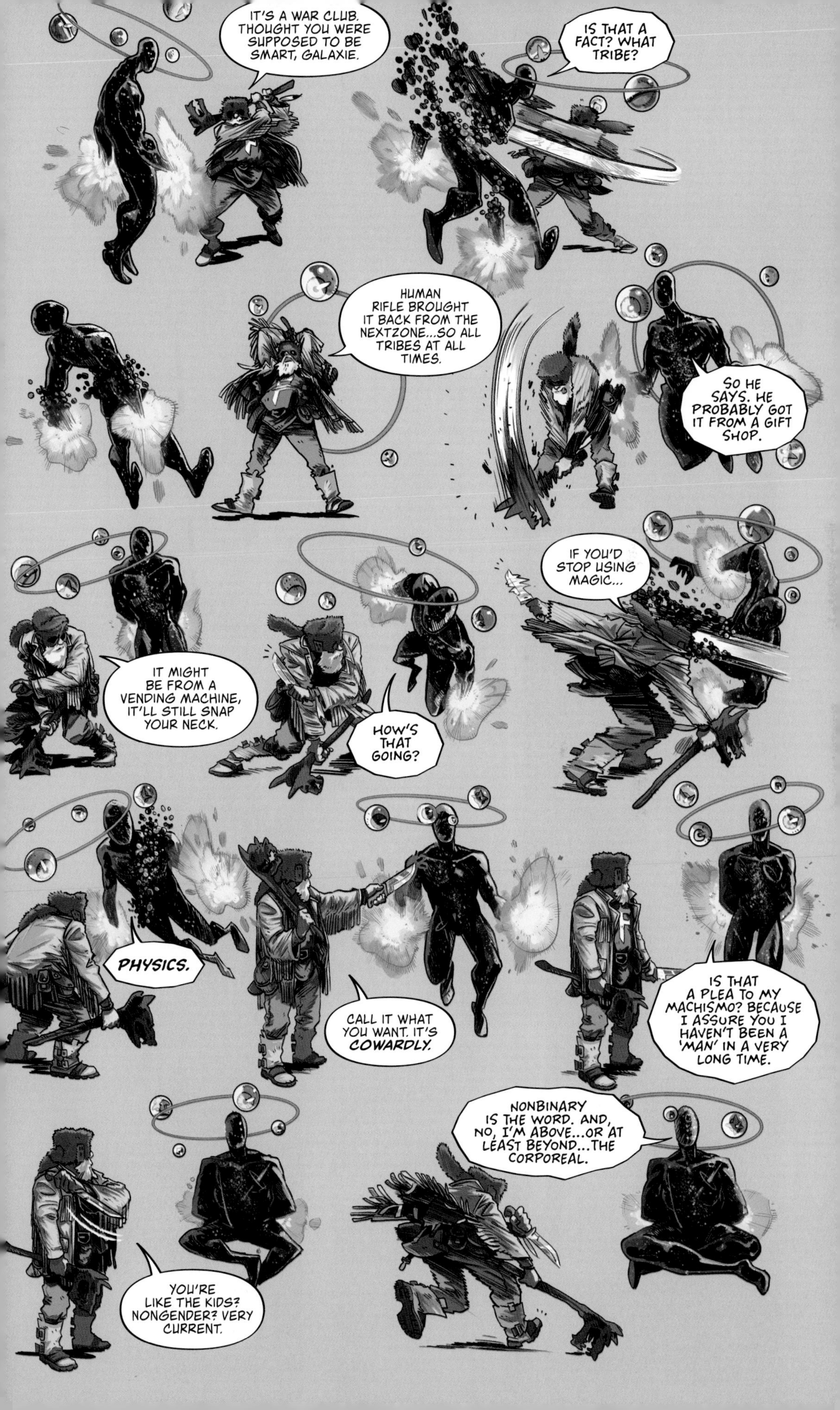
IT'S A WAR CLUB. THOUGHT YOU WERE SUPPOSED TO BE SMART, GALAXIE.
IS THAT A FACT? WHAT TRIBE?
HUMAN RIFLE BROUGHT IT BACK FROM THE NEXTZONE...SO ALL TRIBES AT ALL TIMES.
SO HE SAYS. HE PROBABLY GOT IT FROM A GIFT SHOP.
IT MIGHT BE FROM A VENDING MACHINE, IT'LL STILL SNAP YOUR NECK.
HOW'S THAT GOING?
IF YOU'D STOP USING MAGIC...
PHYSICS.
CALL IT WHAT YOU WANT. IT'S COWARDLY.
IS THAT A PLEA TO MY MACHISMO? BECAUSE I ASSURE YOU I HAVEN'T BEEN A 'MAN' IN A VERY LONG TIME.
YOU'RE LIKE THE KIDS? NONGENDER? VERY CURRENT.
NONBINARY IS THE WORD. AND, NO, I'M ABOVE...OR AT LEAST BEYOND...THE CORPOREAL.

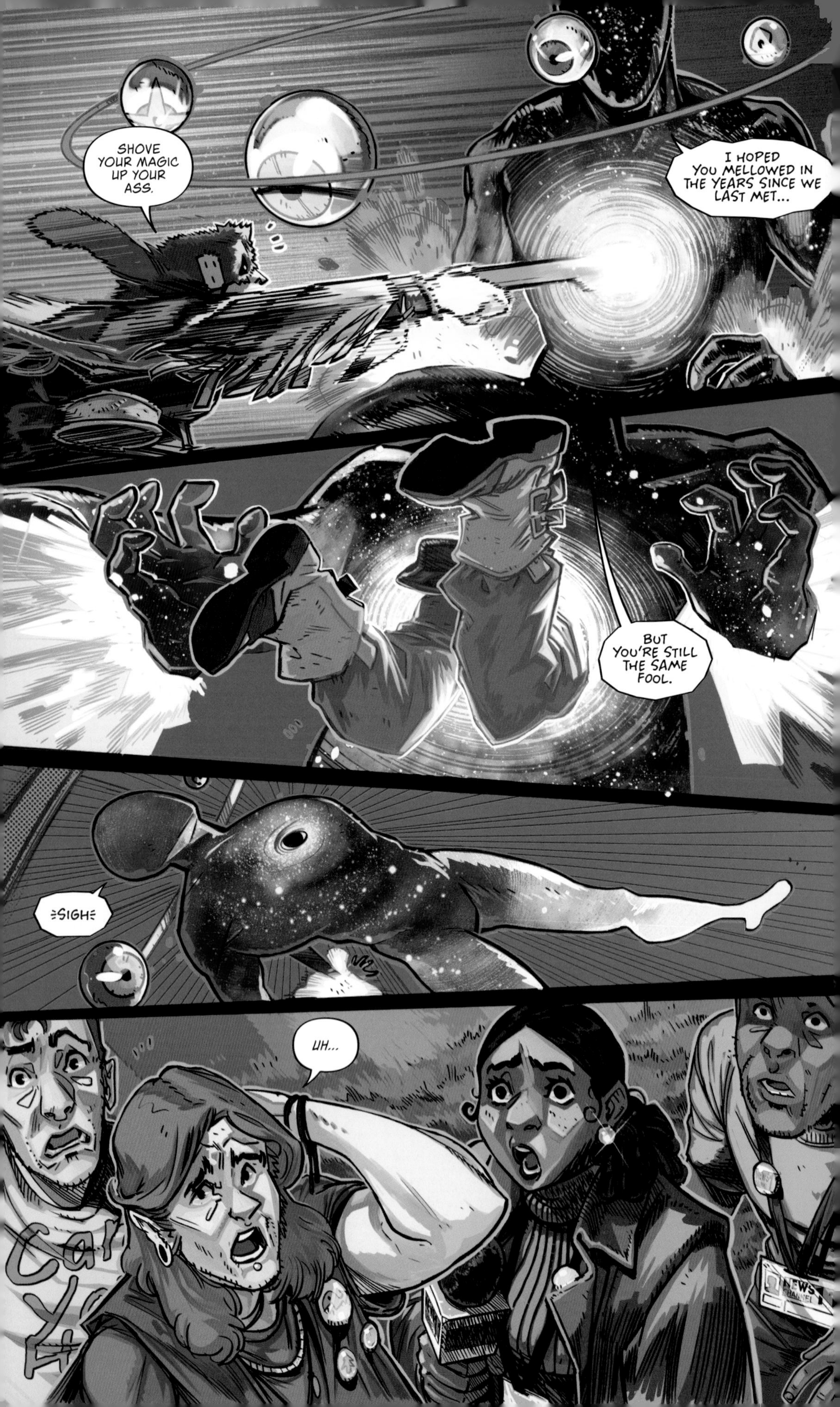
SHOVE YOUR MAGIC UP YOUR ASS.
I HOPED YOU MELLOWED IN THE YEARS SINCE WE LAST MET...
BUT YOU'RE STILL THE SAME FOOL.
=SIGH=
UH...

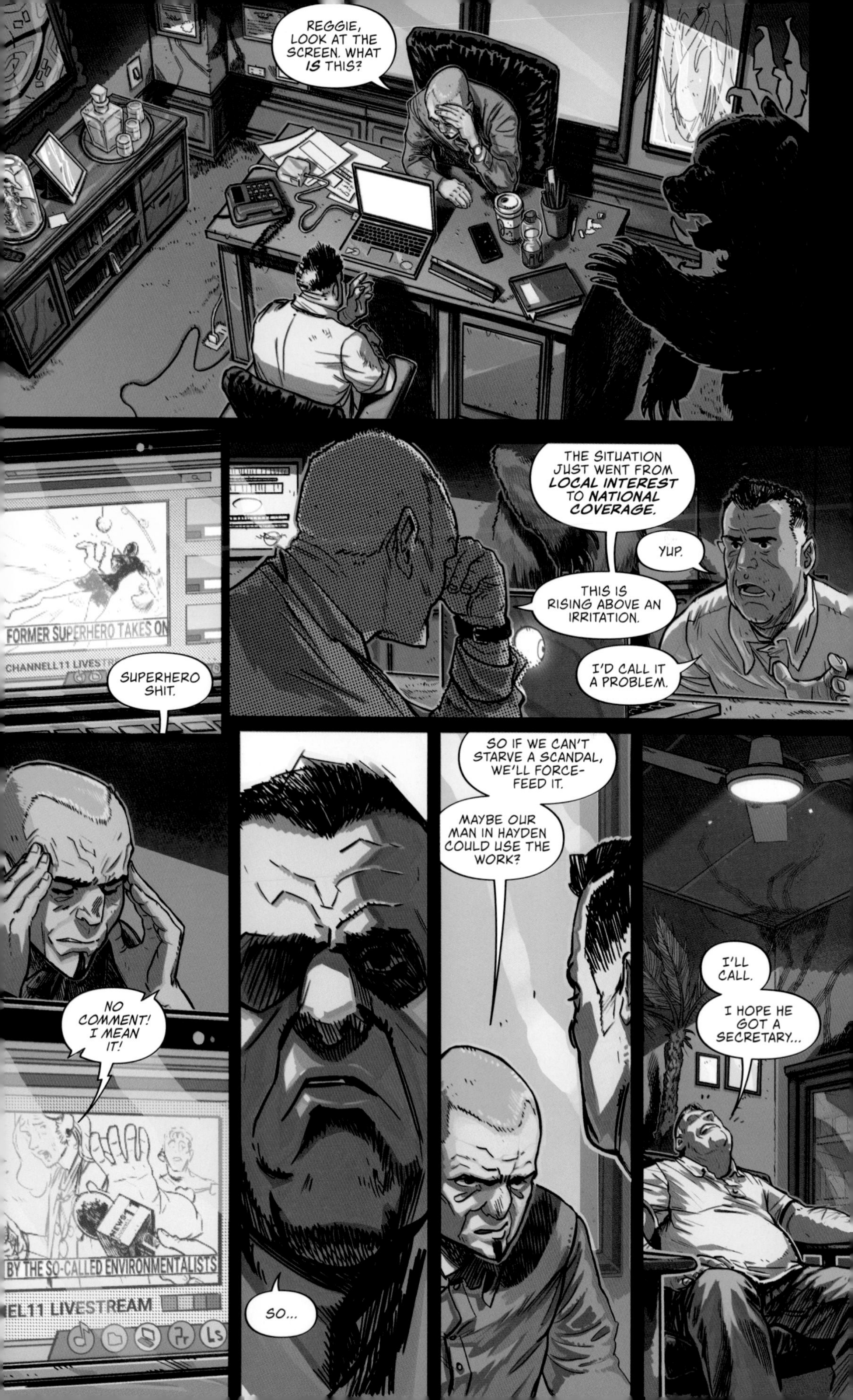
REGGIE, LOOK AT THE SCREEN. WHAT IS THIS?
FORMER SUPERHERO TAKES ON
CHANNELL11 LIVESTR
SUPERHERO SHIT.
THE SITUATION JUST WENT FROM LOCAL INTEREST TO NATIONAL COVERAGE.
YUP.
THIS IS RISING ABOVE AN IRRITATION.
I'D CALL IT A PROBLEM.
NO COMMENT! I MEAN IT!
BY THE SO-CALLED ENVIRONMENTALISTS
EL11 LIVESTREAM
SO...
SO IF WE CAN'T STARVE A SCANDAL, WE'LL FORCE-FEED IT.
MAYBE OUR MAN IN HAYDEN COULD USE THE WORK?
I'LL CALL.
I HOPE HE GOT A SECRETARY...

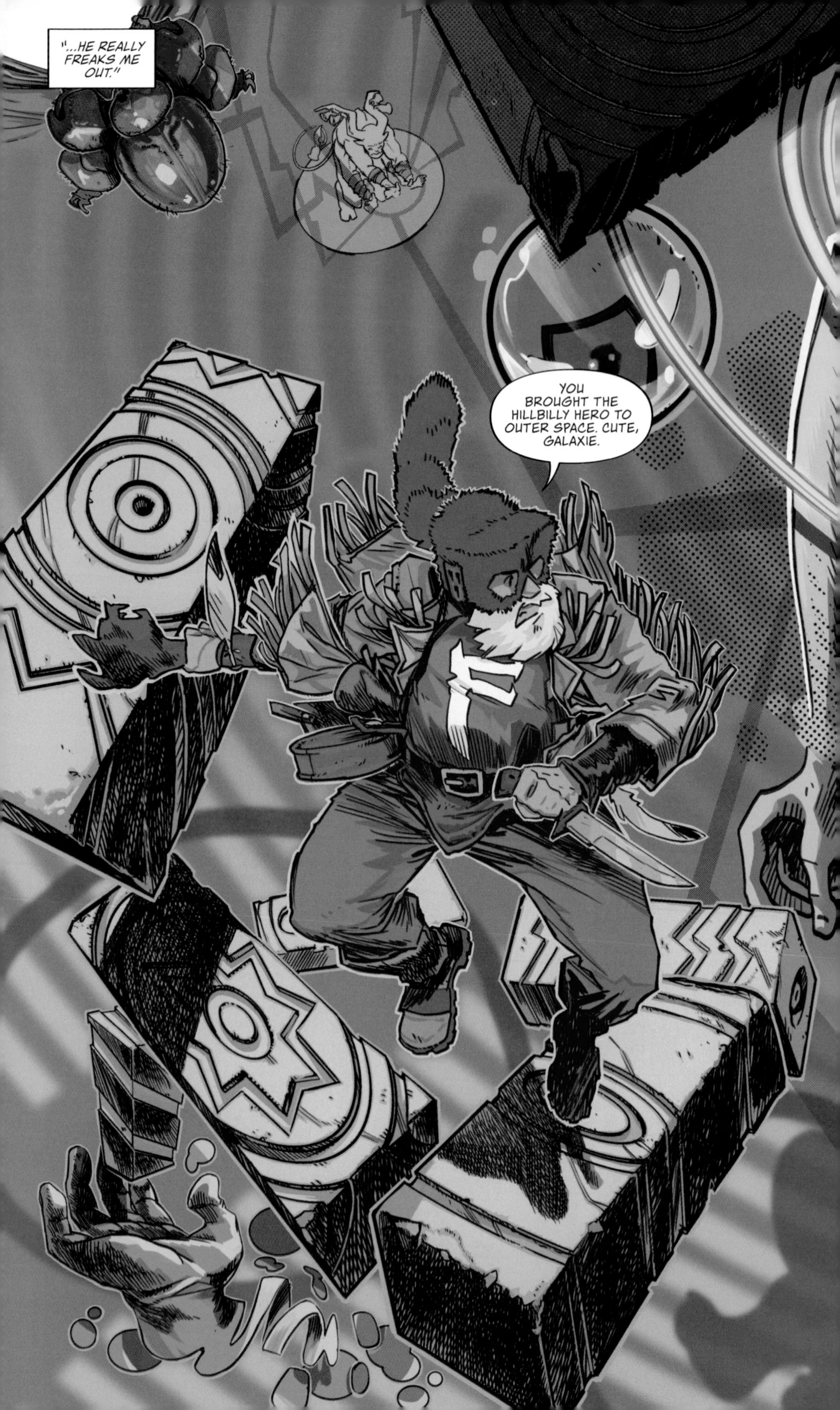
"...HE REALLY FREAKS ME OUT."
YOU BROUGHT THE HILLBILLY HERO TO OUTER SPACE. CUTE, GALAXIE.

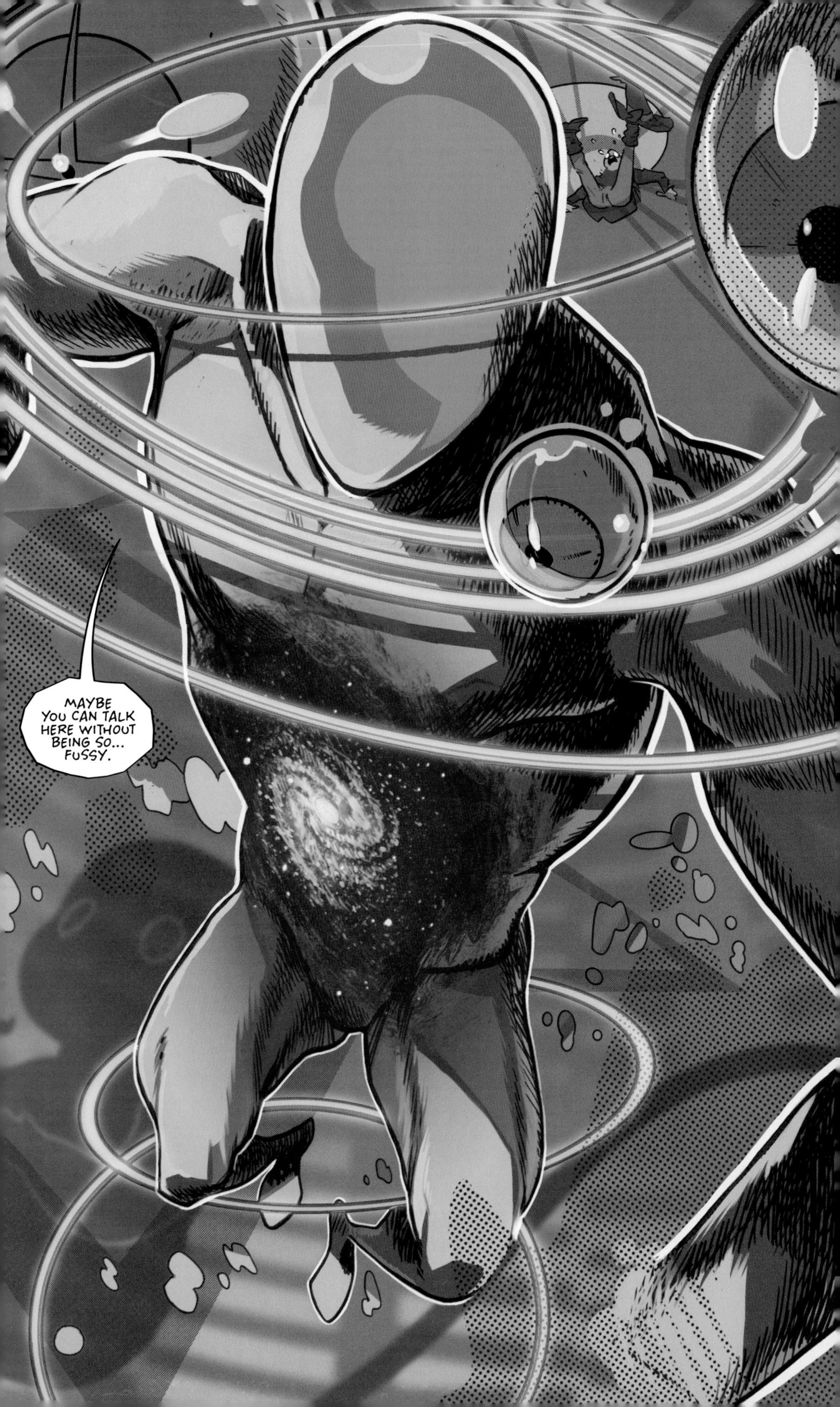
MAYBE YOU CAN TALK HERE WITHOUT BEING SO... FUSSY.

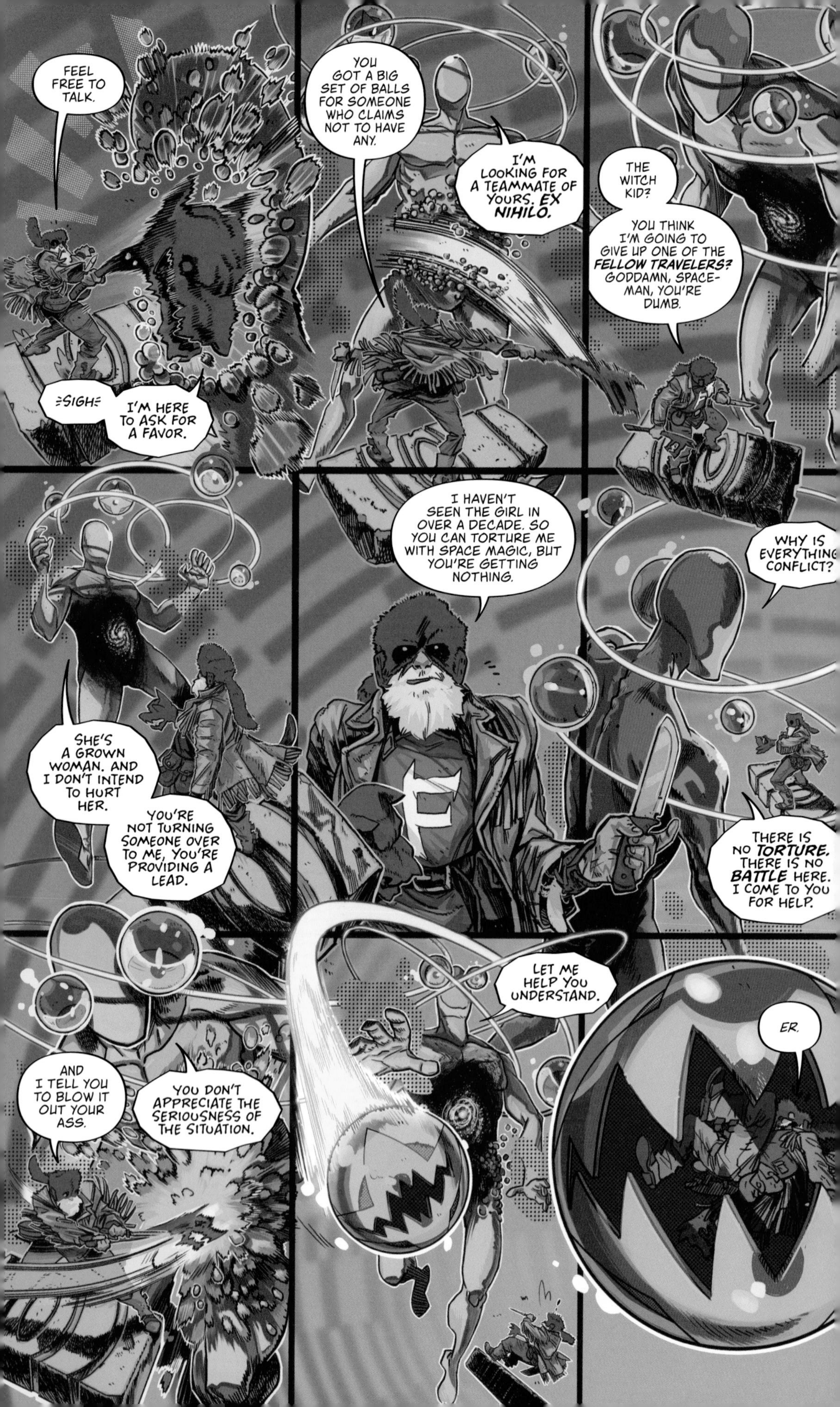
FEEL FREE TO TALK.
≡SIGH≡
I'M HERE TO ASK FOR A FAVOR.
YOU GOT A BIG SET OF BALLS FOR SOMEONE WHO CLAIMS NOT TO HAVE ANY.
I'M LOOKING FOR A TEAMMATE OF YOURS. EX NIHILO.
THE WITCH KID?
YOU THINK I'M GOING TO GIVE UP ONE OF THE FELLOW TRAVELERS? GODDAMN, SPACE-MAN, YOU'RE DUMB.
SHE'S A GROWN WOMAN. AND I DON'T INTEND TO HURT HER.
YOU'RE NOT TURNING SOMEONE OVER TO ME, YOU'RE PROVIDING A LEAD.
I HAVEN'T SEEN THE GIRL IN OVER A DECADE. SO YOU CAN TORTURE ME WITH SPACE MAGIC, BUT YOU'RE GETTING NOTHING.
WHY IS EVERYTHING CONFLICT?
THERE IS NO TORTURE. THERE IS NO BATTLE HERE. I COME TO YOU FOR HELP.
AND I TELL YOU TO BLOW IT OUT YOUR ASS.
YOU DON'T APPRECIATE THE SERIOUSNESS OF THE SITUATION.
LET ME HELP YOU UNDERSTAND.
ER.

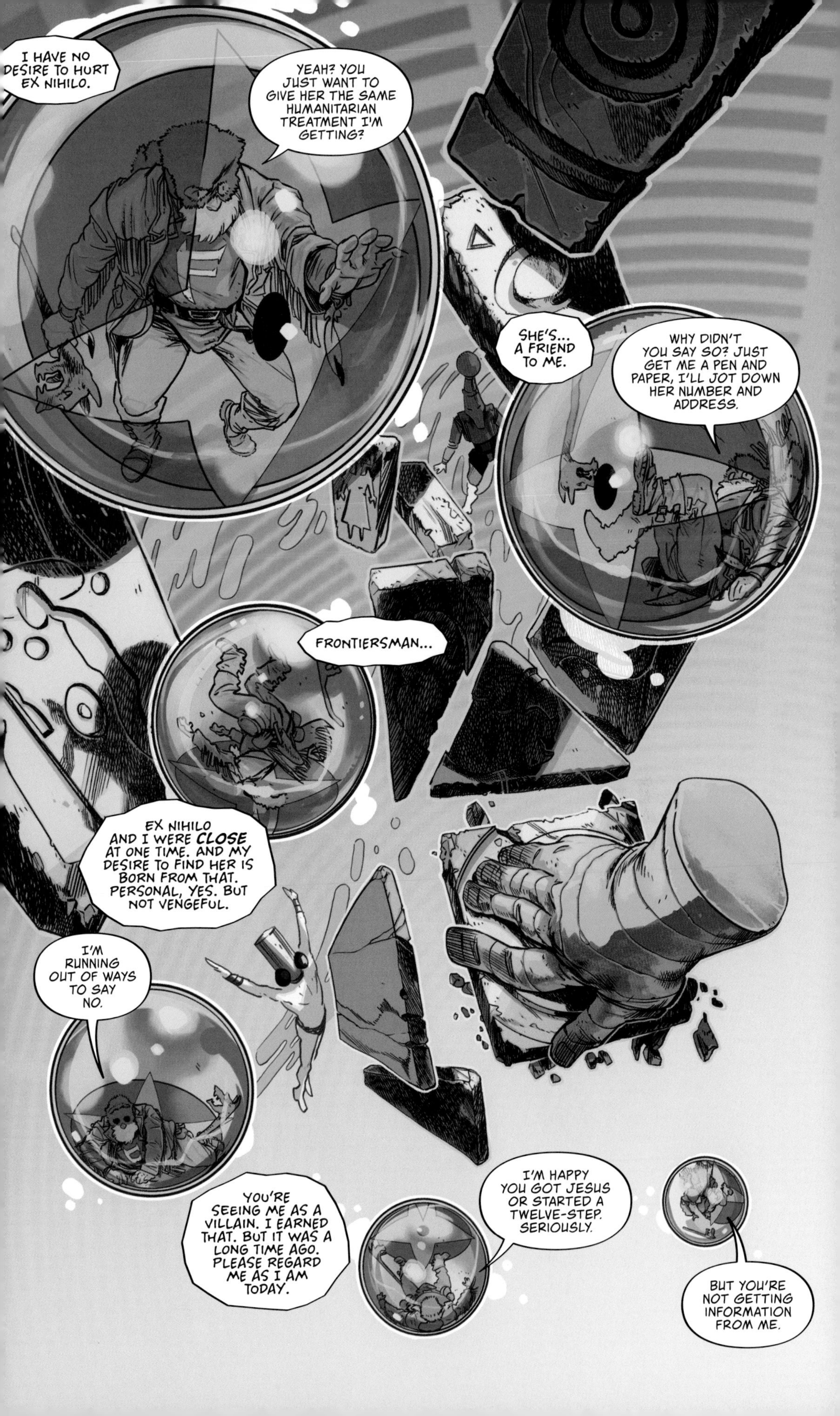
I HAVE NO DESIRE TO HURT EX NIHILO.
YEAH? YOU JUST WANT TO GIVE HER THE SAME HUMANITARIAN TREATMENT I'M GETTING?
SHE'S... A FRIEND TO ME.
WHY DIDN'T YOU SAY SO? JUST GET ME A PEN AND PAPER, I'LL JOT DOWN HER NUMBER AND ADDRESS.
FRONTIERSMAN...
EX NIHILO AND I WERE CLOSE AT ONE TIME. AND MY DESIRE TO FIND HER IS BORN FROM THAT. PERSONAL, YES. BUT NOT VENGEFUL.
I'M RUNNING OUT OF WAYS TO SAY NO.
YOU'RE SEEING ME AS A VILLAIN. I EARNED THAT. BUT IT WAS A LONG TIME AGO. PLEASE REGARD ME AS I AM TODAY.
I'M HAPPY YOU GOT JESUS OR STARTED A TWELVE-STEP. SERIOUSLY.
BUT YOU'RE NOT GETTING INFORMATION FROM ME.

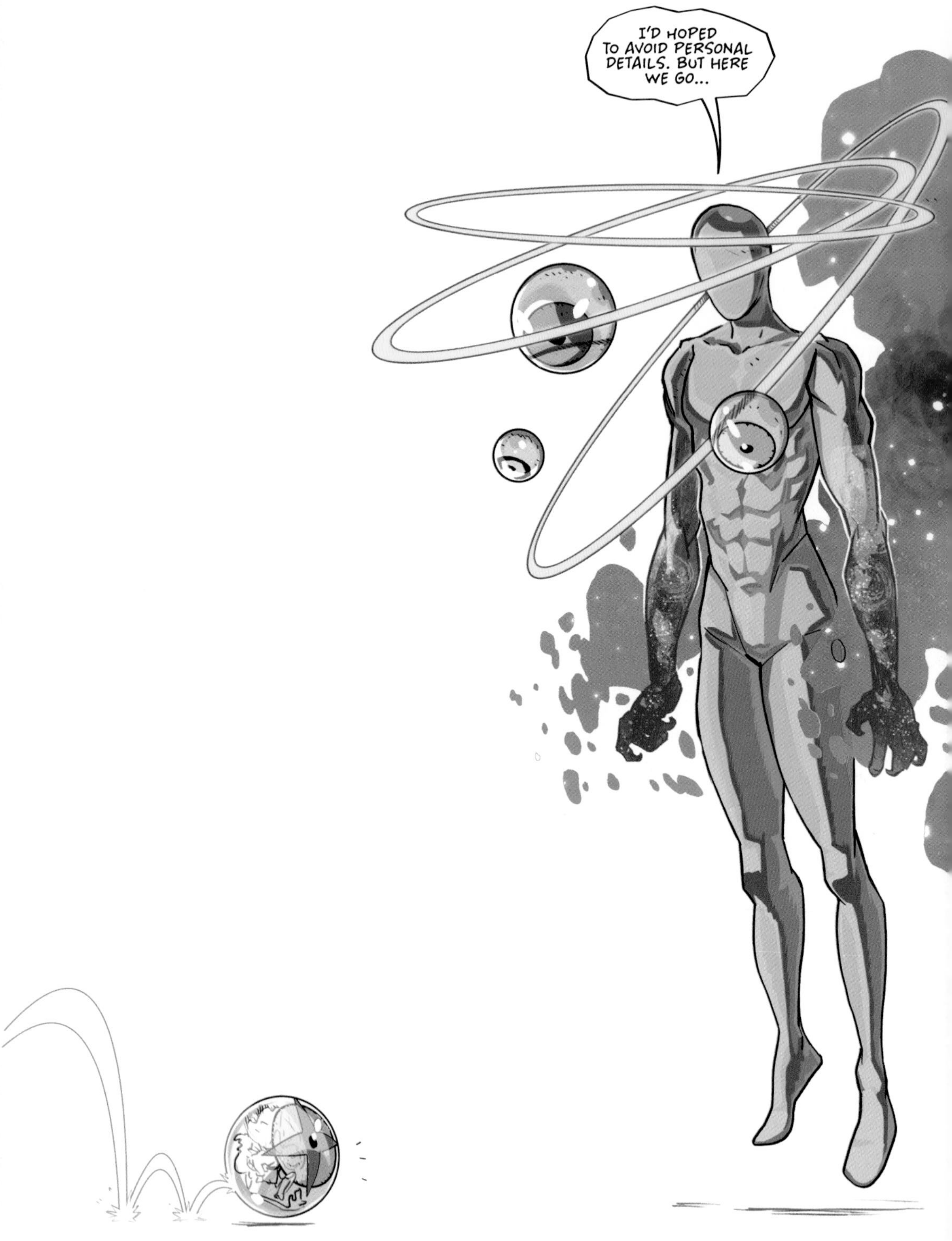
I'D HOPED TO AVOID PERSONAL DETAILS. BUT HERE WE GO...

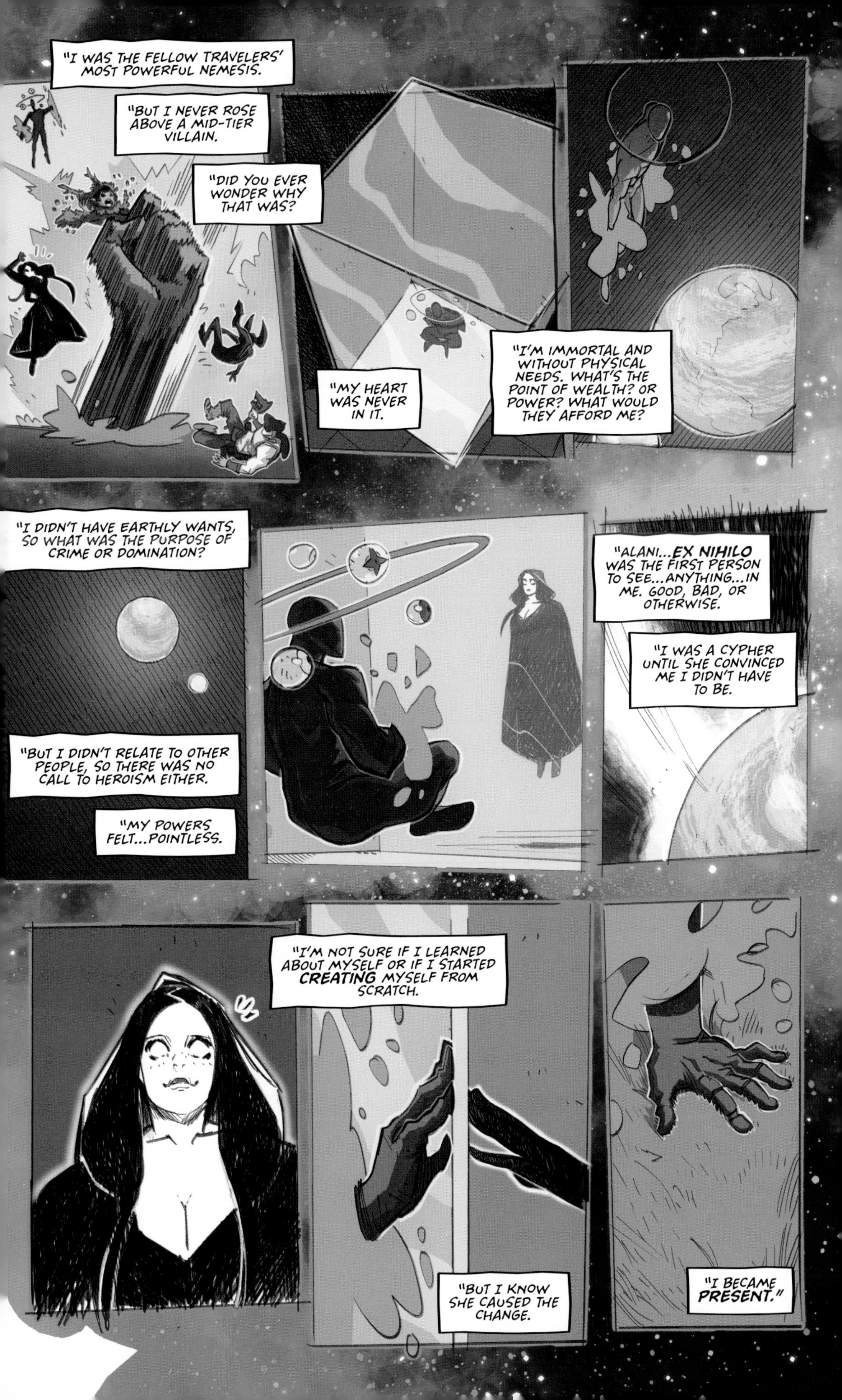
"I WAS THE FELLOW TRAVELERS' MOST POWERFUL NEMESIS.
"BUT I NEVER ROSE ABOVE A MID-TIER VILLAIN.
"DID YOU EVER WONDER WHY THAT WAS?
"MY HEART WAS NEVER IN IT.
"I'M IMMORTAL AND WITHOUT PHYSICAL NEEDS. WHAT'S THE POINT OF WEALTH? OR POWER? WHAT WOULD THEY AFFORD ME?
"I DIDN'T HAVE EARTHLY WANTS, SO WHAT WAS THE PURPOSE OF CRIME OR DOMINATION?
"BUT I DIDN'T RELATE TO OTHER PEOPLE, SO THERE WAS NO CALL TO HEROISM EITHER.
"MY POWERS FELT...POINTLESS.
"ALANI...**EX NIHILO** WAS THE FIRST PERSON TO SEE...ANYTHING...IN ME. GOOD, BAD, OR OTHERWISE.
"I WAS A CYPHER UNTIL SHE CONVINCED ME I DIDN'T HAVE TO BE.
"I'M NOT SURE IF I LEARNED ABOUT MYSELF OR IF I STARTED **CREATING** MYSELF FROM SCRATCH.
"BUT I KNOW SHE CAUSED THE CHANGE.
"I BECAME **PRESENT.**"

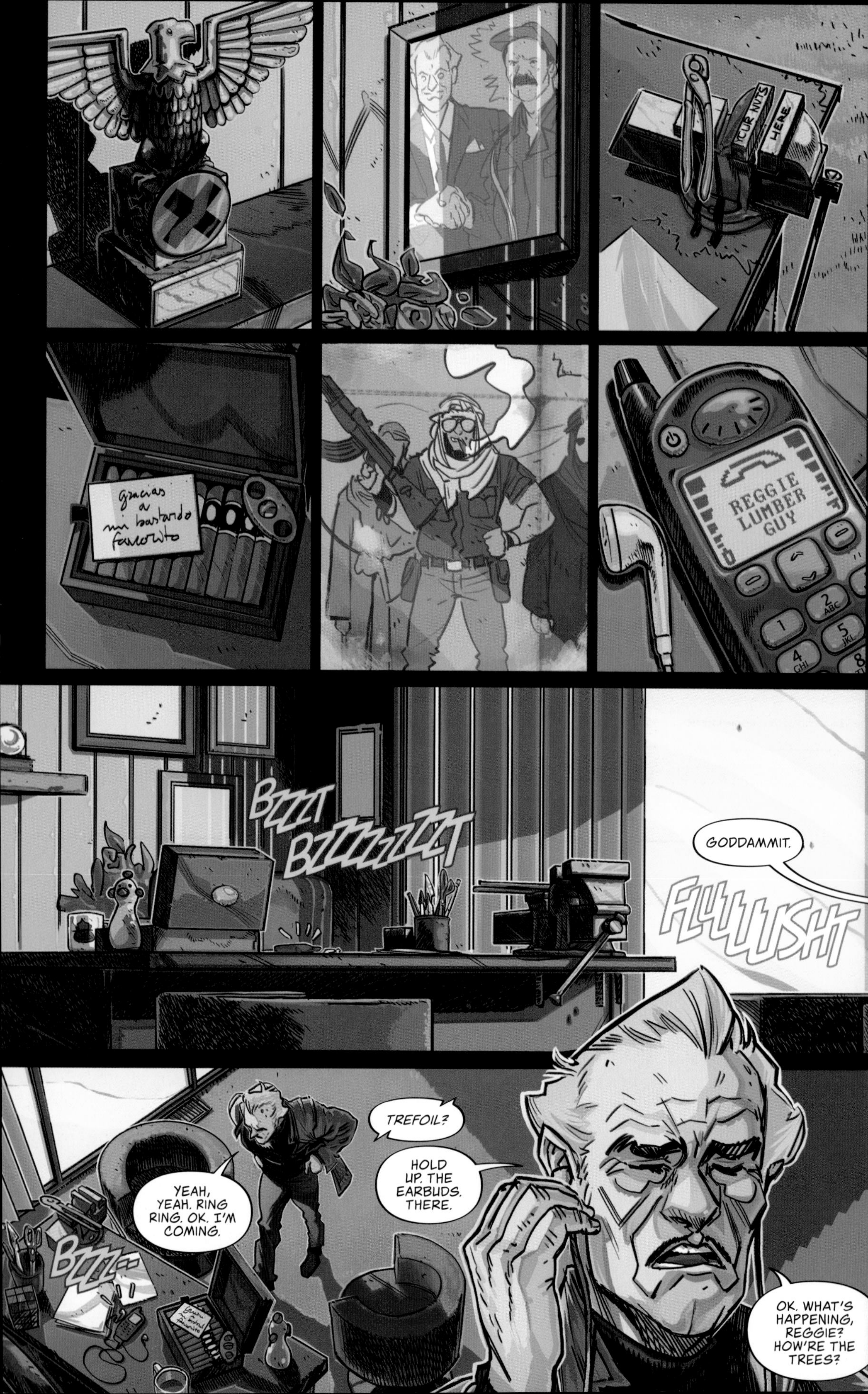
YOUR NUTS
HERE
gracias a mi bastardo favorito
REGGIE LUMBER GUY
BZZZT
BZZZZZZZZT
GODDAMMIT.
FLUUUSHT
YEAH, YEAH. RING RING. OK. I'M COMING.
BZZZ
TREFOIL?
HOLD UP. THE EARBUDS. THERE.
OK. WHAT'S HAPPENING, REGGIE? HOW'RE THE TREES?

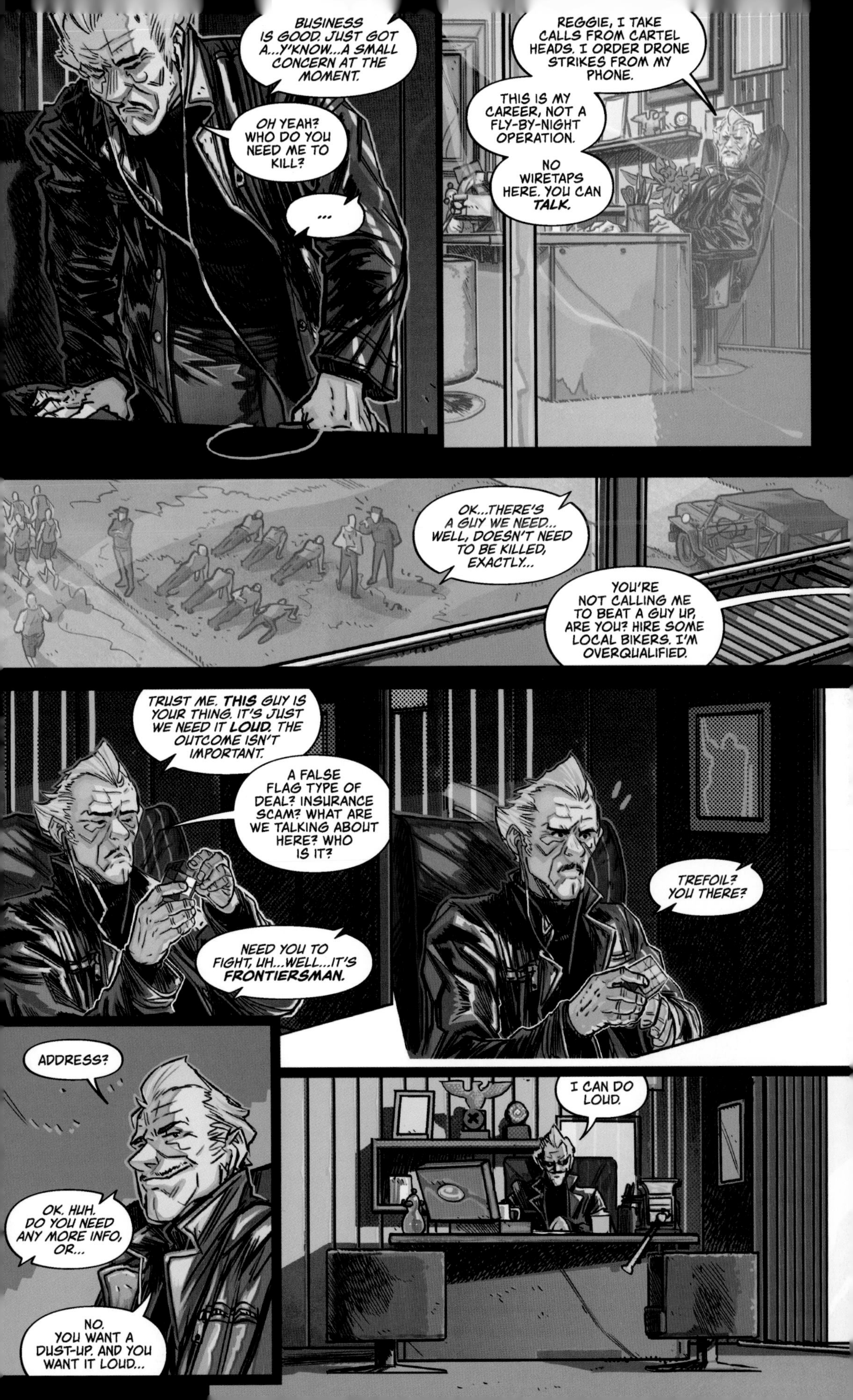
BUSINESS IS GOOD. JUST GOT A...Y'KNOW...A SMALL CONCERN AT THE MOMENT.
OH YEAH? WHO DO YOU NEED ME TO KILL?
...
REGGIE, I TAKE CALLS FROM CARTEL HEADS. I ORDER DRONE STRIKES FROM MY PHONE.
THIS IS MY CAREER, NOT A FLY-BY-NIGHT OPERATION.
NO WIRETAPS HERE. YOU CAN TALK.
OK...THERE'S A GUY WE NEED... WELL, DOESN'T NEED TO BE KILLED, EXACTLY...
YOU'RE NOT CALLING ME TO BEAT A GUY UP, ARE YOU? HIRE SOME LOCAL BIKERS. I'M OVERQUALIFIED.
TRUST ME. THIS GUY IS YOUR THING. IT'S JUST WE NEED IT LOUD. THE OUTCOME ISN'T IMPORTANT.
A FALSE FLAG TYPE OF DEAL? INSURANCE SCAM? WHAT ARE WE TALKING ABOUT HERE? WHO IS IT?
NEED YOU TO FIGHT, UH...WELL...IT'S FRONTIERSMAN.
TREFOIL? YOU THERE?
ADDRESS?
OK. HUH. DO YOU NEED ANY MORE INFO, OR...
NO. YOU WANT A DUST-UP. AND YOU WANT IT LOUD...
I CAN DO LOUD.

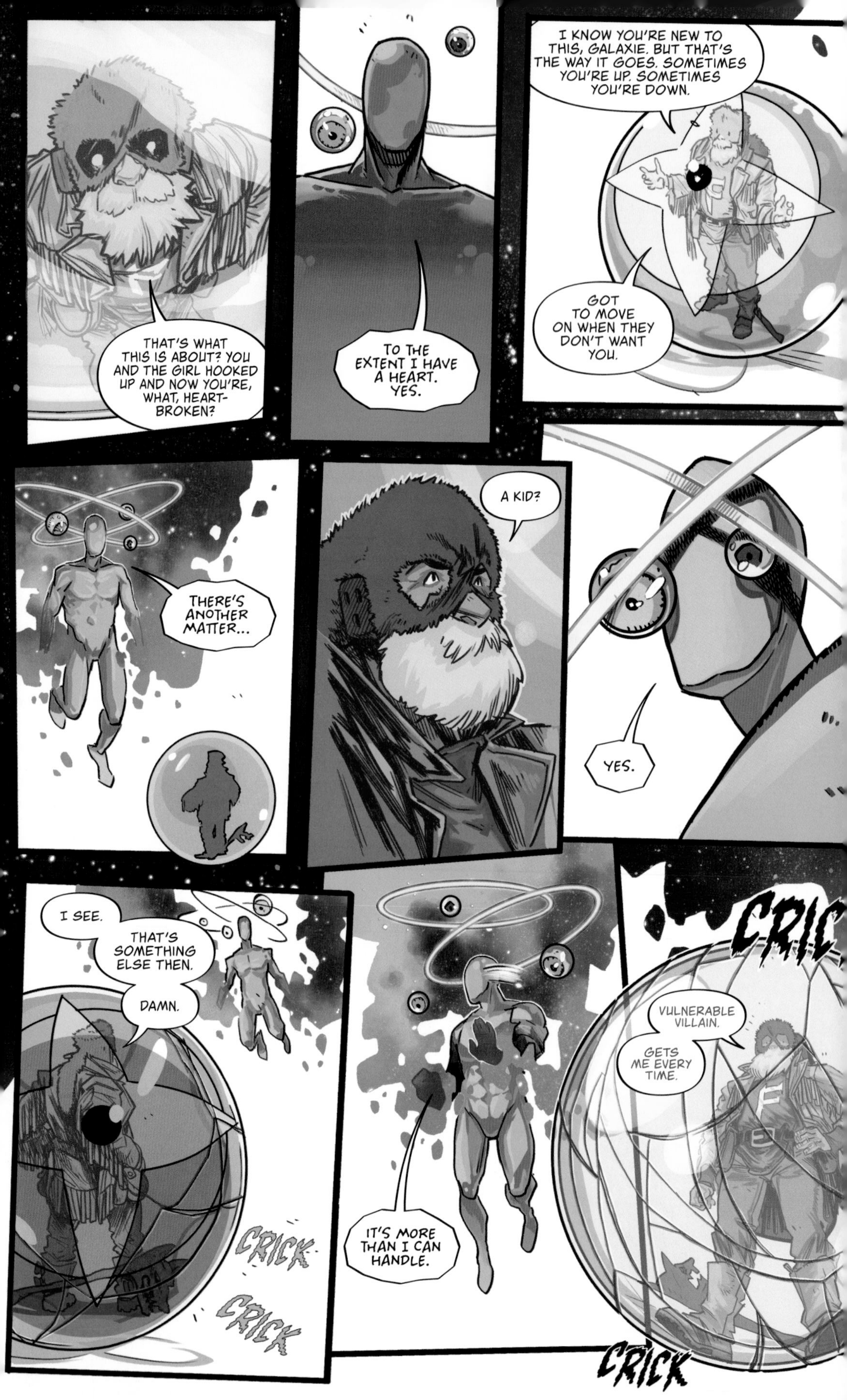
THAT'S WHAT THIS IS ABOUT? YOU AND THE GIRL HOOKED UP AND NOW YOU'RE, WHAT, HEART-BROKEN?
TO THE EXTENT I HAVE A HEART. YES.
I KNOW YOU'RE NEW TO THIS, GALAXIE. BUT THAT'S THE WAY IT GOES. SOMETIMES YOU'RE UP. SOMETIMES YOU'RE DOWN.
GOT TO MOVE ON WHEN THEY DON'T WANT YOU.
THERE'S ANOTHER MATTER...
A KID?
YES.
I SEE.
THAT'S SOMETHING ELSE THEN.
DAMN.
CRICK
CRICK
IT'S MORE THAN I CAN HANDLE.
CRIC
VULNERABLE VILLAIN.
GETS ME EVERY TIME.
CRICK

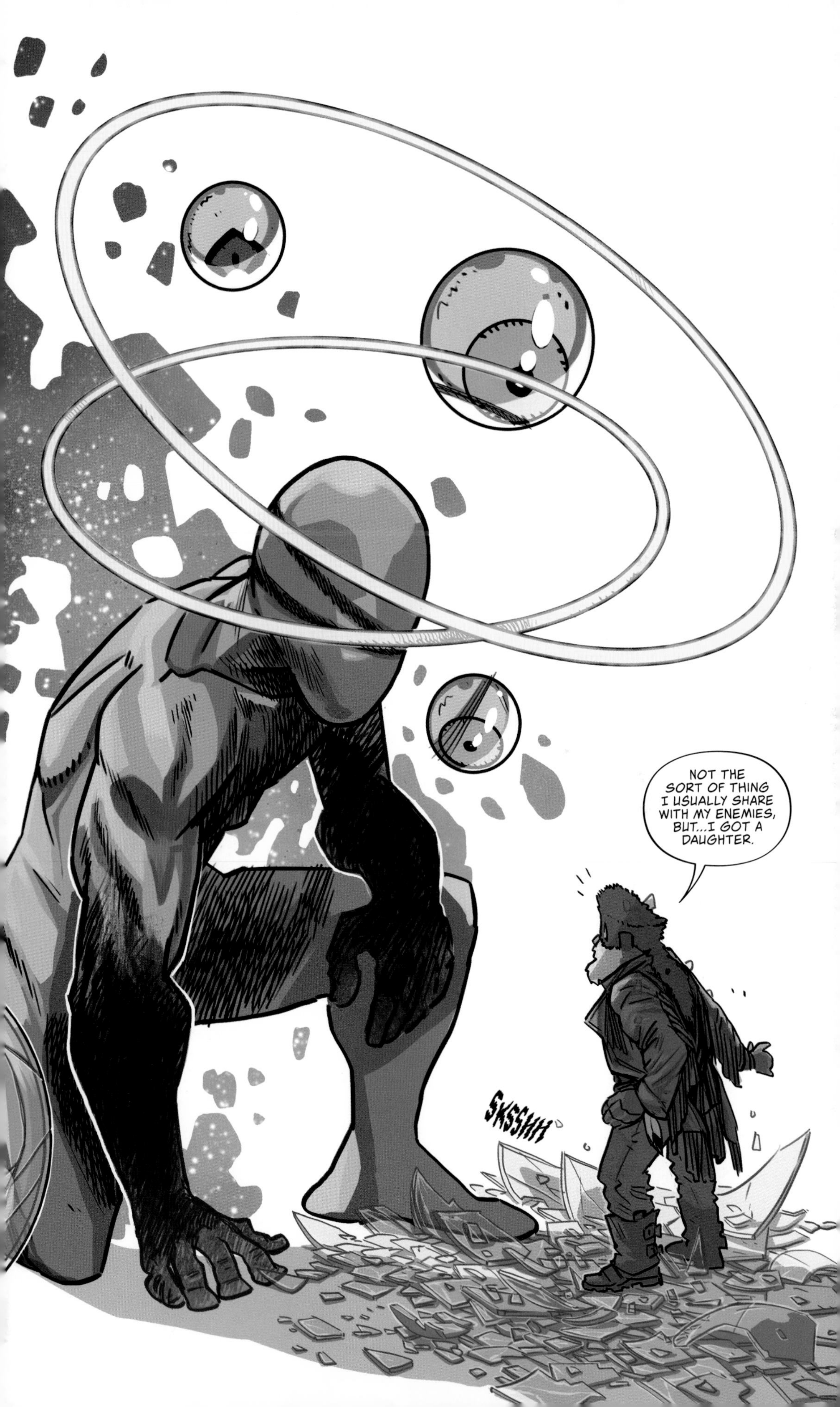
NOT THE SORT OF THING I USUALLY SHARE WITH MY ENEMIES, BUT...I GOT A DAUGHTER.
SKSSHH

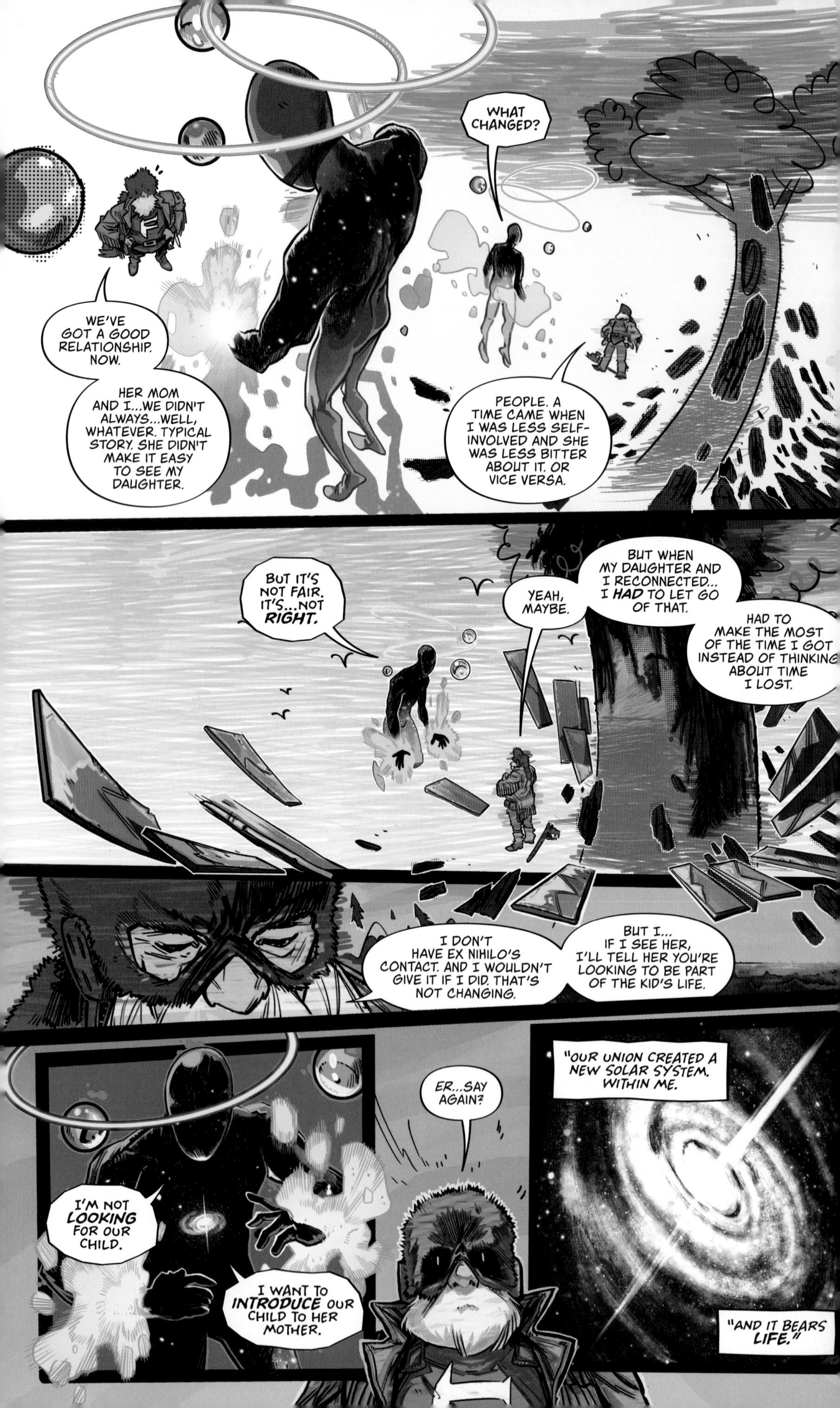

WE'VE GOT A GOOD RELATIONSHIP. NOW.
HER MOM AND I...WE DIDN'T ALWAYS...WELL, WHATEVER. TYPICAL STORY. SHE DIDN'T MAKE IT EASY TO SEE MY DAUGHTER.
WHAT CHANGED?
PEOPLE. A TIME CAME WHEN I WAS LESS SELF-INVOLVED AND SHE WAS LESS BITTER ABOUT IT. OR VICE VERSA.
BUT IT'S NOT FAIR. IT'S...NOT RIGHT.
YEAH, MAYBE.
BUT WHEN MY DAUGHTER AND I RECONNECTED... I HAD TO LET GO OF THAT.
HAD TO MAKE THE MOST OF THE TIME I GOT INSTEAD OF THINKING ABOUT TIME I LOST.
I DON'T HAVE EX NIHILO'S CONTACT. AND I WOULDN'T GIVE IT IF I DID. THAT'S NOT CHANGING.
BUT I... IF I SEE HER, I'LL TELL HER YOU'RE LOOKING TO BE PART OF THE KID'S LIFE.
I'M NOT LOOKING FOR OUR CHILD.
I WANT TO INTRODUCE OUR CHILD TO HER MOTHER.
ER...SAY AGAIN?
"OUR UNION CREATED A NEW SOLAR SYSTEM. WITHIN ME.
"AND IT BEARS LIFE."

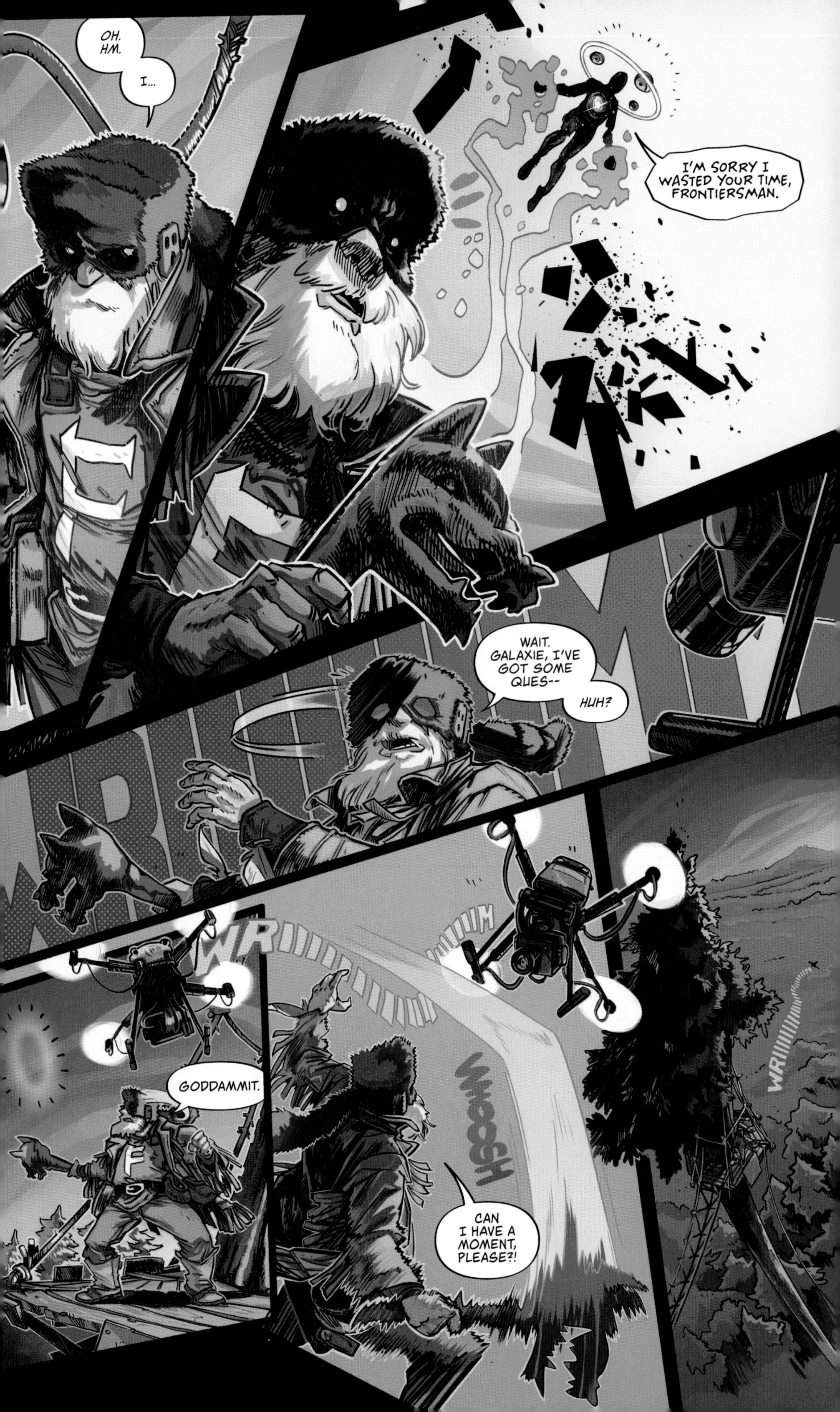

OH. HM.
I...
I'M SORRY I WASTED YOUR TIME, FRONTIERSMAN.
WAIT. GALAXIE, I'VE GOT SOME QUES--
HUH?
WRIIIIIIIIIIM
GODDAMMIT.
WOOOSH
CAN I HAVE A MOMENT, PLEASE?!
WRIIIIIIII

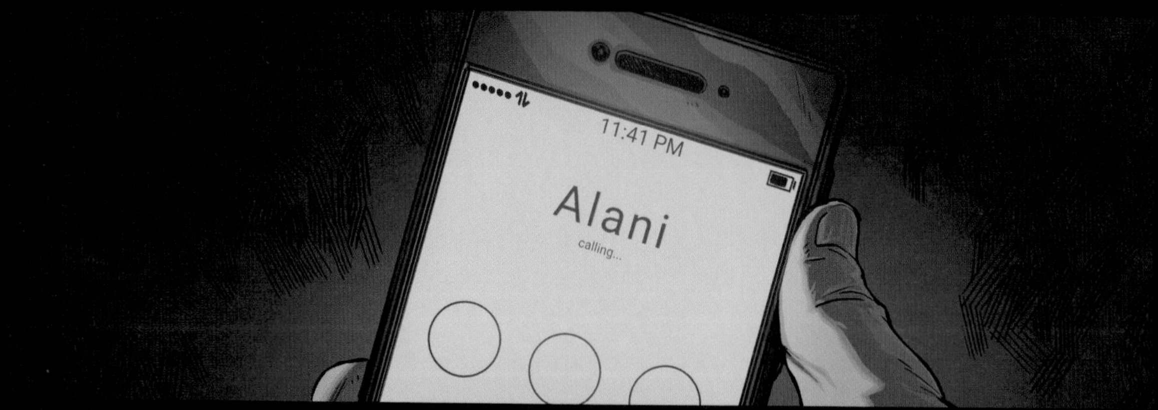
11:41 PM
Alani
calling...

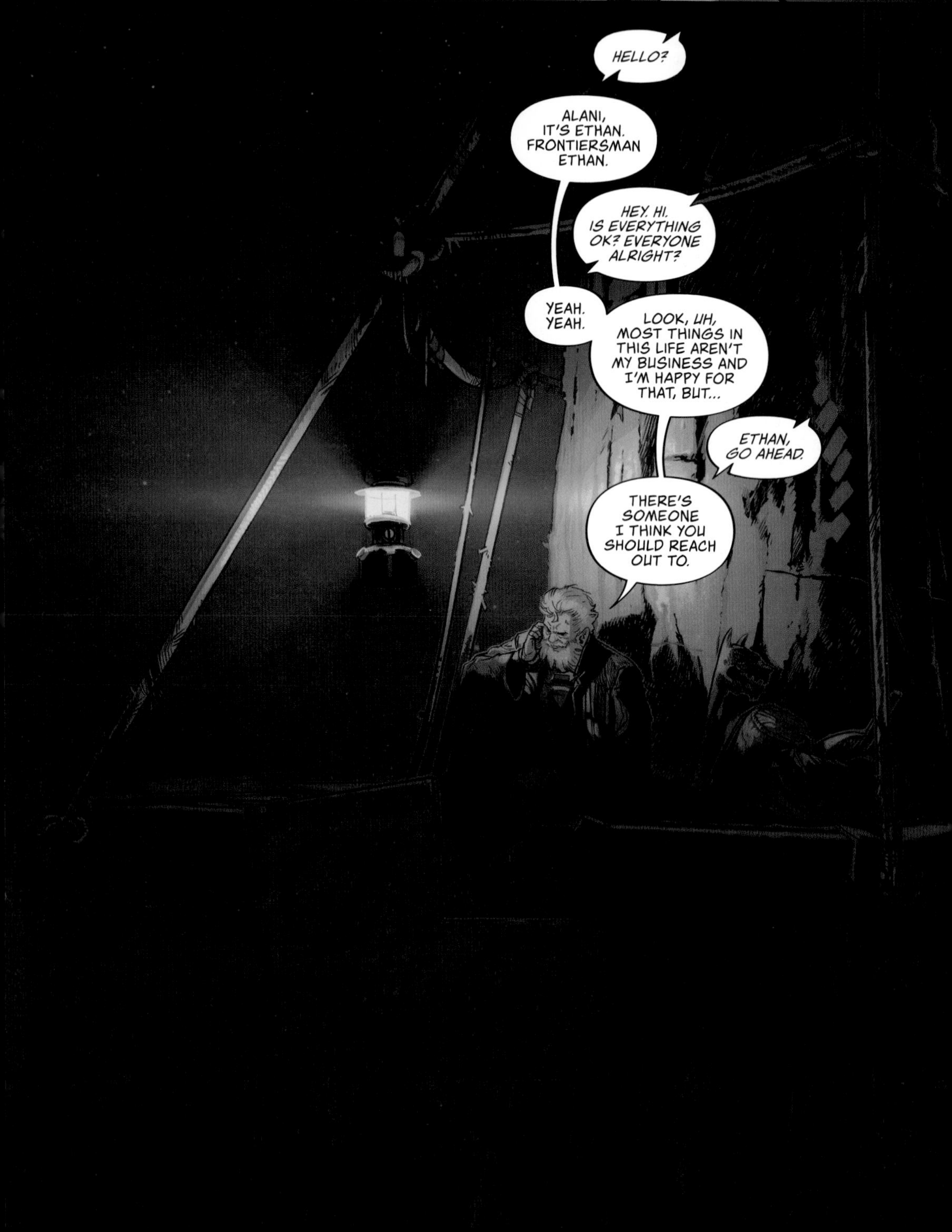
HELLO?
ALANI, IT'S ETHAN. FRONTIERSMAN ETHAN.
HEY. HI. IS EVERYTHING OK? EVERYONE ALRIGHT?
YEAH. YEAH.
LOOK, UH, MOST THINGS IN THIS LIFE AREN'T MY BUSINESS AND I'M HAPPY FOR THAT, BUT...
ETHAN, GO AHEAD.
THERE'S SOMEONE I THINK YOU SHOULD REACH OUT TO.

# ;ALAXIE PRIME

**•al name**: Unknown
**:cupation:** Interdimensional being
**•ntity:** It's unclear if Galaxie Prime's birth me is know to anyone, or if he even has one
**gal status:** Wanted and/or a fugitive across veral star systems and universes
**rmer alises:** The Living All
**•own relatives:** Galaxie Ultra (child)
**oup affiliation:** Raw Reason (former); no Mission Clan (status unknown)
**story:** The being known as Galaxie Prime st appeared as The Living All, a self-appoint- courtroom through which the Inter-Realm en the Intra-Realm) could bring its case ainst Earth. This effort was thwarted by the llow Travelers and The Living All vanished. hen he returned a year later, he was signifi- ntly less powerful. He acted as the team eport for the science-based criminal group, w Reason. Now operating under the name alaxie Prime, he provided the means of cape on a variety of heists.

'he group's goal was to steal the parts quired to build a wormhole generator, ended to break space-time and allow embers to time travel. This intention as withheld from Galaxie Prime, who belled when he found out. Members the superhero team Union Guard ed to intervene but Galaxie Prime anaged to absorb or otherwise abduct of the crew. Since that time, all Raw eason members have been found alive, ough not unscathed- Chaarl was reduced 1/16 his natural size and as of this file's eation has not been returned to normal.

Galaxie Prime was next sighted in the tra-Realm though it's unclear how long he as there or what his intentions were. The tra-Realm warlord Rothchild revealed the two ad crossed paths but provided no details.

When he returned to Earth, Galaxie Prime ayed the role of a minor villain. Often clashing ith the Fellow Travelers, he was time and gain exiled to space and other dimensions. He asn't properly subdued until magic manacles ere forged by the enchanted members of the ellow Travelers. He was later incarcerated eneath The Pylon in South Florida. During this me he forged a connection with Ex Nihilo. ccording to Galaxie Prime, a child was born om this union and he carries it with him.

**eight:** Frequently manfiests as 7ft, but can xpand to the size of a galaxy
**Veight:** Incomprehensible
**yes:** N/A
**air:** N/A
**trength level:** Incalculable, as he can lever- ge the mass of a galaxy when performing hysical tasks
**nown superhuman powers:** It's a matter of ebate what the limits of Galaxie Prime's owers may be. At various times, he's emonstrated an ability to teleport, intraport aking objects and beings into himself), tele- inesis, and matter-bending on the subatomic evel. His psychic abilities are suprisingly lim- ed, however, and it seems he's incapable of ntering a sentient mind. It is unknown why alaxie Prime has appeared more powerful t times and less powerful other times. Pre- umably, it's a mental phenomenon and on ome level self-imposed.

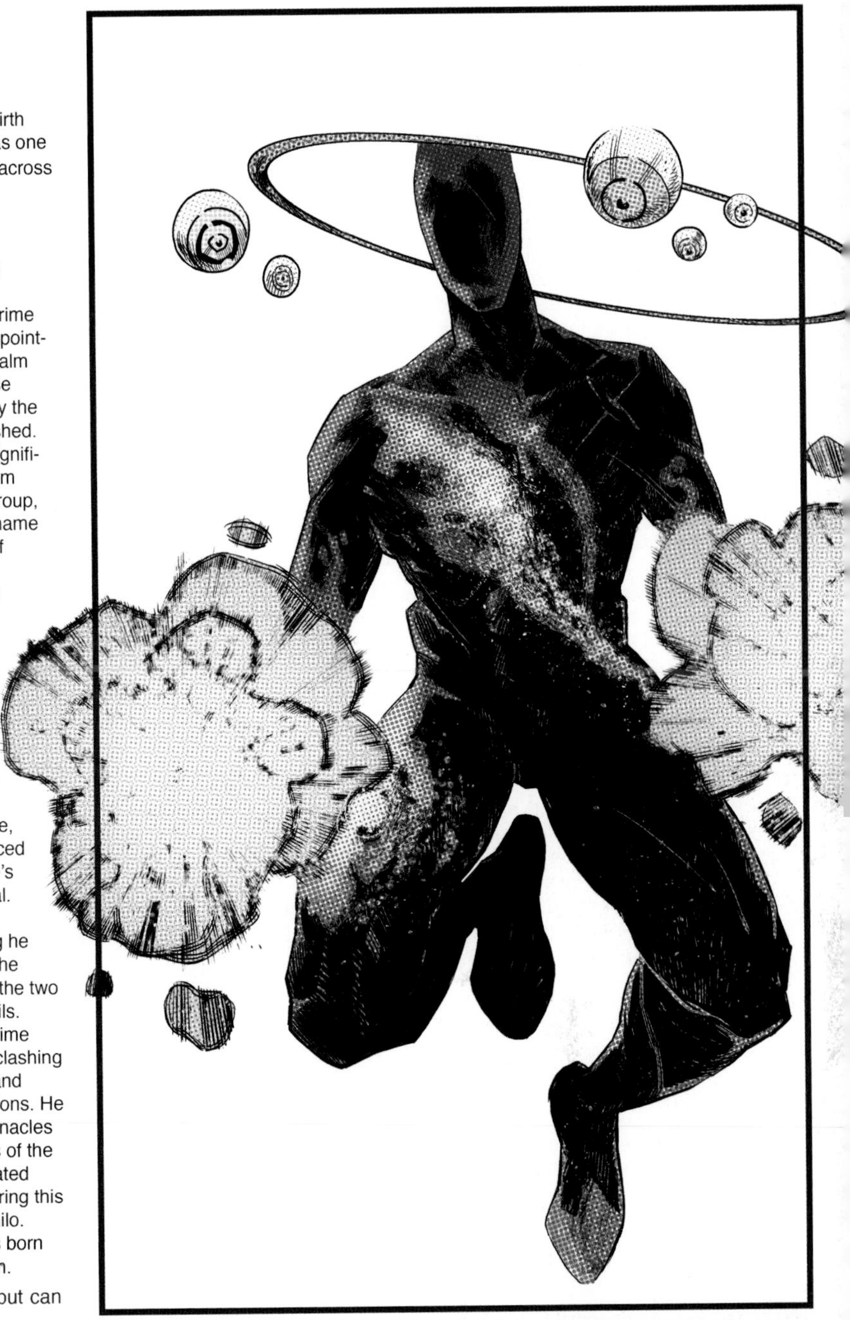

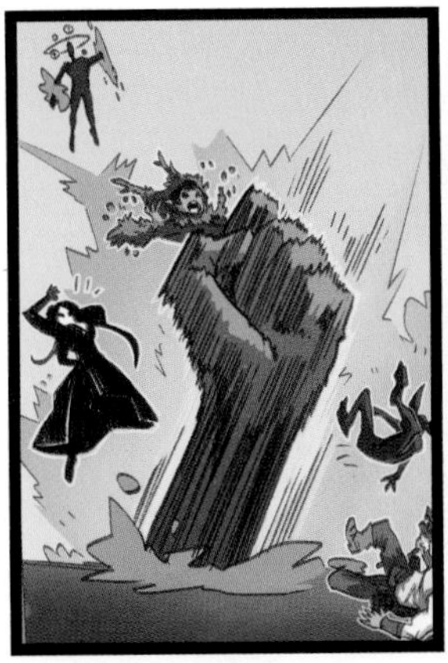

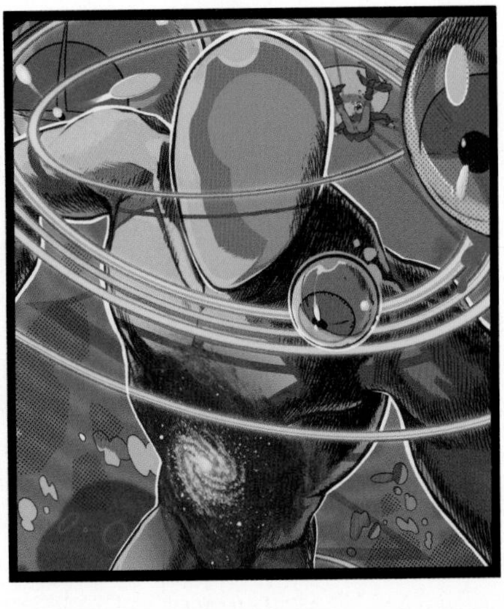

# THE LANCE

**Real name:** Lydia Prescott
**Occupation:** Mercenary
**Identity:** Known within law enforcement circles
**Legal status:** Wanted criminal
**Known relatives:** Layla Prescott (mother)
**Group affiliation:** The Lab
**Alias:** None
**History:** Supervillainry runs in the Prescott family. Lydia's mother, Layla, was a costumed criminal in the 1980s. She operated under the alias Sleep Witch and used a wand with hypnotic power to rob banks. On that stolen money Layla built a life for her daughter, who grew up blissfully unaware of her mother's vocation.

Between high-school and college, Lydia decided to take a year and backpack across Europe. It was on the grassy mortar-made hills of Verdun that she encountered the dying alien Cligès who entrusted her with his lance. Cligès' origins are muddy, but it appears his culture either based itself on Arthurian legend or is itself the basis for that very mythos. In any case, Lydia took the lightweight-but-durable metal weapon to a hostel that night.

And promptly blew a wall of the building into the Meuse River.

It never occurred to Lydia to use the lance for good, as Cligès directed, and she instead took immediately to crime. As she unlocked the lance's abilities one-by-one, she expanded her activities. Starting with simple smash-and-grab heists on jewelry stores, she eventually moved onto robbing commercial jets in midair. Cheap thrills were her real motivation, as the money just came and went. For a time she fashioned herself a type of Robin Hood, raining stolen designer bags on homeless encampments. During this era she fought numerous low-level superheroes, mostly teen teams. It was one of those battles that brought her to the attention of Regionaire.

Convincing Lydia she was better suited to life as a superhuman mercenary rather than a petty criminal, Regionaire rechristened her The Lance. Soon becoming Regionaire's righthand, The Lance engaged in mercenary work across Africa and Asia as well as assisting in domestic terrorism within the US.

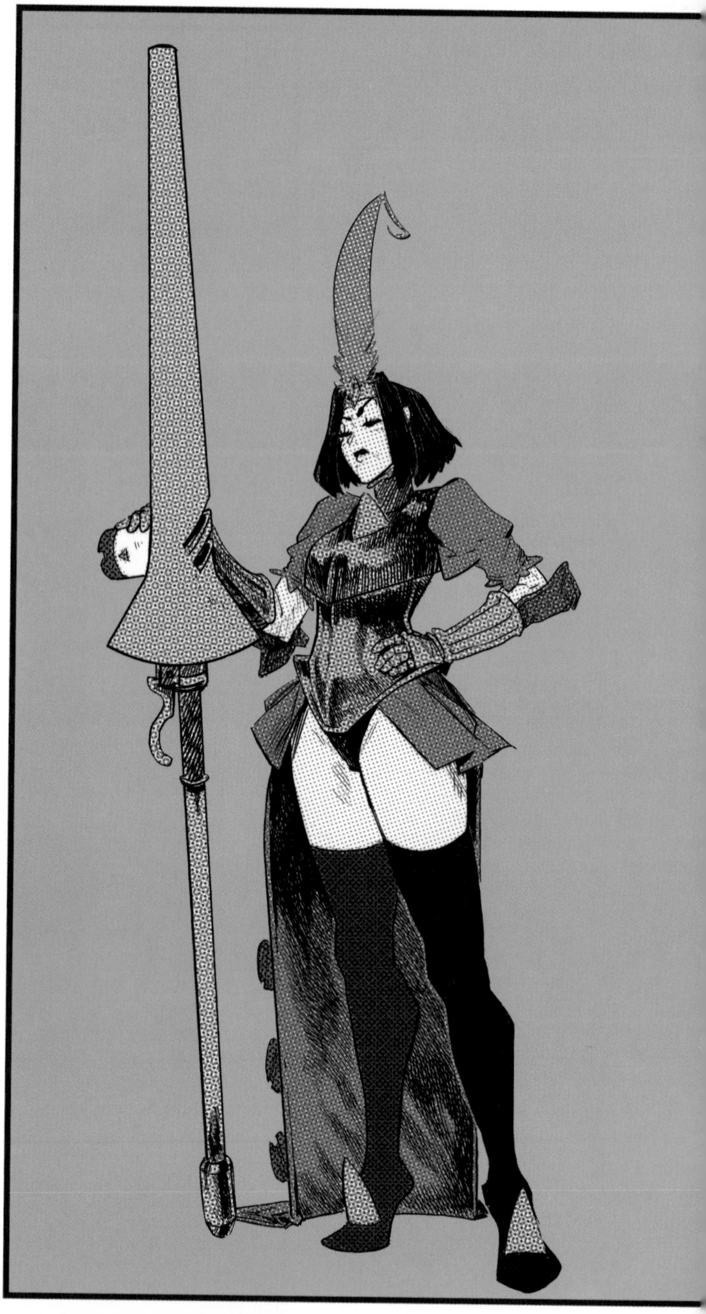

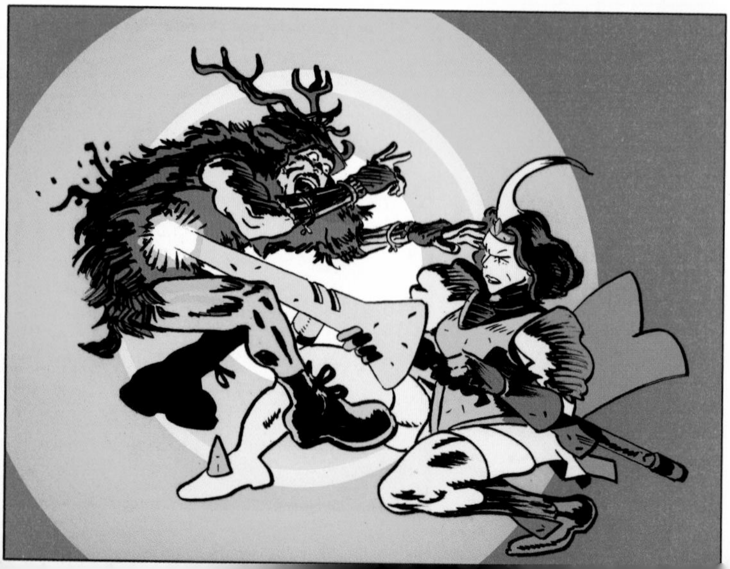

**Height:** 5'10"
**Weight:** 140lbs
**Eyes:** Variable
**Hair:** Blue
**Strength level:** Peak athlete
**Known superhuman powers:** The Lance ha no superhuman abilities of her own and relie on alien technology. Her lance is capable c firing bolts of energy, both in the form of forc blasts and heat waves. The former can b sprayed wide to create a shield of a sor protecting her from projectiles. The lance has magnetic propulsion system that allows it wielder to fly short distances. Regionair modified the lance to accept radioactiv minerals from Earth as a source of fue ensuring the device will work after the alie energy cells have been spent.

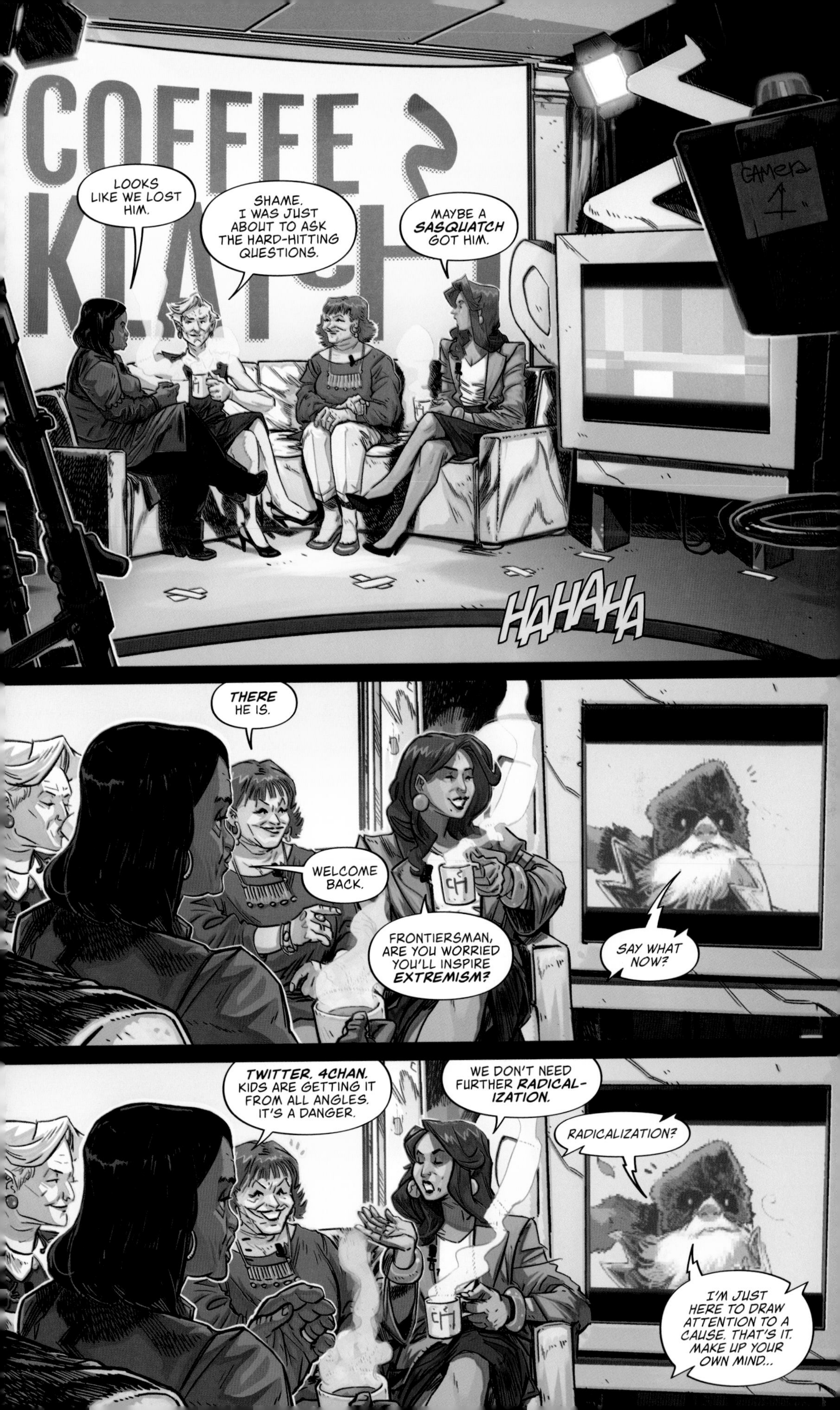
COFFEE
KLATCH
LOOKS LIKE WE LOST HIM.
SHAME. I WAS JUST ABOUT TO ASK THE HARD-HITTING QUESTIONS.
MAYBE A SASQUATCH GOT HIM.
CAMERA 1
HAHAHA
THERE HE IS.
WELCOME BACK.
FRONTIERSMAN, ARE YOU WORRIED YOU'LL INSPIRE EXTREMISM?
SAY WHAT NOW?
TWITTER. 4CHAN. KIDS ARE GETTING IT FROM ALL ANGLES. IT'S A DANGER.
WE DON'T NEED FURTHER RADICAL-IZATION.
RADICALIZATION?
I'M JUST HERE TO DRAW ATTENTION TO A CAUSE. THAT'S IT. MAKE UP YOUR OWN MIND...

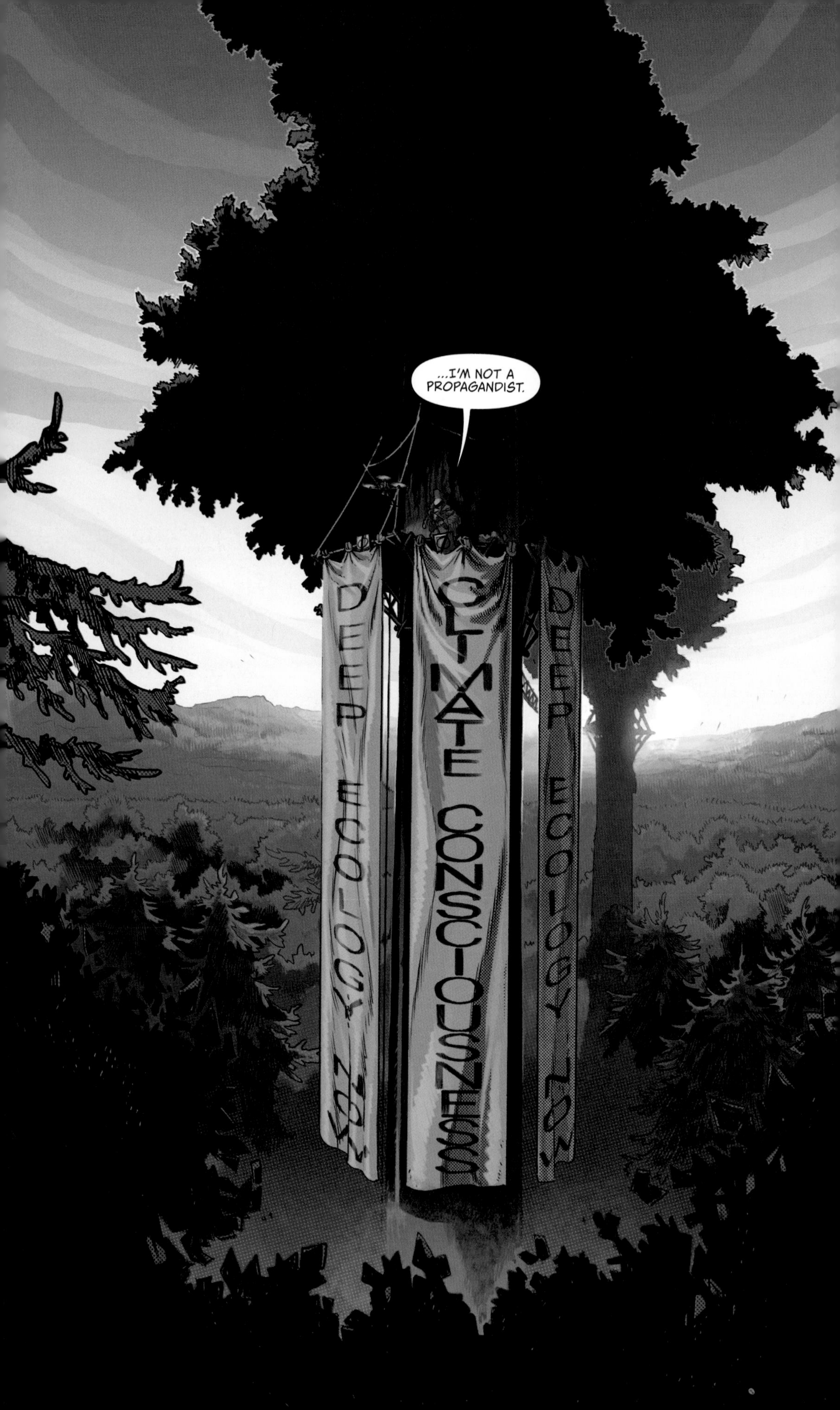
...I'M NOT A PROPAGANDIST.
DEEP ECOLOGY NOW
ULTIMATE CONSCIOUSNESS
DEEP ECOLOGY NOW

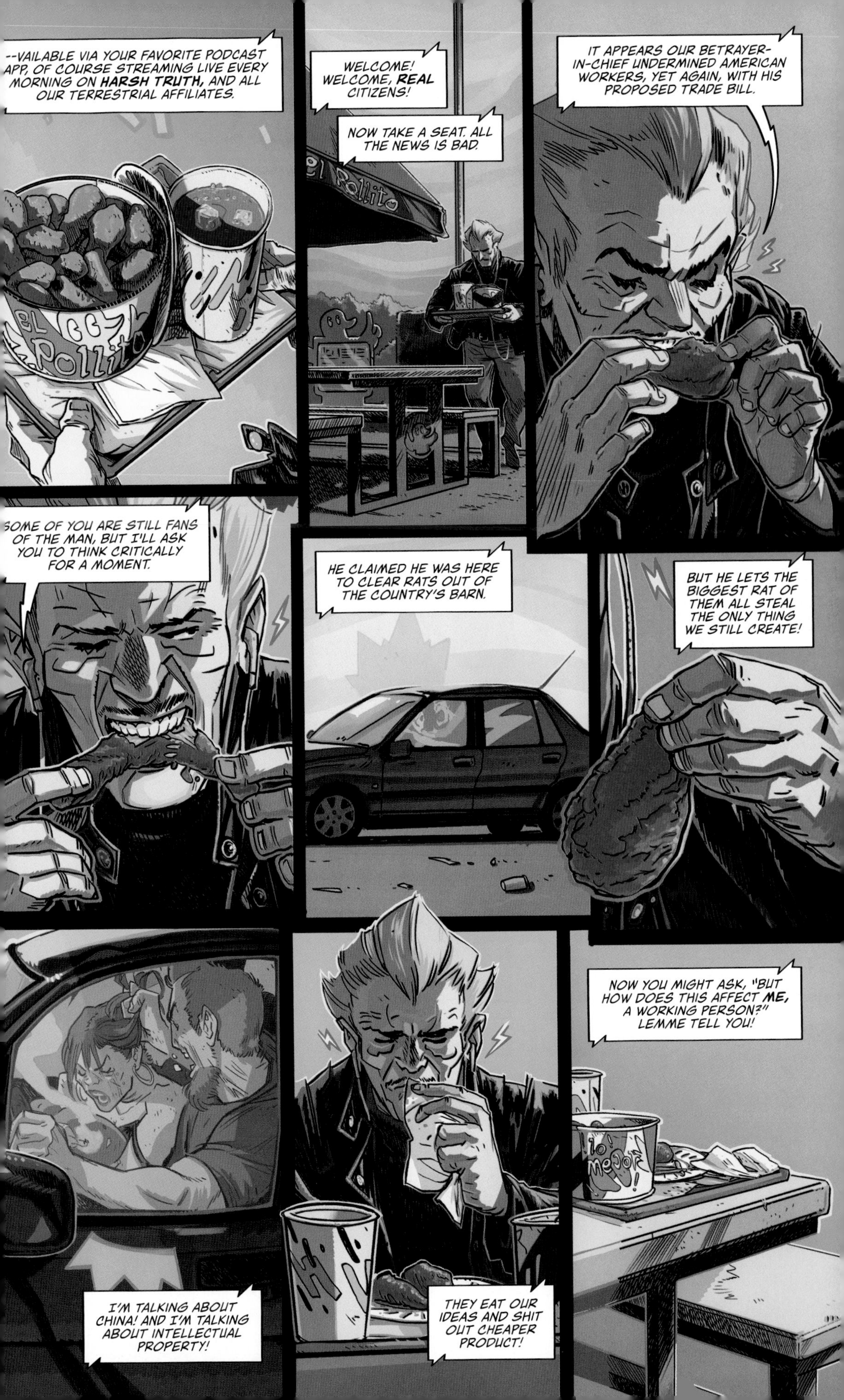
--VAILABLE VIA YOUR FAVORITE PODCAST APP, OF COURSE STREAMING LIVE EVERY MORNING ON HARSH TRUTH, AND ALL OUR TERRESTRIAL AFFILIATES.
EL POLLITO
WELCOME! WELCOME, REAL CITIZENS!
NOW TAKE A SEAT. ALL THE NEWS IS BAD.
EL POLLITO
IT APPEARS OUR BETRAYER-IN-CHIEF UNDERMINED AMERICAN WORKERS, YET AGAIN, WITH HIS PROPOSED TRADE BILL.
SOME OF YOU ARE STILL FANS OF THE MAN, BUT I'LL ASK YOU TO THINK CRITICALLY FOR A MOMENT.
HE CLAIMED HE WAS HERE TO CLEAR RATS OUT OF THE COUNTRY'S BARN.
BUT HE LETS THE BIGGEST RAT OF THEM ALL STEAL THE ONLY THING WE STILL CREATE!
I'M TALKING ABOUT CHINA! AND I'M TALKING ABOUT INTELLECTUAL PROPERTY!
THEY EAT OUR IDEAS AND SHIT OUT CHEAPER PRODUCT!
NOW YOU MIGHT ASK, "BUT HOW DOES THIS AFFECT ME, A WORKING PERSON?" LEMME TELL YOU!
¡LO MEJOR!

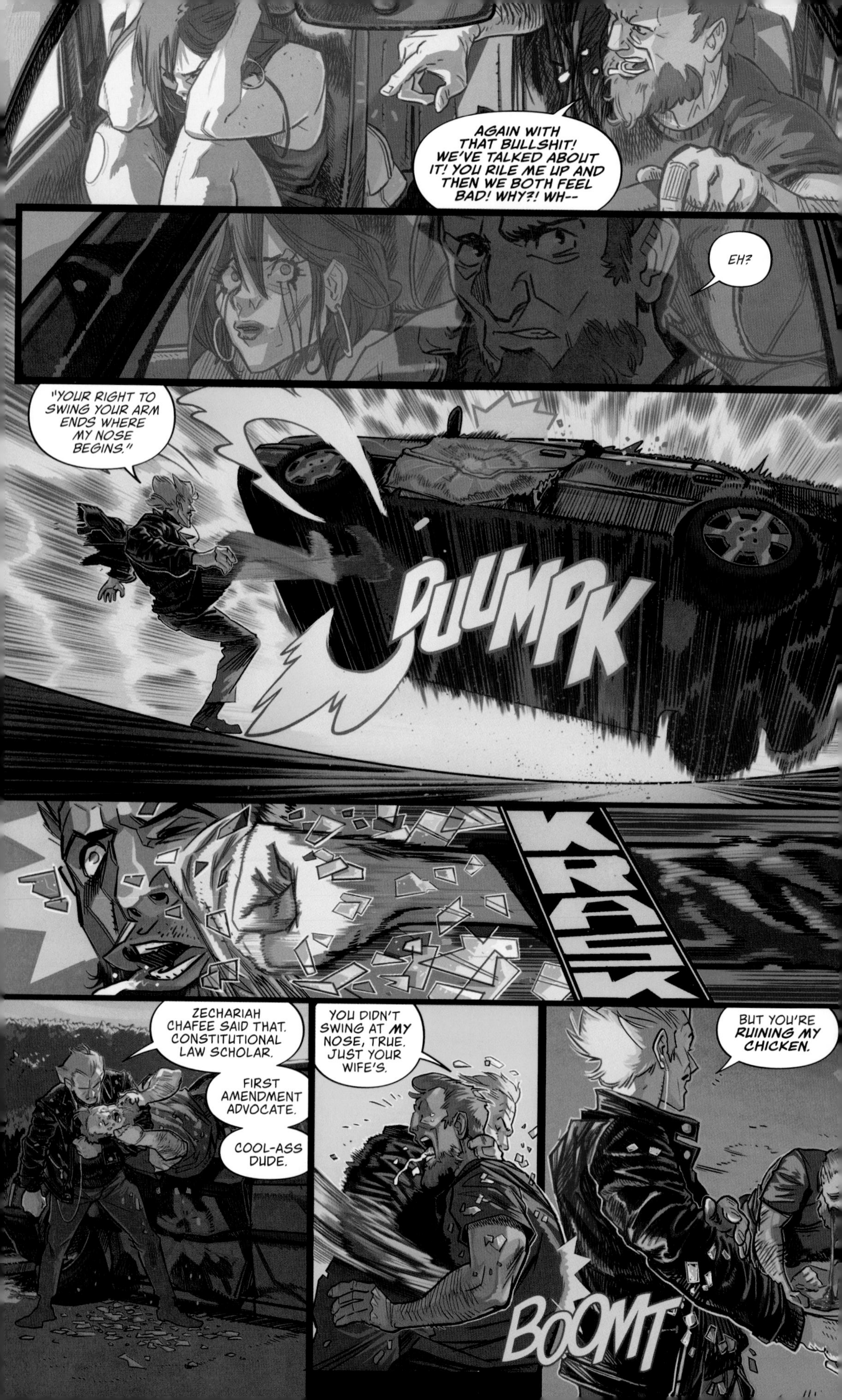
AGAIN WITH THAT BULLSHIT! WE'VE TALKED ABOUT IT! YOU RILE ME UP AND THEN WE BOTH FEEL BAD! WHY?! WH--
EH?
"YOUR RIGHT TO SWING YOUR ARM ENDS WHERE MY NOSE BEGINS."
DUUMPK
KRASK
ZECHARIAH CHAFEE SAID THAT. CONSTITUTIONAL LAW SCHOLAR.
FIRST AMENDMENT ADVOCATE.
COOL-ASS DUDE.
YOU DIDN'T SWING AT MY NOSE, TRUE. JUST YOUR WIFE'S.
BUT YOU'RE RUINING MY CHICKEN.
BOOMT

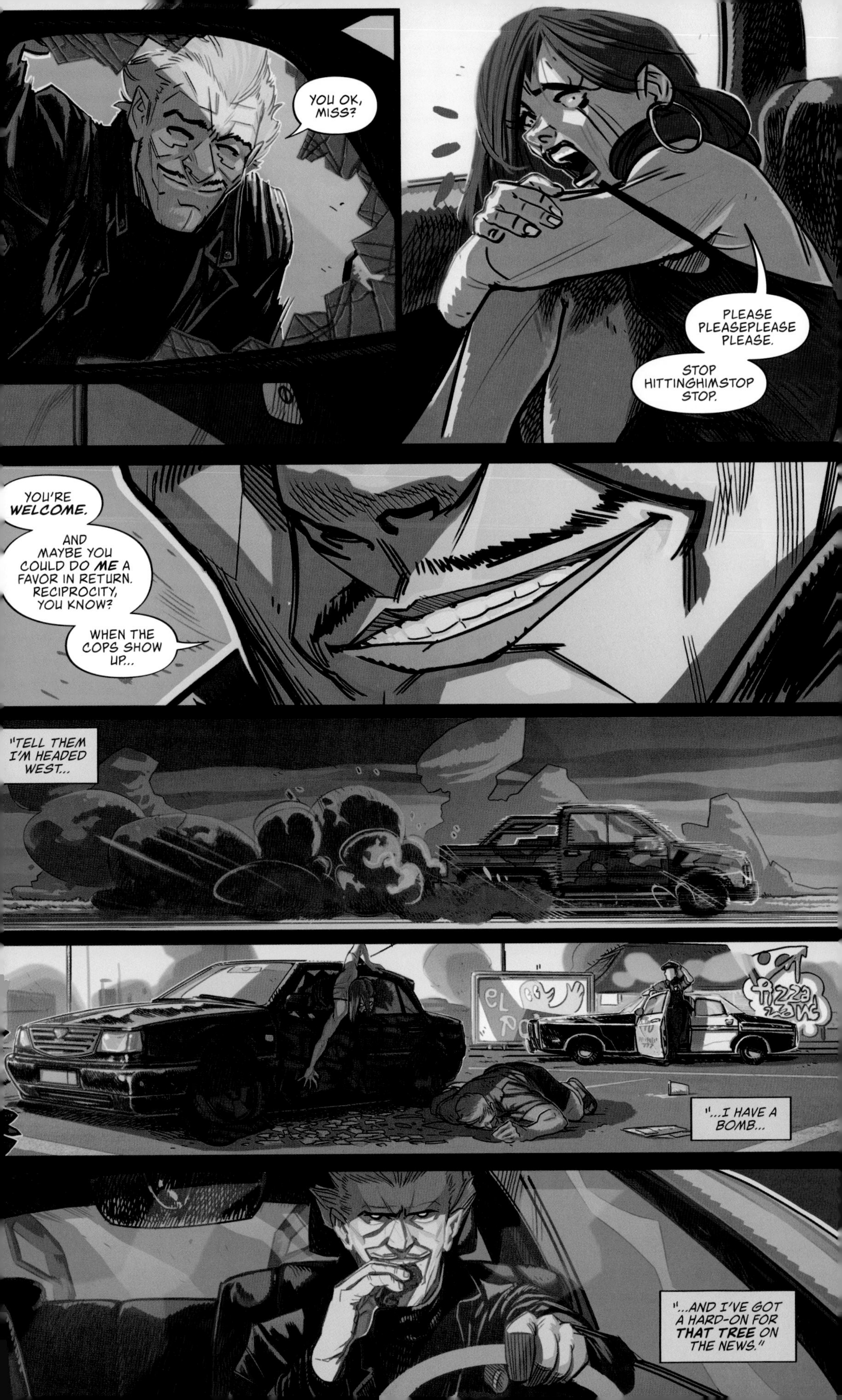
YOU OK, MISS?
PLEASE PLEASEPLEASE PLEASE.
STOP HITTINGHIMSTOP STOP.
YOU'RE **WELCOME.**
AND MAYBE YOU COULD DO **ME** A FAVOR IN RETURN. RECIPROCITY, YOU KNOW?
WHEN THE COPS SHOW UP...
"TELL THEM I'M HEADED WEST...
"...I HAVE A BOMB...
"...AND I'VE GOT A HARD-ON FOR **THAT TREE** ON THE NEWS."

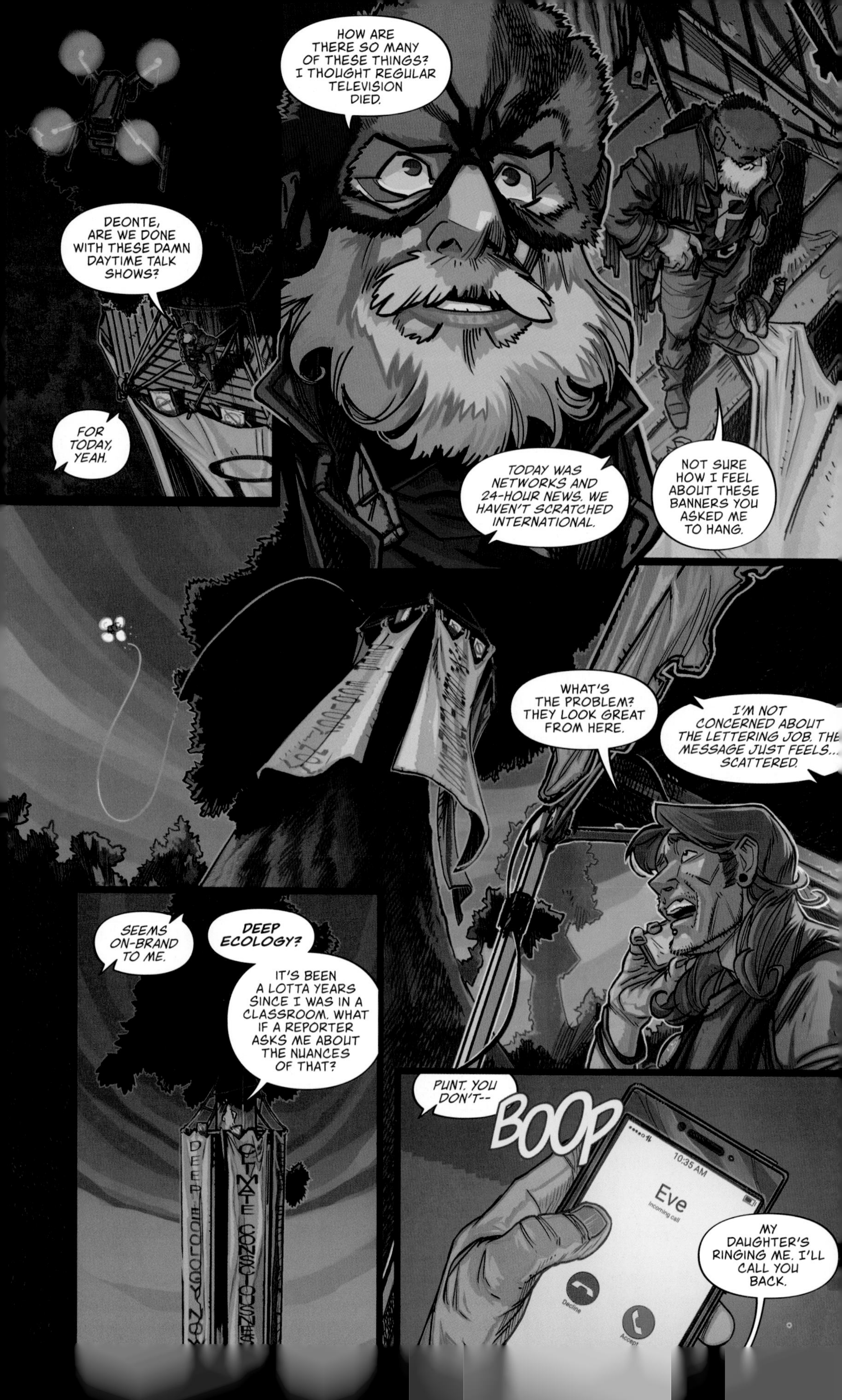
HOW ARE THERE SO MANY OF THESE THINGS? I THOUGHT REGULAR TELEVISION DIED.
DEONTE, ARE WE DONE WITH THESE DAMN DAYTIME TALK SHOWS?
FOR TODAY, YEAH.
TODAY WAS NETWORKS AND 24-HOUR NEWS. WE HAVEN'T SCRATCHED INTERNATIONAL.
NOT SURE HOW I FEEL ABOUT THESE BANNERS YOU ASKED ME TO HANG.
WHAT'S THE PROBLEM? THEY LOOK GREAT FROM HERE.
I'M NOT CONCERNED ABOUT THE LETTERING JOB. THE MESSAGE JUST FEELS... SCATTERED.
SEEMS ON-BRAND TO ME.
DEEP ECOLOGY?
IT'S BEEN A LOTTA YEARS SINCE I WAS IN A CLASSROOM. WHAT IF A REPORTER ASKS ME ABOUT THE NUANCES OF THAT?
DEEP ECOLOGY
CLIMATE CONSCIOUSNESS
PUNT. YOU DON'T--
BOOP
10:35 AM
Eve
Incoming call
Decline
Accept
MY DAUGHTER'S RINGING ME. I'LL CALL YOU BACK.

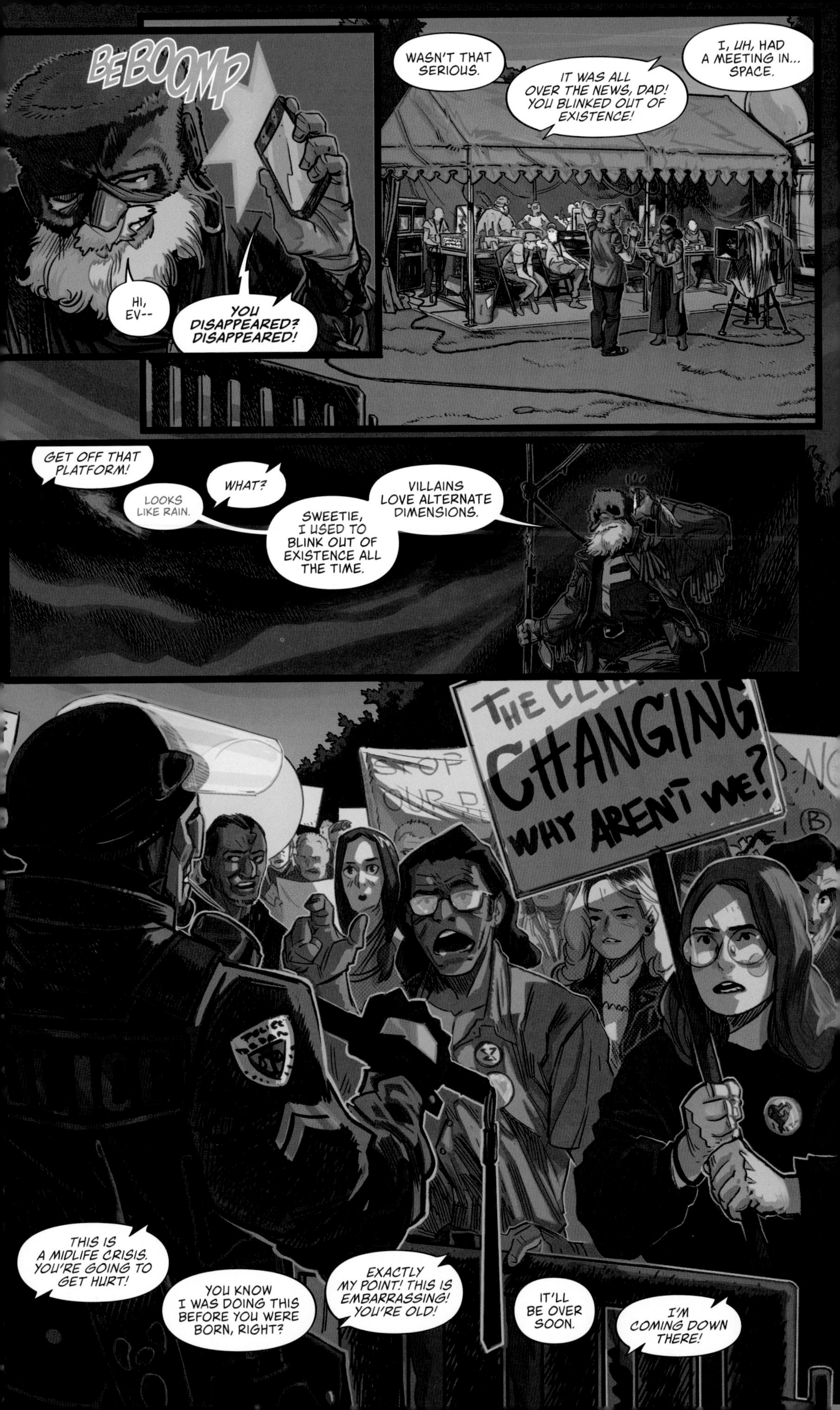
BEBOOMP
HI, EV--
YOU DISAPPEARED? DISAPPEARED!
WASN'T THAT SERIOUS.
IT WAS ALL OVER THE NEWS, DAD! YOU BLINKED OUT OF EXISTENCE!
I, UH, HAD A MEETING IN... SPACE.
GET OFF THAT PLATFORM!
LOOKS LIKE RAIN.
WHAT?
SWEETIE, I USED TO BLINK OUT OF EXISTENCE ALL THE TIME.
VILLAINS LOVE ALTERNATE DIMENSIONS.
CHANGING
WHY AREN'T WE?
THIS IS A MIDLIFE CRISIS. YOU'RE GOING TO GET HURT!
YOU KNOW I WAS DOING THIS BEFORE YOU WERE BORN, RIGHT?
EXACTLY MY POINT! THIS IS EMBARRASSING! YOU'RE OLD!
IT'LL BE OVER SOON.
I'M COMING DOWN THERE!

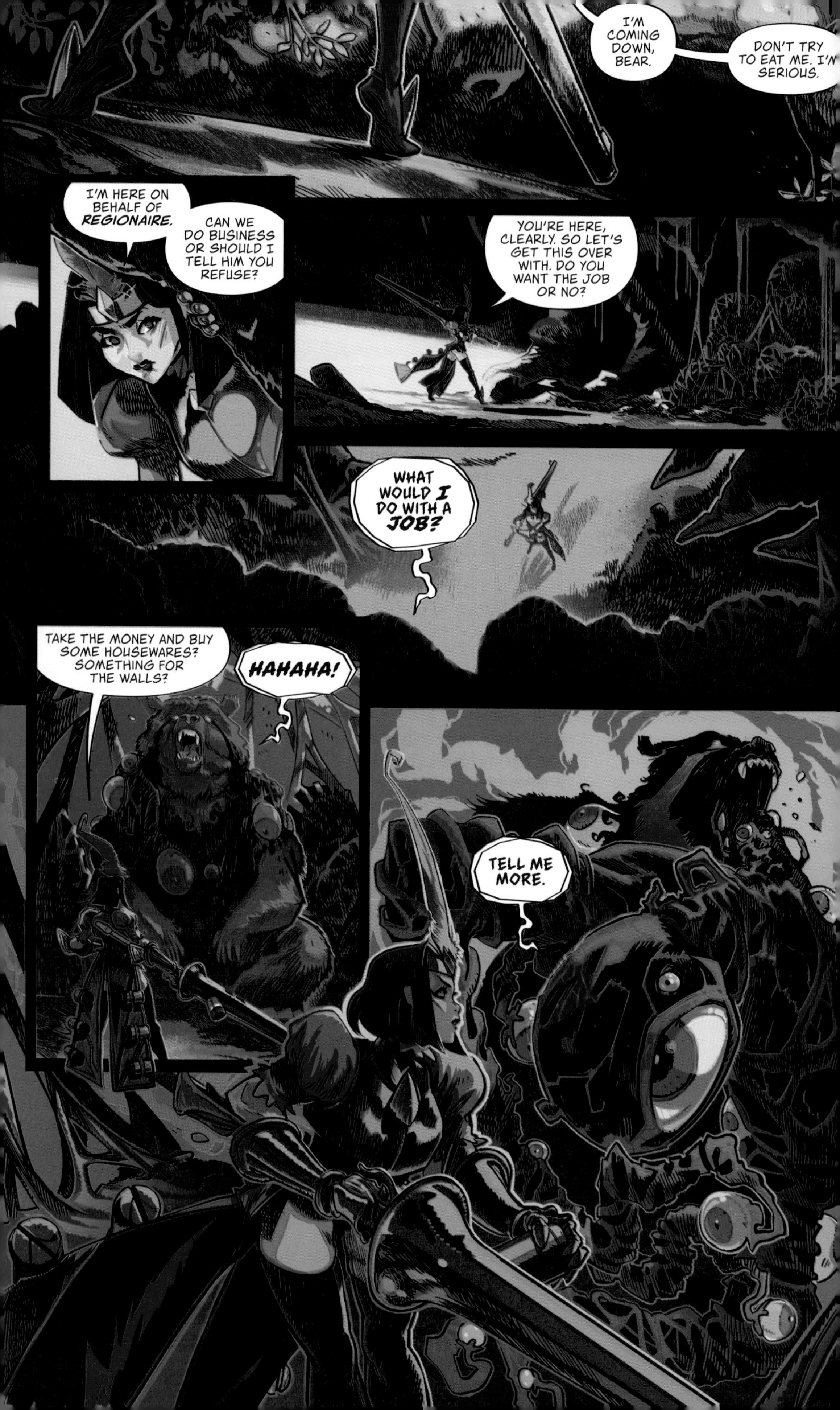

I'M COMING DOWN, BEAR.
DON'T TRY TO EAT ME. I'M SERIOUS.
I'M HERE ON BEHALF OF **REGIONAIRE.**
CAN WE DO BUSINESS OR SHOULD I TELL HIM YOU REFUSE?
YOU'RE HERE, CLEARLY. SO LET'S GET THIS OVER WITH. DO YOU WANT THE JOB OR NO?
WHAT WOULD *I* DO WITH A *JOB?*
TAKE THE MONEY AND BUY SOME HOUSEWARES? SOMETHING FOR THE WALLS?
HAHAHA!
TELL ME MORE.

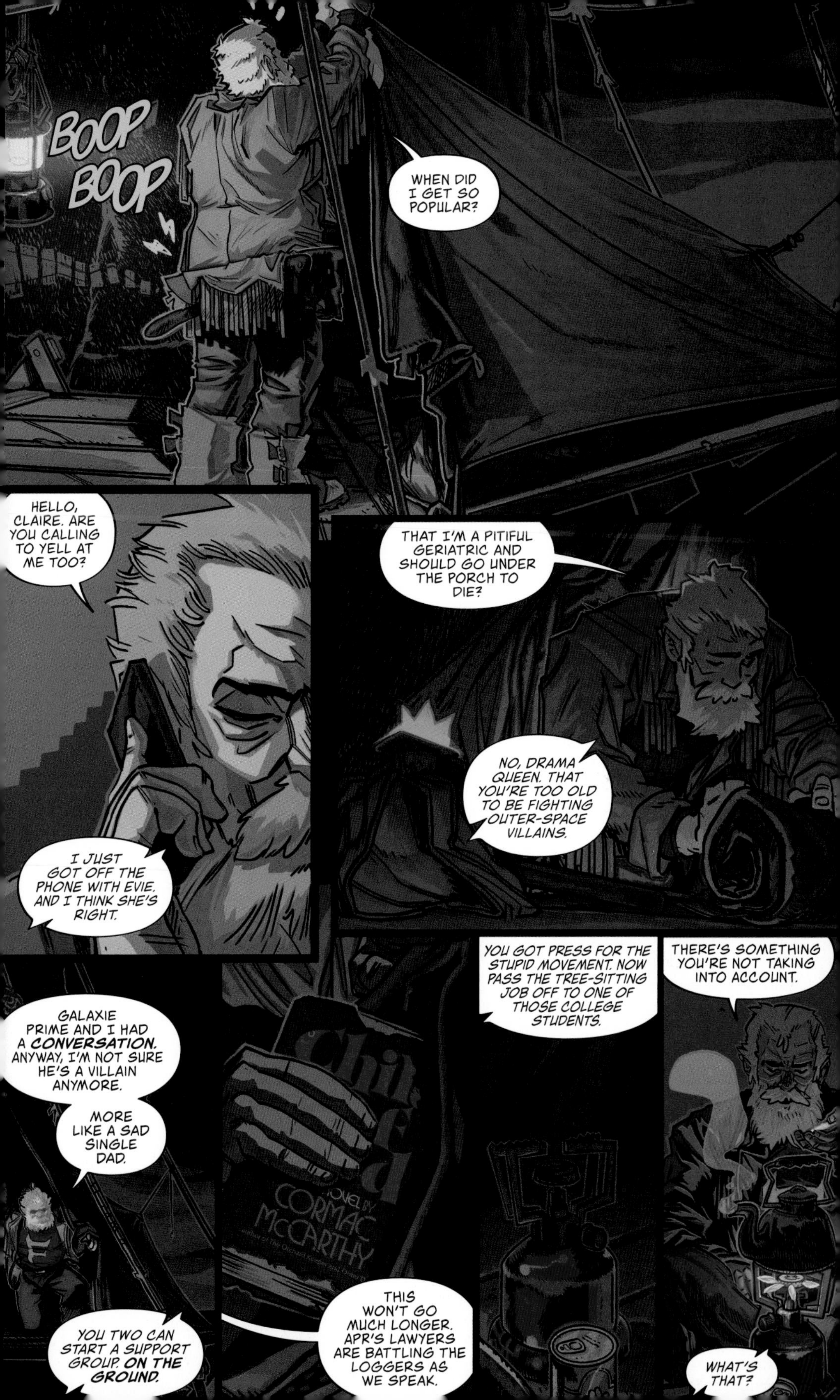
BOOP BOOP
WHEN DID I GET SO POPULAR?
HELLO, CLAIRE. ARE YOU CALLING TO YELL AT ME TOO?
THAT I'M A PITIFUL GERIATRIC AND SHOULD GO UNDER THE PORCH TO DIE?
NO, DRAMA QUEEN. THAT YOU'RE TOO OLD TO BE FIGHTING OUTER-SPACE VILLAINS.
I JUST GOT OFF THE PHONE WITH EVIE. AND I THINK SHE'S RIGHT.
GALAXIE PRIME AND I HAD A **CONVERSATION.** ANYWAY, I'M NOT SURE HE'S A VILLAIN ANYMORE.
MORE LIKE A SAD SINGLE DAD.
YOU TWO CAN START A SUPPORT GROUP. **ON THE GROUND.**
CORMAC McCARTHY
THIS WON'T GO MUCH LONGER. APR'S LAWYERS ARE BATTLING THE LOGGERS AS WE SPEAK.
YOU GOT PRESS FOR THE STUPID MOVEMENT. NOW PASS THE TREE-SITTING JOB OFF TO ONE OF THOSE COLLEGE STUDENTS.
THERE'S SOMETHING YOU'RE NOT TAKING INTO ACCOUNT.
WHAT'S THAT?

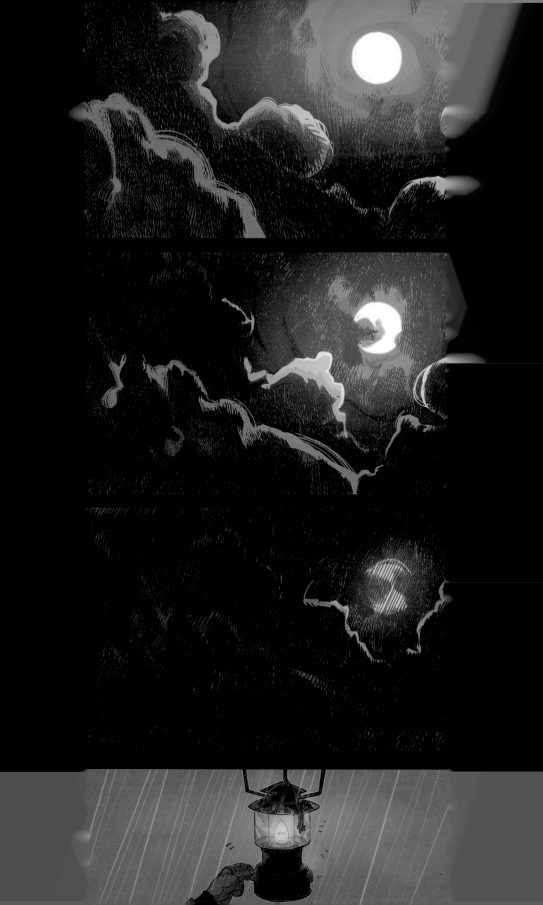

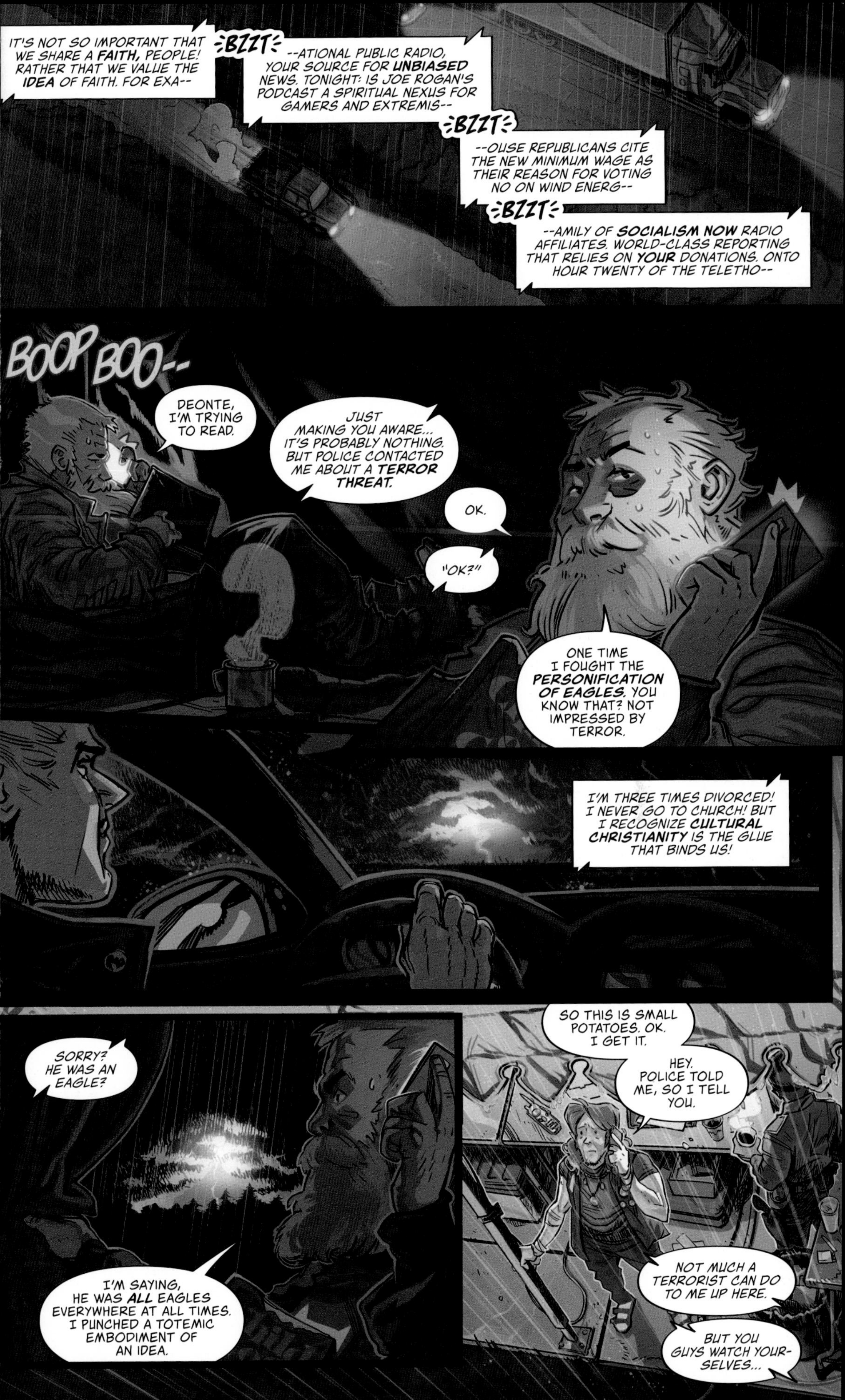
IT'S NOT SO IMPORTANT THAT WE SHARE A FAITH, PEOPLE! RATHER THAT WE VALUE THE IDEA OF FAITH. FOR EXA--
BZZT
--ATIONAL PUBLIC RADIO, YOUR SOURCE FOR UNBIASED NEWS. TONIGHT: IS JOE ROGAN'S PODCAST A SPIRITUAL NEXUS FOR GAMERS AND EXTREMIS--
BZZT
--OUSE REPUBLICANS CITE THE NEW MINIMUM WAGE AS THEIR REASON FOR VOTING NO ON WIND ENERG--
BZZT
--AMILY OF SOCIALISM NOW RADIO AFFILIATES. WORLD-CLASS REPORTING THAT RELIES ON YOUR DONATIONS. ONTO HOUR TWENTY OF THE TELETHO--
BOOP BOO--
DEONTE, I'M TRYING TO READ.
JUST MAKING YOU AWARE... IT'S PROBABLY NOTHING. BUT POLICE CONTACTED ME ABOUT A TERROR THREAT.
OK.
"OK?"
ONE TIME I FOUGHT THE PERSONIFICATION OF EAGLES. YOU KNOW THAT? NOT IMPRESSED BY TERROR.
I'M THREE TIMES DIVORCED! I NEVER GO TO CHURCH! BUT I RECOGNIZE CULTURAL CHRISTIANITY IS THE GLUE THAT BINDS US!
SORRY? HE WAS AN EAGLE?
I'M SAYING, HE WAS ALL EAGLES EVERYWHERE AT ALL TIMES. I PUNCHED A TOTEMIC EMBODIMENT OF AN IDEA.
SO THIS IS SMALL POTATOES. OK. I GET IT.
HEY. POLICE TOLD ME, SO I TELL YOU.
NOT MUCH A TERRORIST CAN DO TO ME UP HERE.
BUT YOU GUYS WATCH YOUR-SELVES...

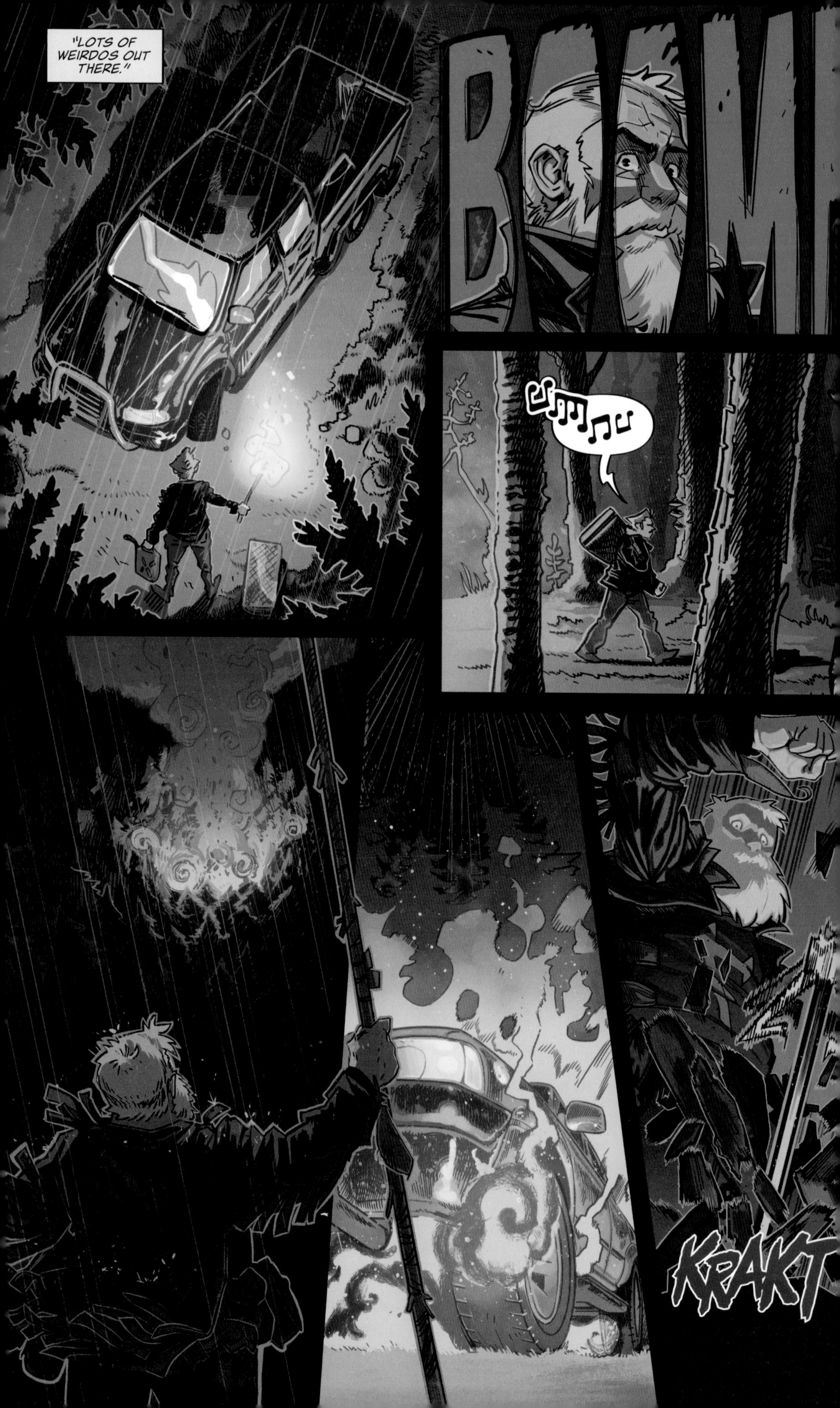
"LOTS OF WEIRDOS OUT THERE."
KRAKT

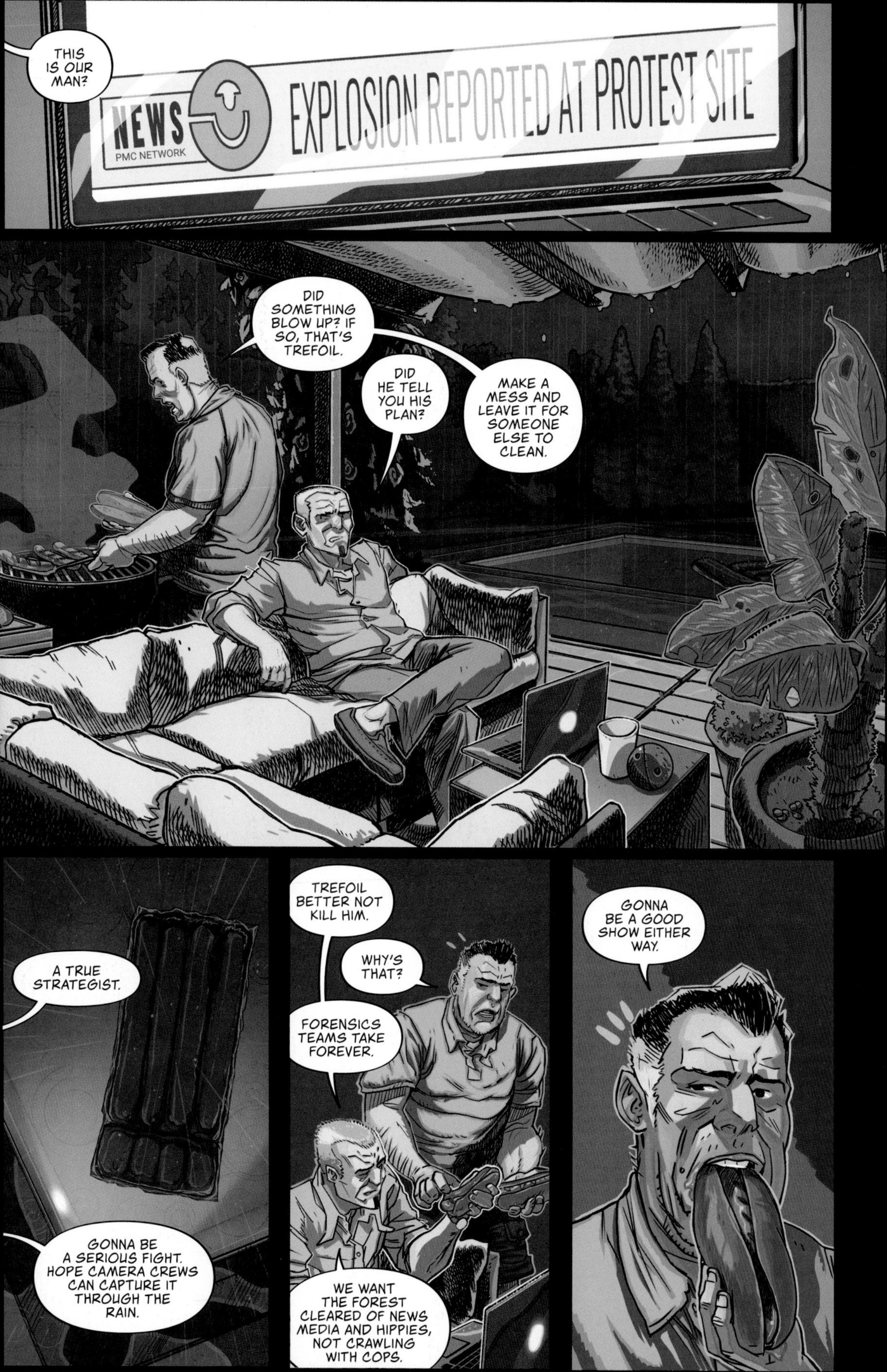
THIS IS OUR MAN?
NEWS PMC NETWORK
EXPLOSION REPORTED AT PROTEST SITE
DID SOMETHING BLOW UP? IF SO, THAT'S TREFOIL.
MAKE A MESS AND LEAVE IT FOR SOMEONE ELSE TO CLEAN.
DID HE TELL YOU HIS PLAN?
A TRUE STRATEGIST.
GONNA BE A SERIOUS FIGHT. HOPE CAMERA CREWS CAN CAPTURE IT THROUGH THE RAIN.
TREFOIL BETTER NOT KILL HIM.
WHY'S THAT?
FORENSICS TEAMS TAKE FOREVER.
WE WANT THE FOREST CLEARED OF NEWS MEDIA AND HIPPIES, NOT CRAWLING WITH COPS.
GONNA BE A GOOD SHOW EITHER WAY.

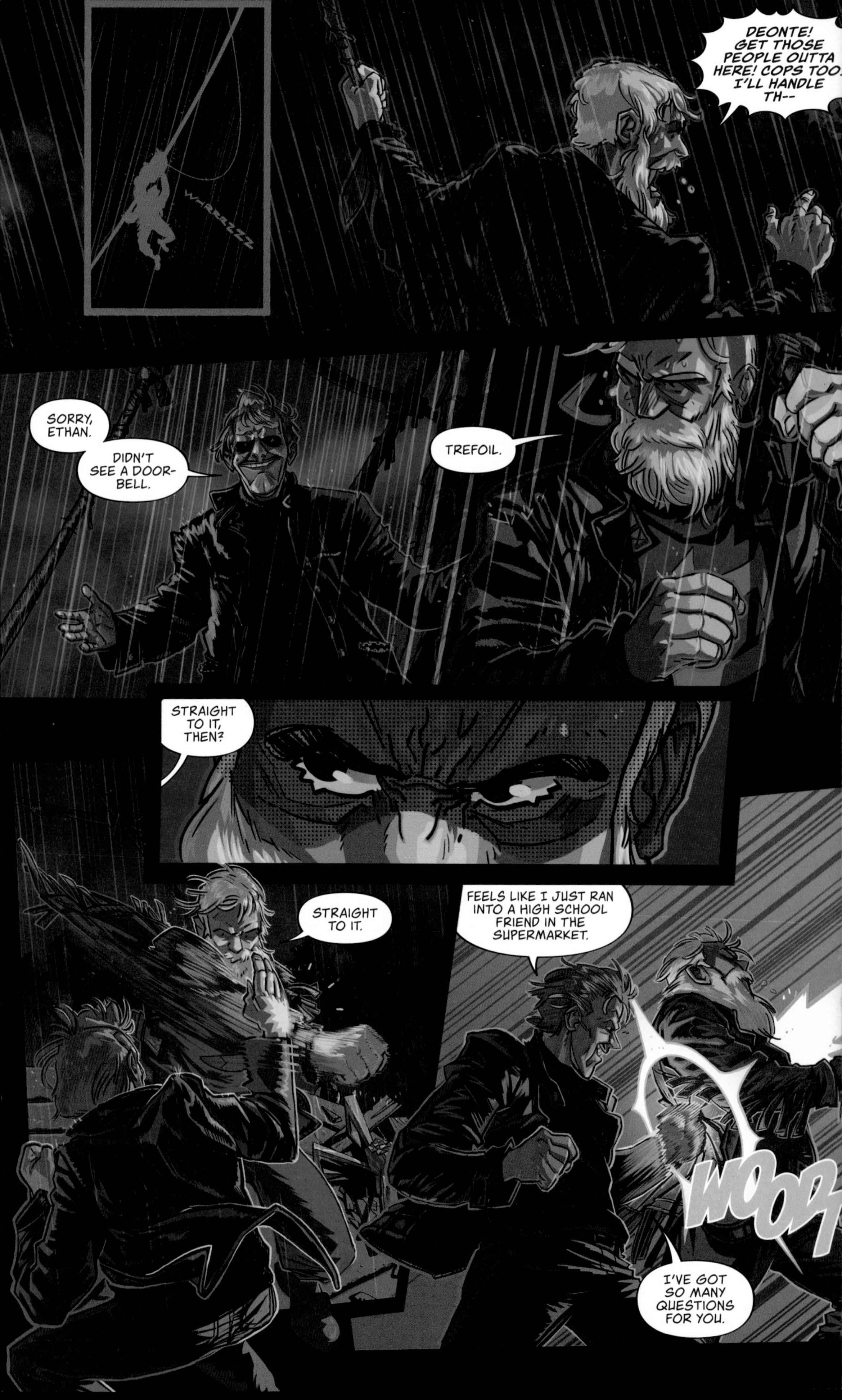
WHRRRZZZZ
DEONTE! GET THOSE PEOPLE OUTTA HERE! COPS TOO! I'LL HANDLE TH--
SORRY, ETHAN.
DIDN'T SEE A DOOR-BELL.
TREFOIL.
STRAIGHT TO IT, THEN?
STRAIGHT TO IT.
FEELS LIKE I JUST RAN INTO A HIGH SCHOOL FRIEND IN THE SUPERMARKET.
WOOD
I'VE GOT SO MANY QUESTIONS FOR YOU.

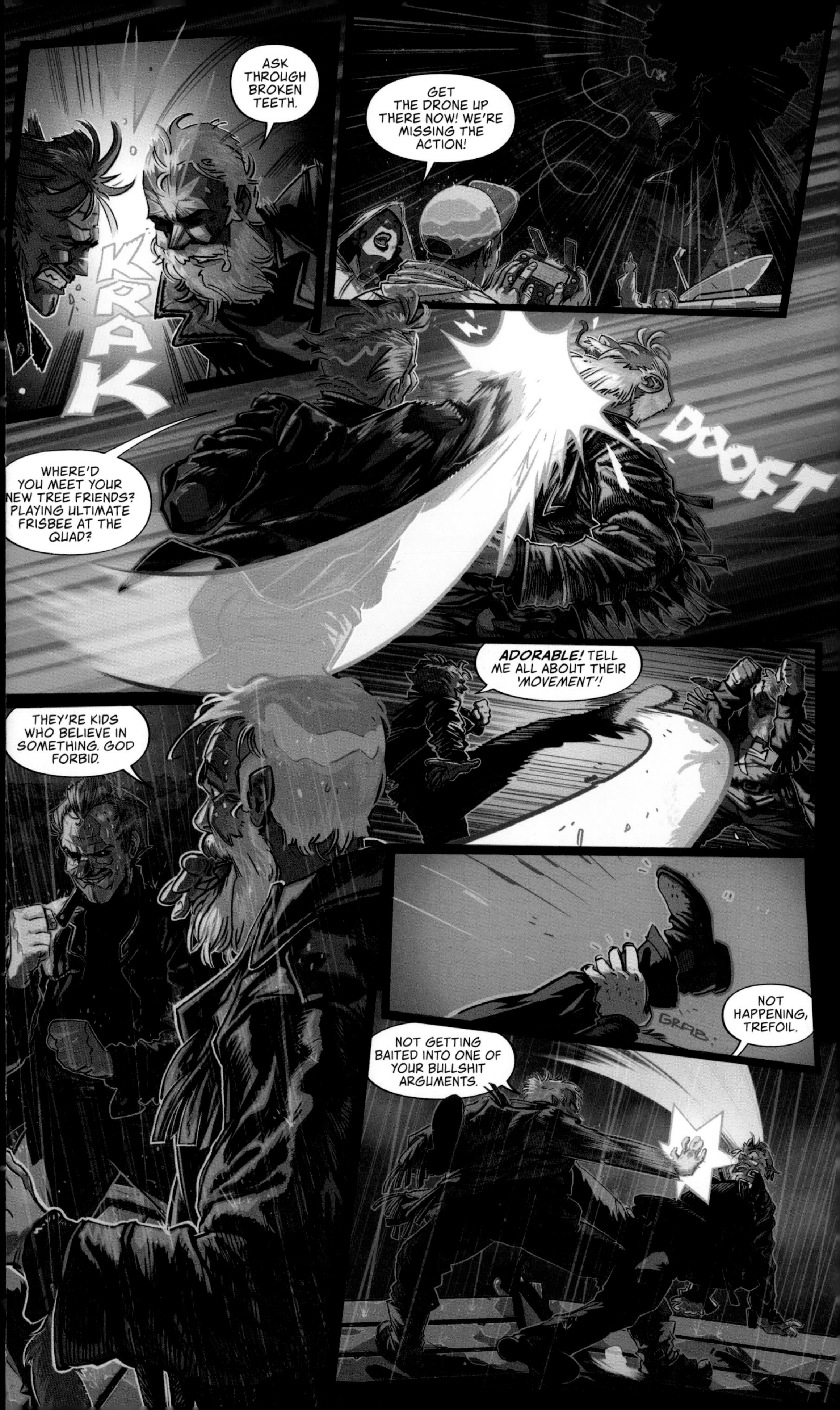
ASK THROUGH BROKEN TEETH.
KRAK
GET THE DRONE UP THERE NOW! WE'RE MISSING THE ACTION!
DOOFT
WHERE'D YOU MEET YOUR NEW TREE FRIENDS? PLAYING ULTIMATE FRISBEE AT THE QUAD?
ADORABLE! TELL ME ALL ABOUT THEIR 'MOVEMENT'!
THEY'RE KIDS WHO BELIEVE IN SOMETHING. GOD FORBID.
GRAB
NOT HAPPENING, TREFOIL.
NOT GETTING BAITED INTO ONE OF YOUR BULLSHIT ARGUMENTS.

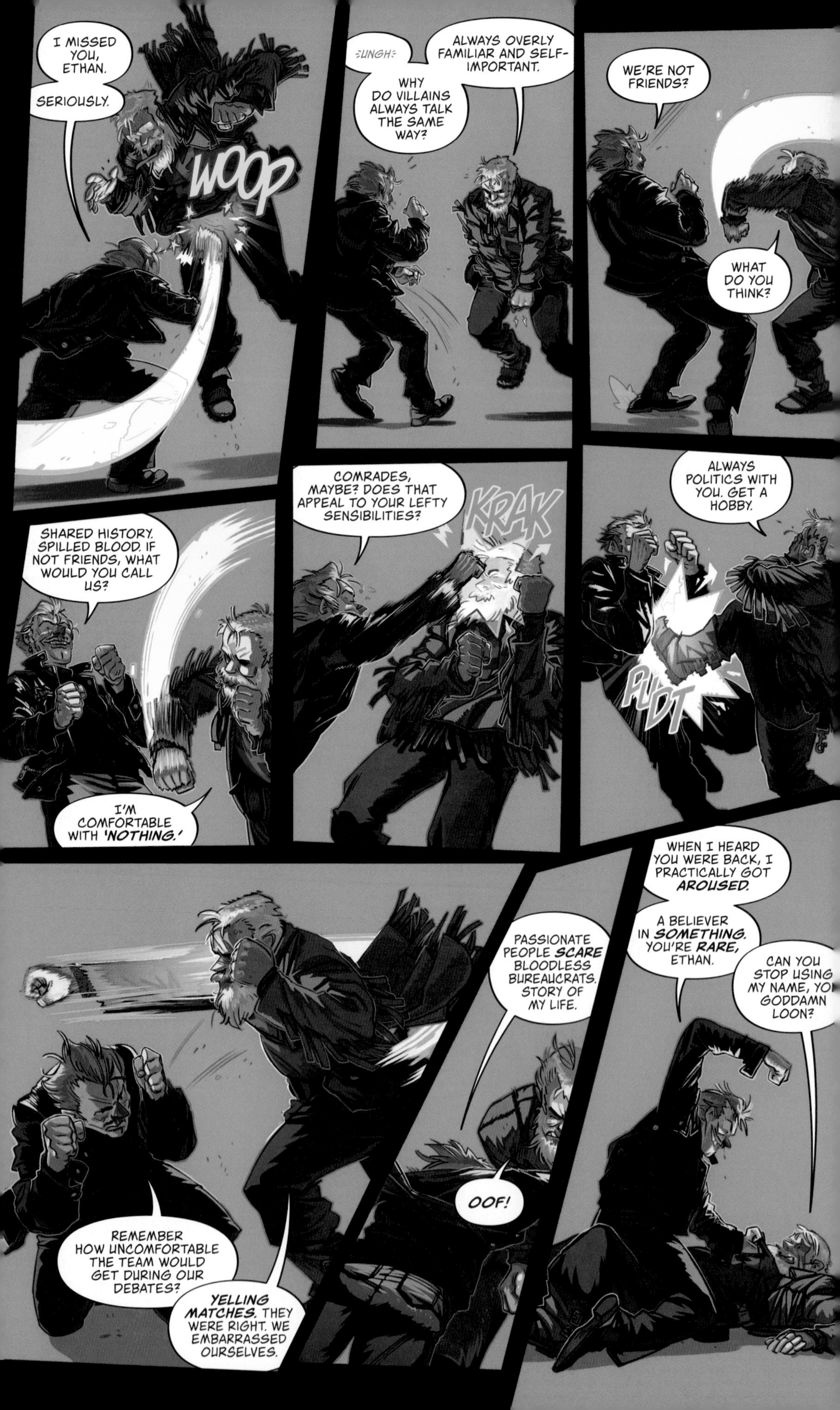
I MISSED YOU, ETHAN.
SERIOUSLY.
WOOP
UNGH
ALWAYS OVERLY FAMILIAR AND SELF-IMPORTANT.
WHY DO VILLAINS ALWAYS TALK THE SAME WAY?
WE'RE NOT FRIENDS?
WHAT DO YOU THINK?
SHARED HISTORY. SPILLED BLOOD. IF NOT FRIENDS, WHAT WOULD YOU CALL US?
I'M COMFORTABLE WITH 'NOTHING.'
COMRADES, MAYBE? DOES THAT APPEAL TO YOUR LEFTY SENSIBILITIES?
KRAK
ALWAYS POLITICS WITH YOU. GET A HOBBY.
PUDT
REMEMBER HOW UNCOMFORTABLE THE TEAM WOULD GET DURING OUR DEBATES?
YELLING MATCHES. THEY WERE RIGHT. WE EMBARRASSED OURSELVES.
PASSIONATE PEOPLE SCARE BLOODLESS BUREAUCRATS. STORY OF MY LIFE.
OOF!
WHEN I HEARD YOU WERE BACK, I PRACTICALLY GOT AROUSED.
A BELIEVER IN SOMETHING. YOU'RE RARE, ETHAN.
CAN YOU STOP USING MY NAME, YO GODDAMN LOON?

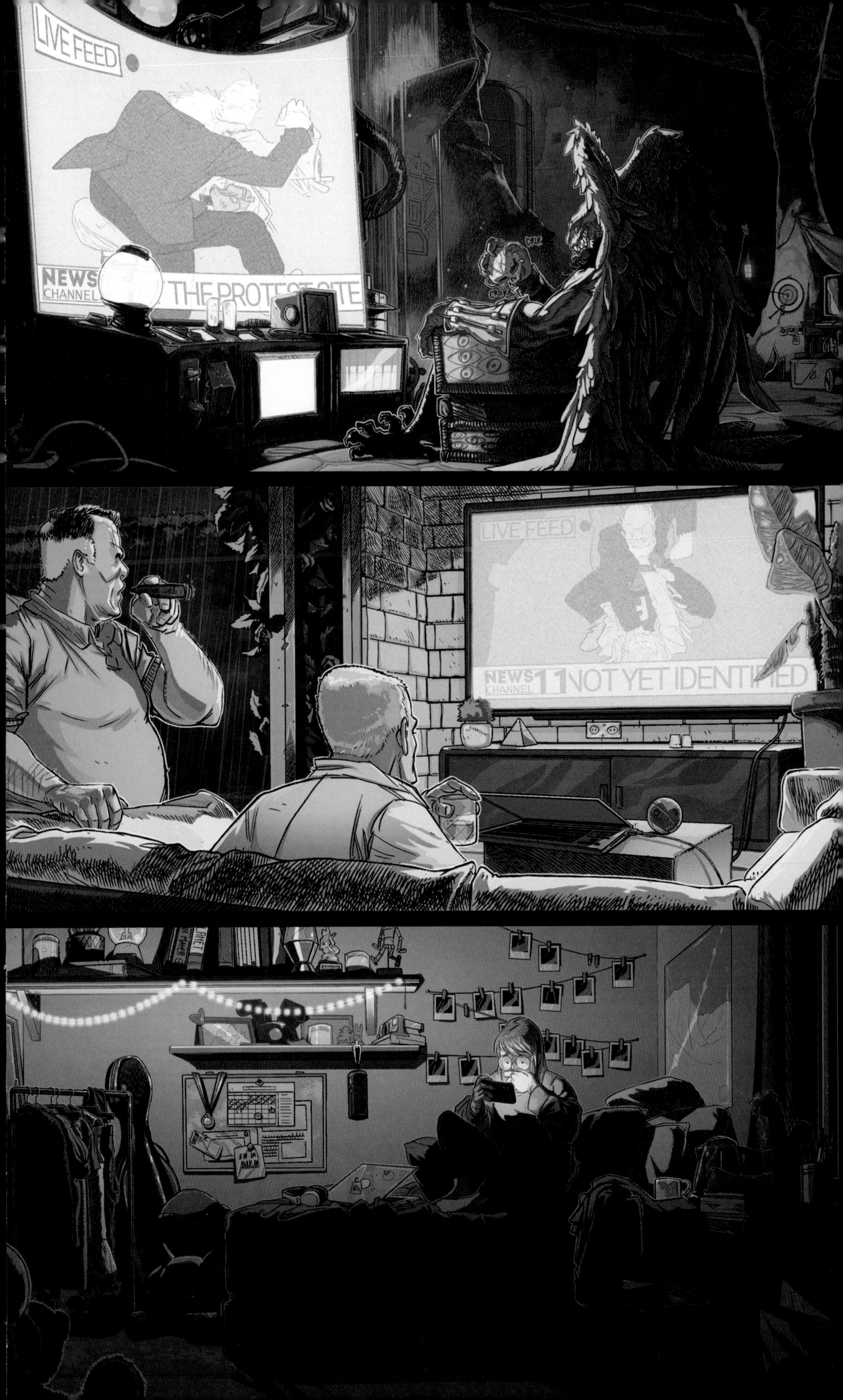
LIVE FEED
NEWS CHANNEL
THE PROTEST SITE
CRIK
LIVE FEED
NEWS CHANNEL 11
NOT YET IDENTIFIED

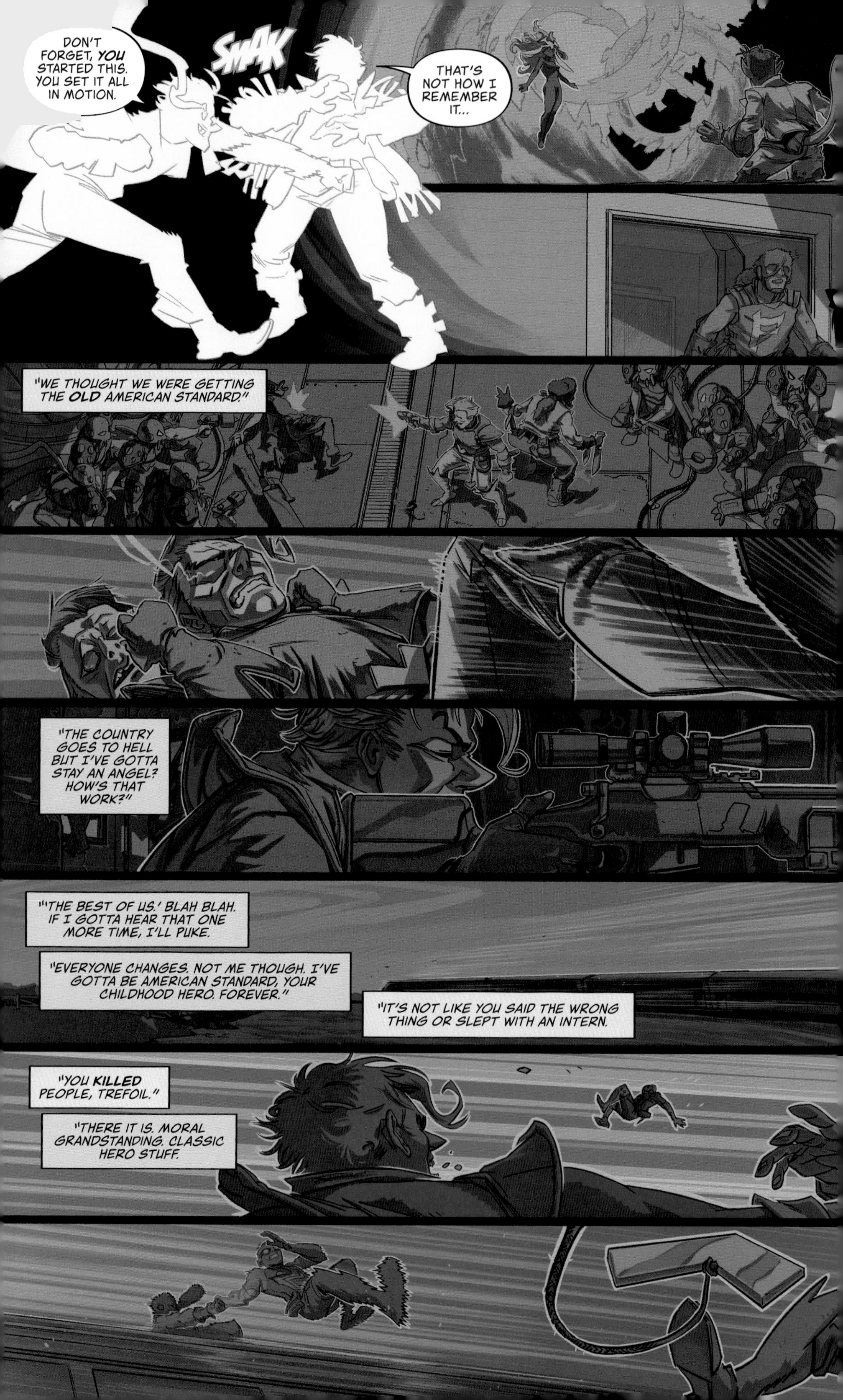
DON'T FORGET, YOU STARTED THIS. YOU SET IT ALL IN MOTION.
SMAK
THAT'S NOT HOW I REMEMBER IT...
"WE THOUGHT WE WERE GETTING THE OLD AMERICAN STANDARD."
"THE COUNTRY GOES TO HELL BUT I'VE GOTTA STAY AN ANGEL? HOW'S THAT WORK?"
"'THE BEST OF US.' BLAH BLAH. IF I GOTTA HEAR THAT ONE MORE TIME, I'LL PUKE.
"EVERYONE CHANGES. NOT ME THOUGH. I'VE GOTTA BE AMERICAN STANDARD, YOUR CHILDHOOD HERO. FOREVER."
"IT'S NOT LIKE YOU SAID THE WRONG THING OR SLEPT WITH AN INTERN.
"YOU KILLED PEOPLE, TREFOIL."
"THERE IT IS. MORAL GRANDSTANDING. CLASSIC HERO STUFF.

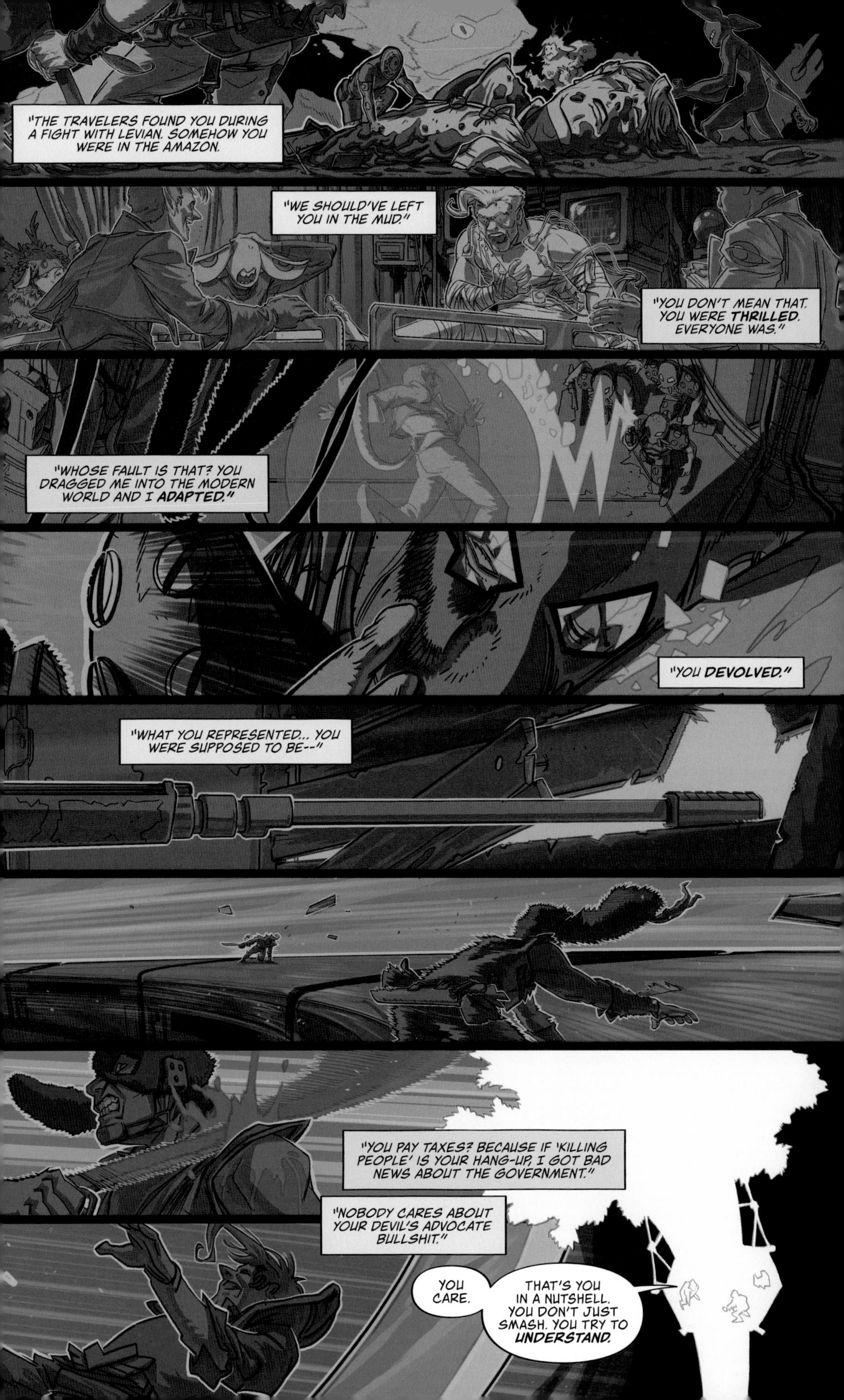
"THE TRAVELERS FOUND YOU DURING A FIGHT WITH LEVIAN. SOMEHOW YOU WERE IN THE AMAZON.
"WE SHOULD'VE LEFT YOU IN THE MUD."
"YOU DON'T MEAN THAT. YOU WERE **THRILLED**. EVERYONE WAS."
"WHOSE FAULT IS THAT? YOU DRAGGED ME INTO THE MODERN WORLD AND I **ADAPTED**."
"YOU **DEVOLVED**."
"WHAT YOU REPRESENTED... YOU WERE SUPPOSED TO BE--"
"YOU PAY TAXES? BECAUSE IF 'KILLING PEOPLE' IS YOUR HANG-UP, I GOT BAD NEWS ABOUT THE GOVERNMENT."
"NOBODY CARES ABOUT YOUR DEVIL'S ADVOCATE BULLSHIT."
YOU CARE.
THAT'S YOU IN A NUTSHELL. YOU DON'T JUST SMASH. YOU TRY TO ***UNDERSTAND***.

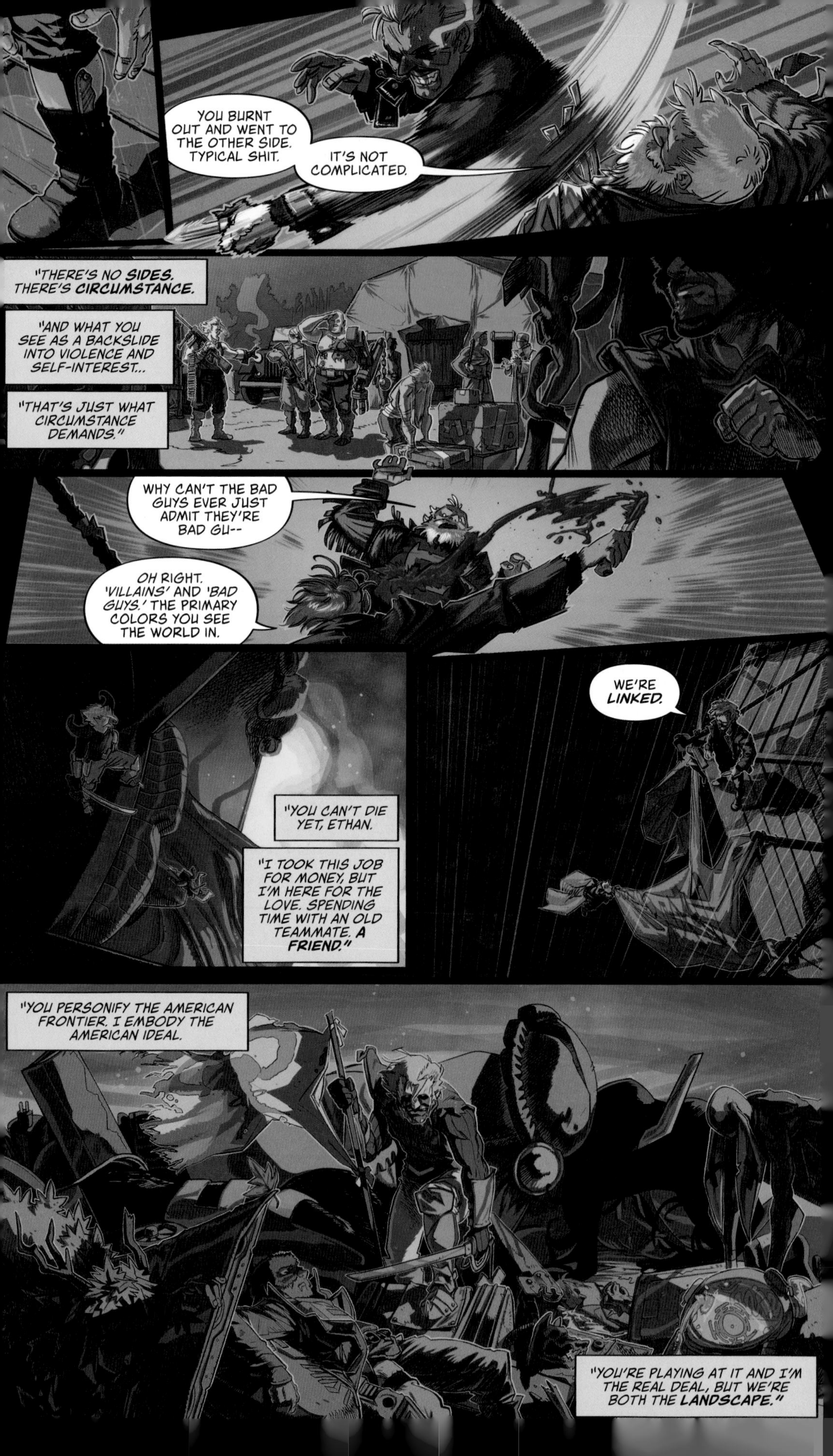
YOU BURNT OUT AND WENT TO THE OTHER SIDE. TYPICAL SHIT.
IT'S NOT COMPLICATED.
"THERE'S NO SIDES. THERE'S CIRCUMSTANCE.
"AND WHAT YOU SEE AS A BACKSLIDE INTO VIOLENCE AND SELF-INTEREST...
"THAT'S JUST WHAT CIRCUMSTANCE DEMANDS."
WHY CAN'T THE BAD GUYS EVER JUST ADMIT THEY'RE BAD GU--
OH RIGHT. 'VILLAINS' AND 'BAD GUYS.' THE PRIMARY COLORS YOU SEE THE WORLD IN.
"YOU CAN'T DIE YET, ETHAN.
"I TOOK THIS JOB FOR MONEY, BUT I'M HERE FOR THE LOVE. SPENDING TIME WITH AN OLD TEAMMATE. A FRIEND."
WE'RE LINKED.
"YOU PERSONIFY THE AMERICAN FRONTIER. I EMBODY THE AMERICAN IDEAL.
"YOU'RE PLAYING AT IT AND I'M THE REAL DEAL, BUT WE'RE BOTH THE LANDSCAPE."

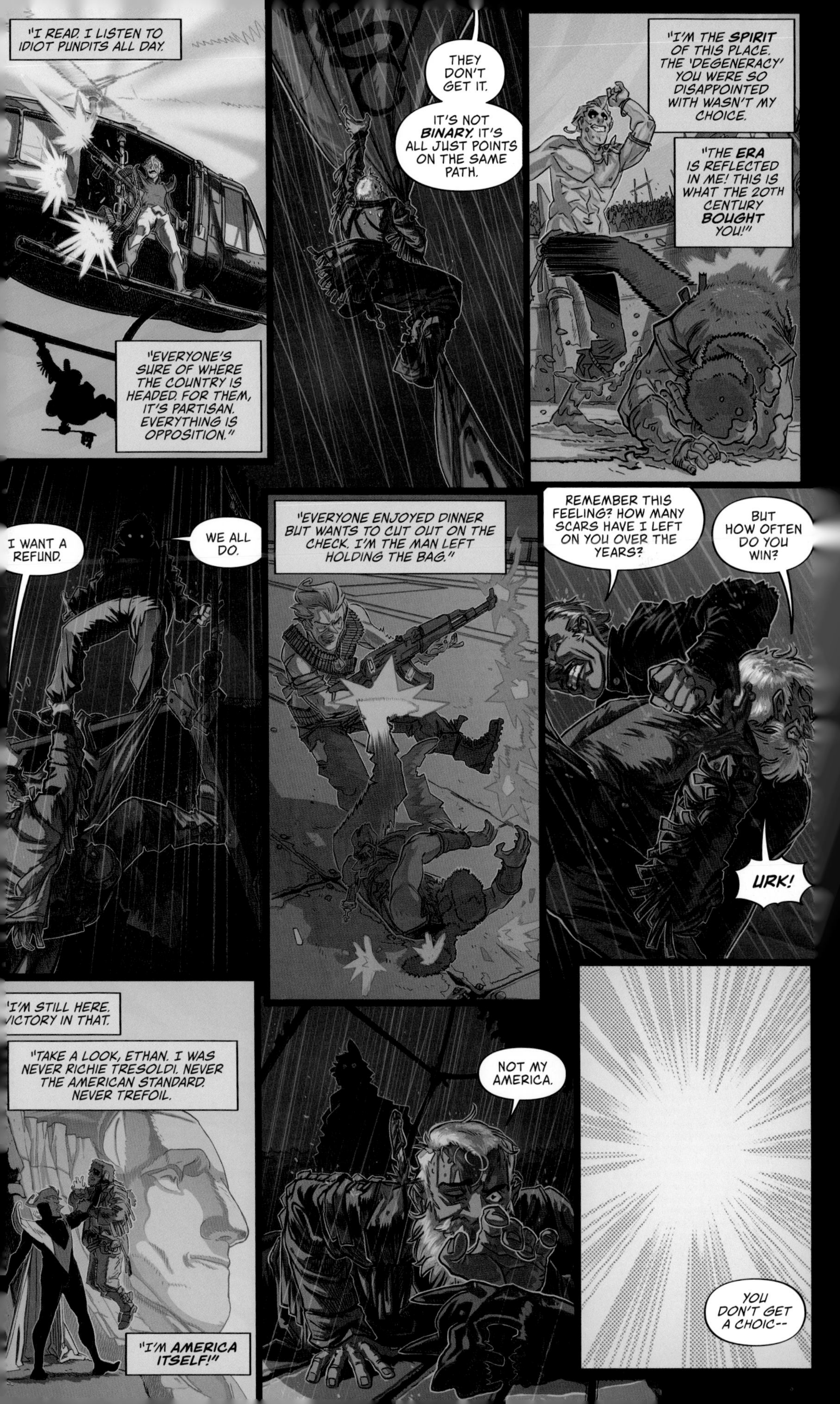
"I READ. I LISTEN TO IDIOT PUNDITS ALL DAY.
"EVERYONE'S SURE OF WHERE THE COUNTRY IS HEADED. FOR THEM, IT'S PARTISAN. EVERYTHING IS OPPOSITION."
THEY DON'T GET IT.
IT'S NOT BINARY. IT'S ALL JUST POINTS ON THE SAME PATH.
"I'M THE SPIRIT OF THIS PLACE. THE 'DEGENERACY' YOU WERE SO DISAPPOINTED WITH WASN'T MY CHOICE.
"THE ERA IS REFLECTED IN ME! THIS IS WHAT THE 20TH CENTURY BOUGHT YOU!"
I WANT A REFUND.
WE ALL DO.
"EVERYONE ENJOYED DINNER BUT WANTS TO CUT OUT ON THE CHECK. I'M THE MAN LEFT HOLDING THE BAG."
REMEMBER THIS FEELING? HOW MANY SCARS HAVE I LEFT ON YOU OVER THE YEARS?
BUT HOW OFTEN DO YOU WIN?
URK!
"I'M STILL HERE. VICTORY IN THAT.
"TAKE A LOOK, ETHAN. I WAS NEVER RICHIE TRESOLDI. NEVER THE AMERICAN STANDARD. NEVER TREFOIL.
"I'M AMERICA ITSELF!"
NOT MY AMERICA.
YOU DON'T GET A CHOIC--

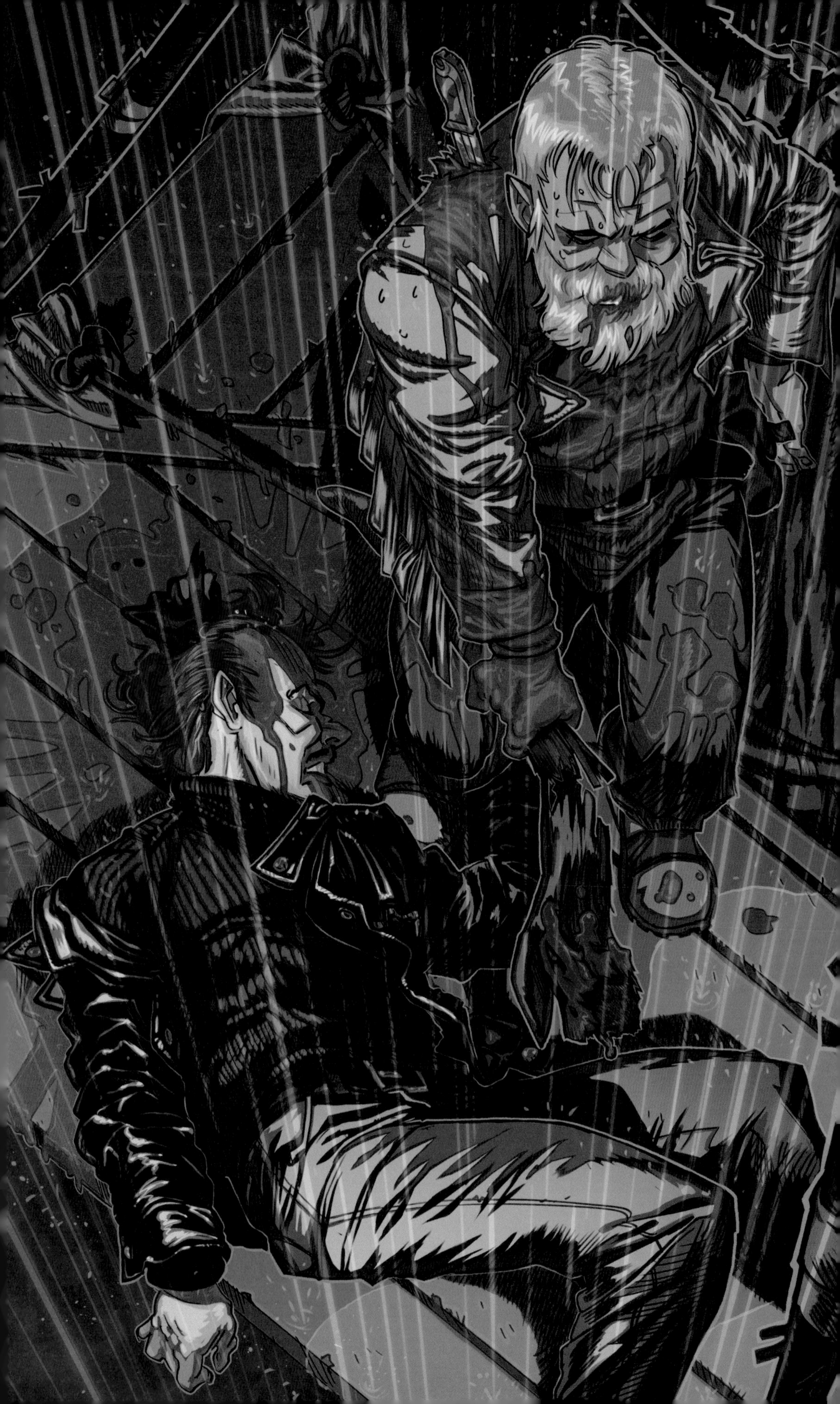

# 'ALOR

**eal name**: Richard Tresoldi
**ccupation:** Mercenary
**entity:** Widely known
**egal status:** Citizen of the United States ith extensive criminal record
**nown relatives:** None
**roup affiliation:** Bold Travelers (former); ellow Travelers (former); Maulers US (fomer)
**ias:** American Standard (former); Trefoil (present)
**istory:** Often referred to as America's First ero, Richard Tresoldi was actually the sixth persoldier the US put into combat. A petty ficer in the Navy at the time of his recruitment the supersoldier program, Office L, Tresoldi as chosen for his bravery and enthusiasm for mbat. He proved a real asset for the nerican fighting forces until the bombing of roshima, which he attempted to stop and as subsequently court-martialed. Put back to action, Tresoldi never fully recovered from e experience and his work in the field flected that. He saw action in the Korean War it disappeared around the Vietnam War.
Tresoldi has provided conflicting accounts of s whereabouts during this period, ranging om a military prison to an intersteller pleasure aft. There are unsubstantiated sightings of a an meeting his description operating in Laos nd later across Central and South America. ne truth remains unknown.
He was found by the Fellow Travelers in the ud of the Amazon during a battle with Levian. ollowing his discovery, Tresoldi shed the nerican Standard moniker and adopted Valor s his hero name.
n his first missions with the Fellow Travelers e lived up to his reputation and proved a great ammate. As time went on, however, his ctics became more brutal. Tresoldi was put n adminstrative leave from the team pending n investigation into the death of the ipervillain Admin.
He went missing during this period and is ssumed to have been building a mercenary rmy inside the rogue nation of Conquista. The ext time he was sighted, it was during a failed oup of Bolivia. He escaped prosecution for nat incusion but again disappeared.
In his next battle with Fellow Travelers, resoldi called himself Trefoil. It's unclear what xactly that is in reference to. During this fight, resoldi spared the life of the superhero Glib, ut vowed it would be the last courtesy he xtends to his former teammates.

**eight:** 6'
**Veight:** 200lbs
**yes:** Blue
**air:** Blonde
**trength level:** Valor is considered an nhanced human rather than a proper uperhuman. His strength is several times that f a normal human, but he falls short of the on-lift' marker.
**nown superhuman powers:** All of resoldi's physical attributes are enhanced, cluding his agility, strength, and endurance. is senses are likewise elevated, allowing him ) see in low light and track by scent. As he ever received an IQ test prior to his time in ffice L, it's unclear if the supersoldier rogram enhanced his intelligence, but it ppears Tresoldi has an above-average ntellect.

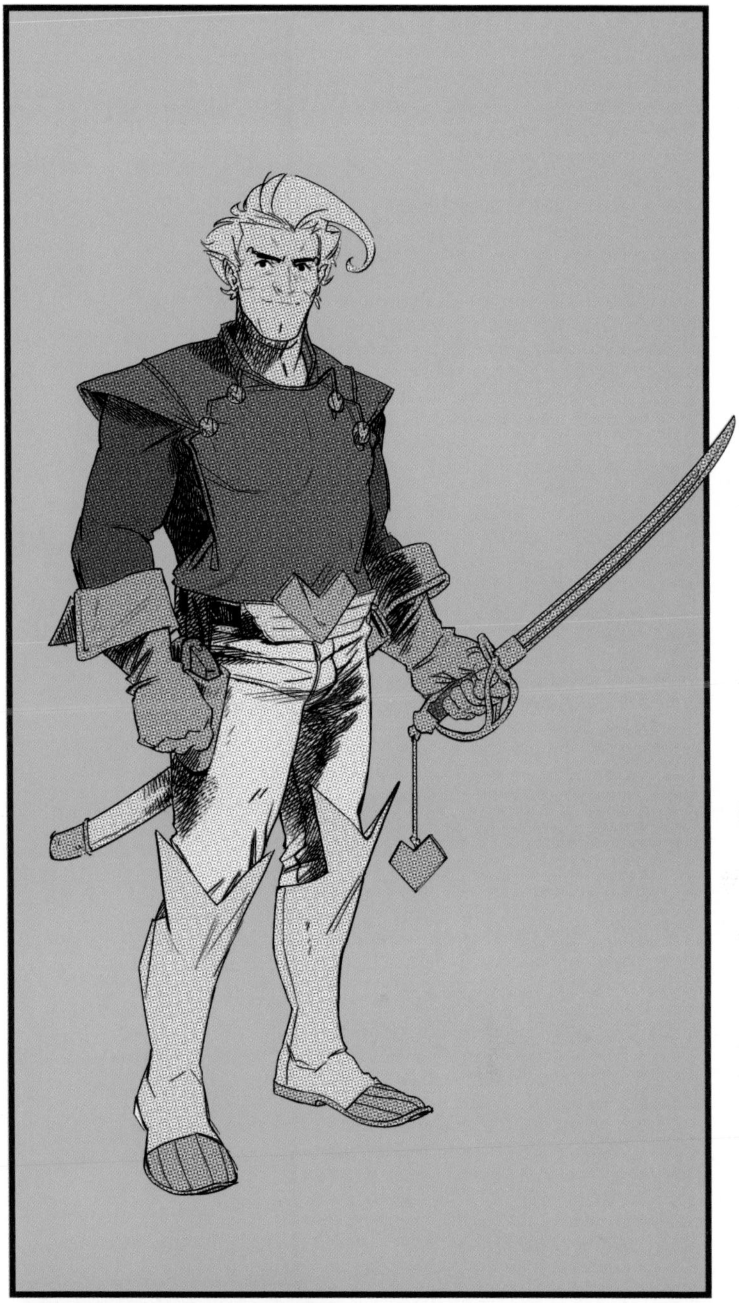

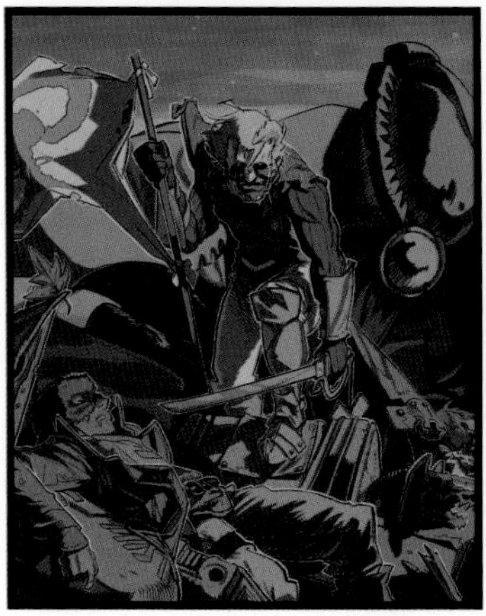

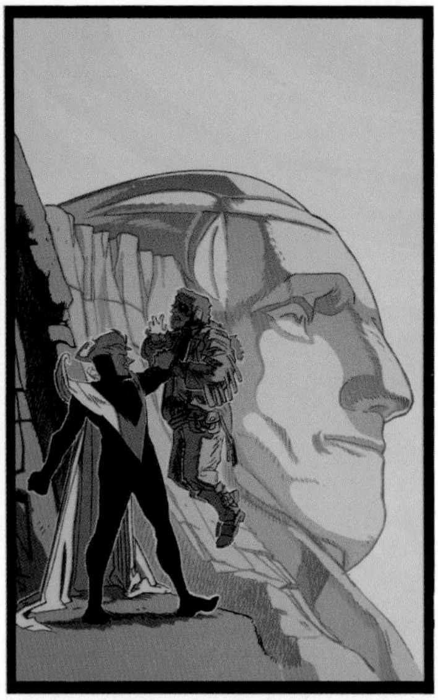

# SHOGGOTHBEAR

**Real name:** None
**Occupation:** None
**Identity:** N/A
**Legal status:** Wanted criminal
**Known relatives:** None
**Group affiliation:** None
**Alias:** Bear; Emperor Ursidae; Hastur
**History:** Shoggothbear's first modern appearance was in the commuter rail tunnel linking New Jersey and New York. Sightings of a monstrous beast and the disappearance of multiple railway workers led to the intervention of Manhattan-based supernatural investigators Team Creep. Shoggothbear fled to the pine barrens of New Jersey after the battle with Team Creep ruptured a gas line.

A few months later, the beast was spotted sapping the power lines outside Woodbine, New Jersey. This time Team Creep was assisted by the costumed hero Public Defender, who had been displaced to the Pine Barrens after the events of Kali Yuga. The group managed to defeat Shoggothbear using the forest's uniquely flammable underbrush.

The monster, temporarily referring to himself as Emperor Ursidae, next appeared at the upstate New York wedding of Glibb and Miss Dint. Crashing the event seeking revenge on Public Defender, he instead found himself up against fifty of the world's strongest heroes. The battle did not last long and Shoggothbear disappeared into the depths of Lake George.

Though it's unclear if he's reliable, Shoggothbear claims to have hunted humans since the beginning of recorded history. His exact origins are unclear, but he's suggested that he's older than Earth itself and arrived from another solar system or dimension. Through oral histories and art there is some confirmation of a long history with the native peoples of the Americas. But the exact nature of the relationship or level of contact is impossible to determine. Additionally, Dr. Deltag Delcourt, a historian of Scandinavian folk tradition and professor at Ann Arbor University, asserts there is a bear-like monster fitting Shoggothbear's description in the pre-written histories of Iceland and Greenland.

**Height:** 8ft (bear form)
**Weight:** 800lbs
**Eyes:** Variable
**Hair:** Brown
**Strength level:** Unknown; presumed to be superhuman level or greater
**Known superhuman powers:** Shoggothbear is a extradimensional being whose physiology doesn't correspond with Earth animals. His cells can expand, contract, or multiply at will. While Shoggothbear roughly maintains the shape of his host animal -a particularly large grizzly- he will forfeit this camouflage whenever necessary. During this time in his 'real' shape, Shoggothbear appears malleable, fluid, and almost formless. In this form, he can absorb other beings into himself, devouring their consciousness and adding their mass to his own.

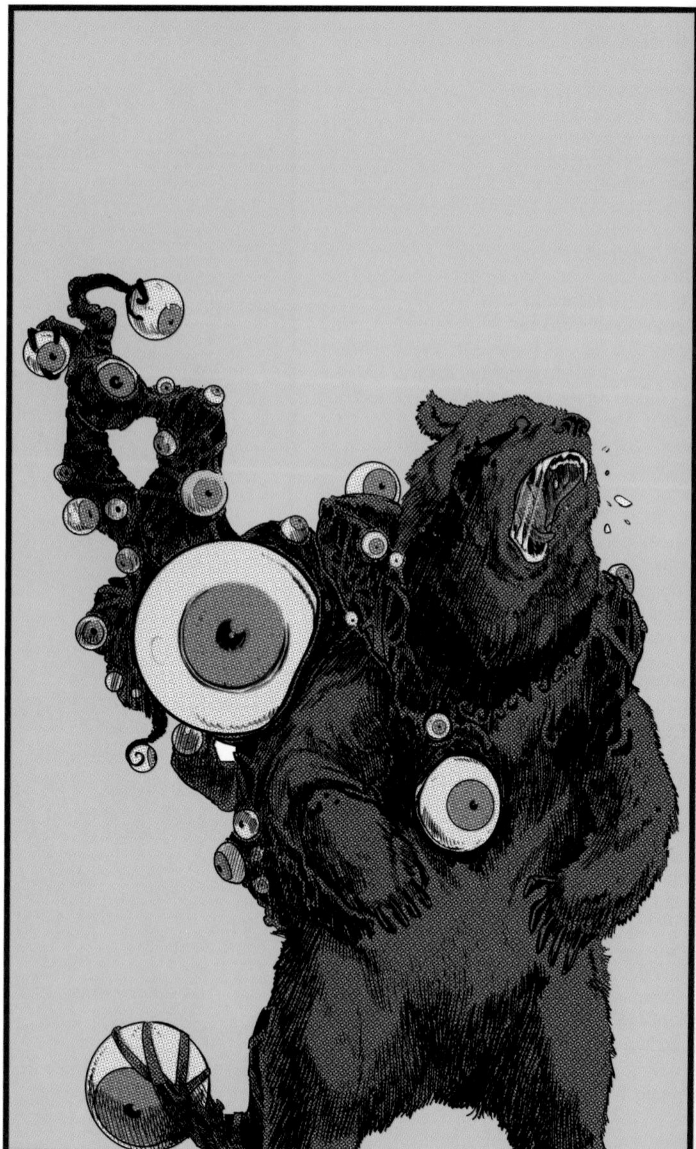

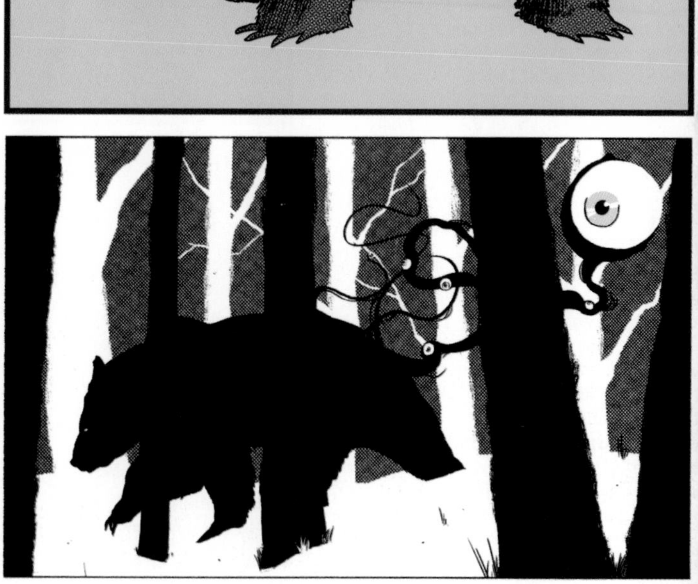

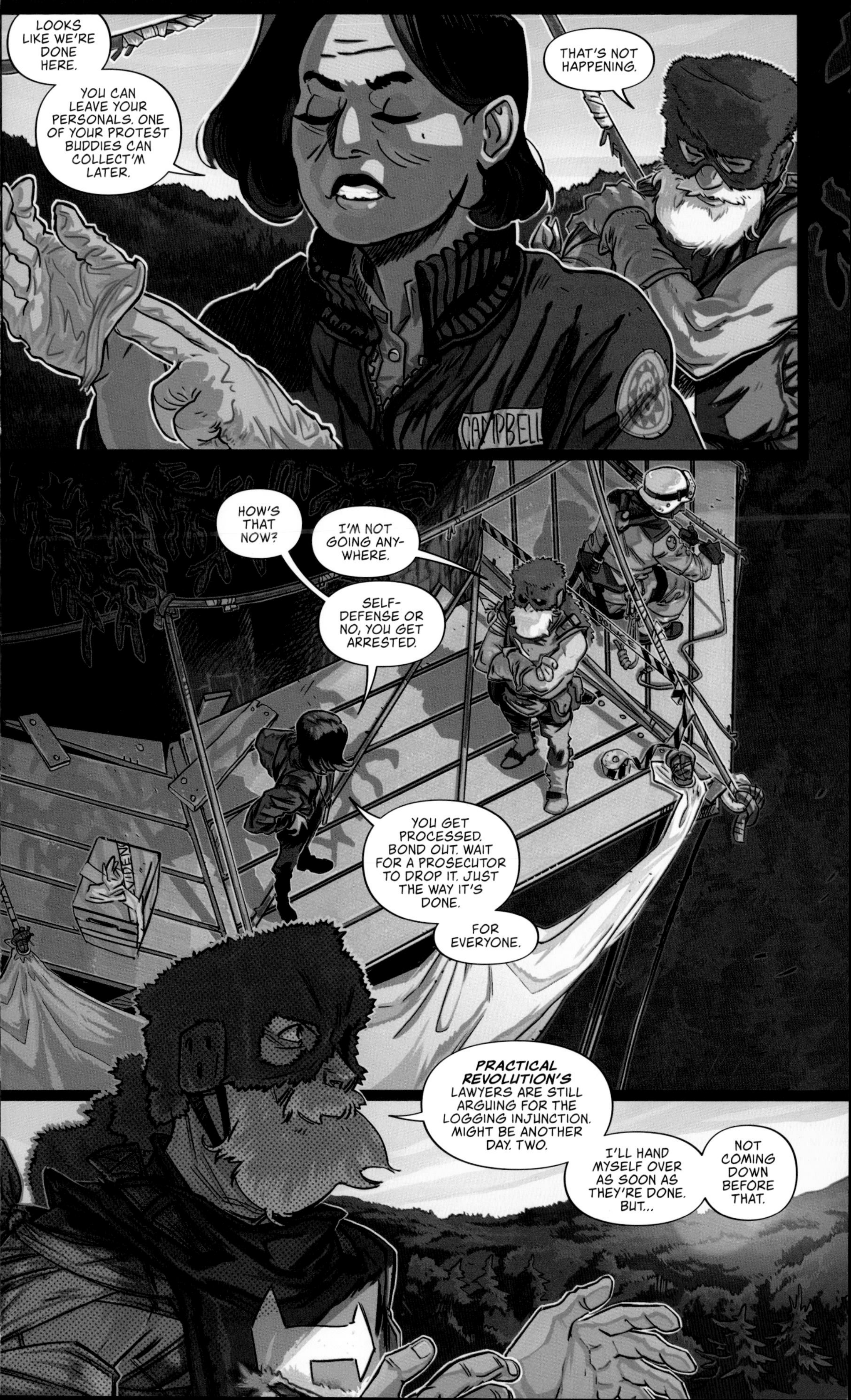
LOOKS LIKE WE'RE DONE HERE.
YOU CAN LEAVE YOUR PERSONALS. ONE OF YOUR PROTEST BUDDIES CAN COLLECT'M LATER.
THAT'S NOT HAPPENING.
CAMPBELL
HOW'S THAT NOW?
I'M NOT GOING ANY-WHERE.
SELF-DEFENSE OR NO, YOU GET ARRESTED.
YOU GET PROCESSED. BOND OUT. WAIT FOR A PROSECUTOR TO DROP IT. JUST THE WAY IT'S DONE.
FOR EVERYONE.
*PRACTICAL REVOLUTION'S* LAWYERS ARE STILL ARGUING FOR THE LOGGING INJUNCTION. MIGHT BE ANOTHER DAY. TWO.
I'LL HAND MYSELF OVER AS SOON AS THEY'RE DONE. BUT...
NOT COMING DOWN BEFORE THAT.

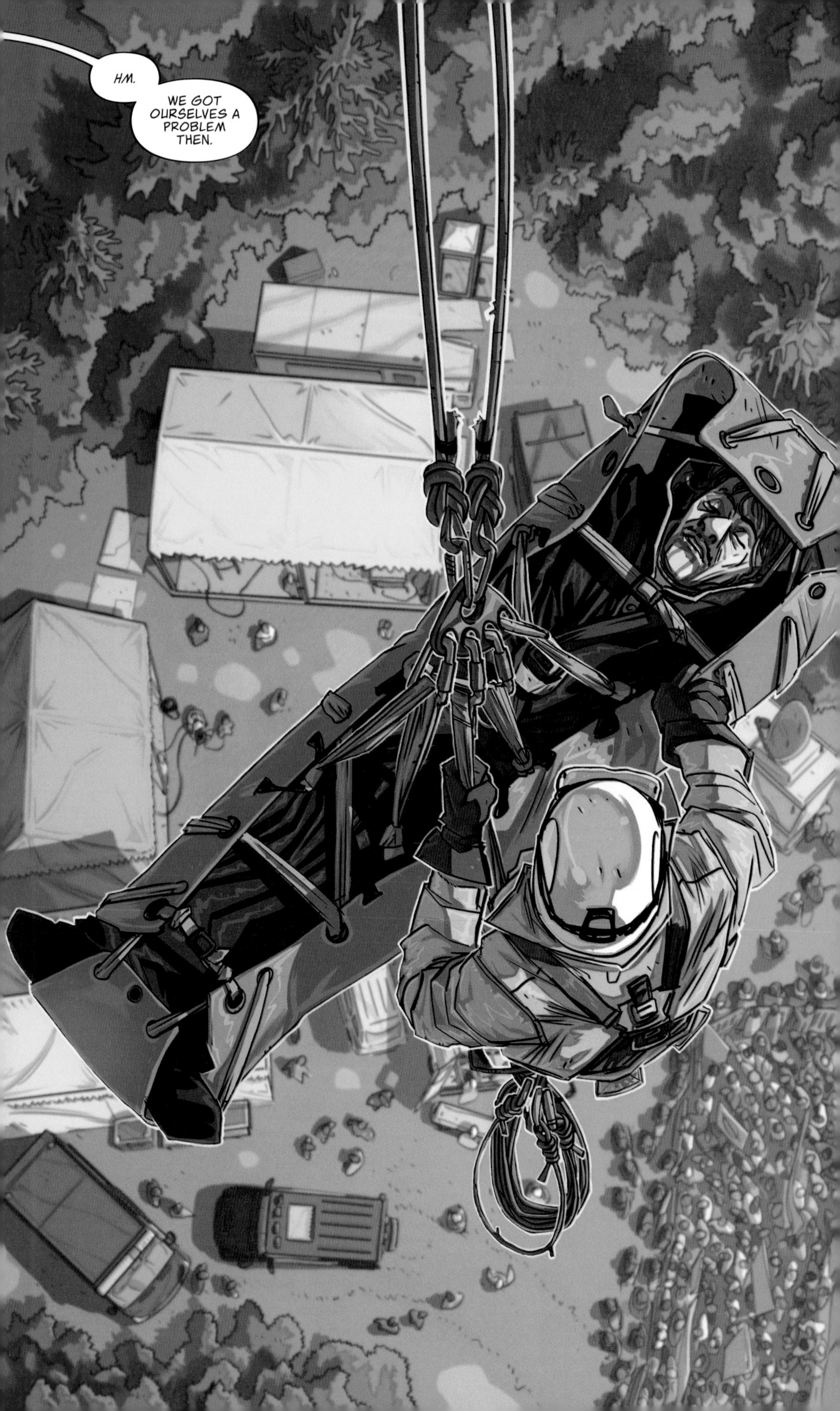
HM.
WE GOT OURSELVES A PROBLEM THEN.

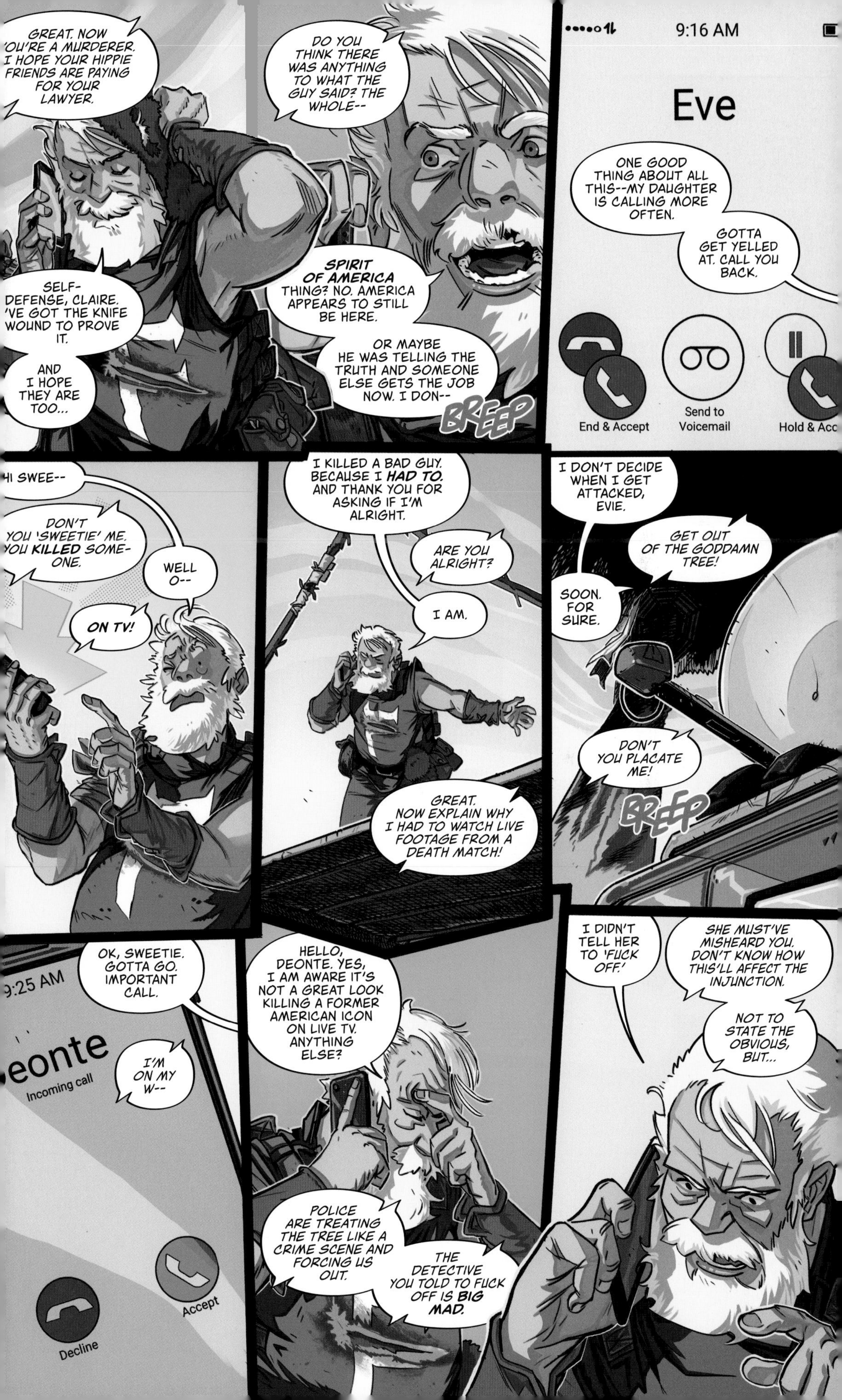
GREAT. NOW YOU'RE A MURDERER. I HOPE YOUR HIPPIE FRIENDS ARE PAYING FOR YOUR LAWYER.
SELF-DEFENSE, CLAIRE. I'VE GOT THE KNIFE WOUND TO PROVE IT.
AND I HOPE THEY ARE TOO...
DO YOU THINK THERE WAS ANYTHING TO WHAT THE GUY SAID? THE WHOLE--
SPIRIT OF AMERICA THING? NO. AMERICA APPEARS TO STILL BE HERE.
OR MAYBE HE WAS TELLING THE TRUTH AND SOMEONE ELSE GETS THE JOB NOW. I DON--
BREEP
9:16 AM
Eve
ONE GOOD THING ABOUT ALL THIS--MY DAUGHTER IS CALLING MORE OFTEN.
GOTTA GET YELLED AT. CALL YOU BACK.
End & Accept
Send to Voicemail
Hold & Acc
HI SWEE--
DON'T YOU 'SWEETIE' ME. YOU KILLED SOME-ONE.
WELL O--
ON TV!
I KILLED A BAD GUY. BECAUSE I HAD TO. AND THANK YOU FOR ASKING IF I'M ALRIGHT.
ARE YOU ALRIGHT?
I AM.
GREAT. NOW EXPLAIN WHY I HAD TO WATCH LIVE FOOTAGE FROM A DEATH MATCH!
I DON'T DECIDE WHEN I GET ATTACKED, EVIE.
GET OUT OF THE GODDAMN TREE!
SOON. FOR SURE.
DON'T YOU PLACATE ME!
BREEP
9:25 AM
eonte
Incoming call
OK, SWEETIE. GOTTA GO. IMPORTANT CALL.
I'M ON MY W--
Decline
Accept
HELLO, DEONTE. YES, I AM AWARE IT'S NOT A GREAT LOOK KILLING A FORMER AMERICAN ICON ON LIVE TV. ANYTHING ELSE?
POLICE ARE TREATING THE TREE LIKE A CRIME SCENE AND FORCING US OUT.
THE DETECTIVE YOU TOLD TO FUCK OFF IS BIG MAD.
I DIDN'T TELL HER TO 'FUCK OFF.'
SHE MUST'VE MISHEARD YOU. DON'T KNOW HOW THIS'LL AFFECT THE INJUNCTION.
NOT TO STATE THE OBVIOUS, BUT...

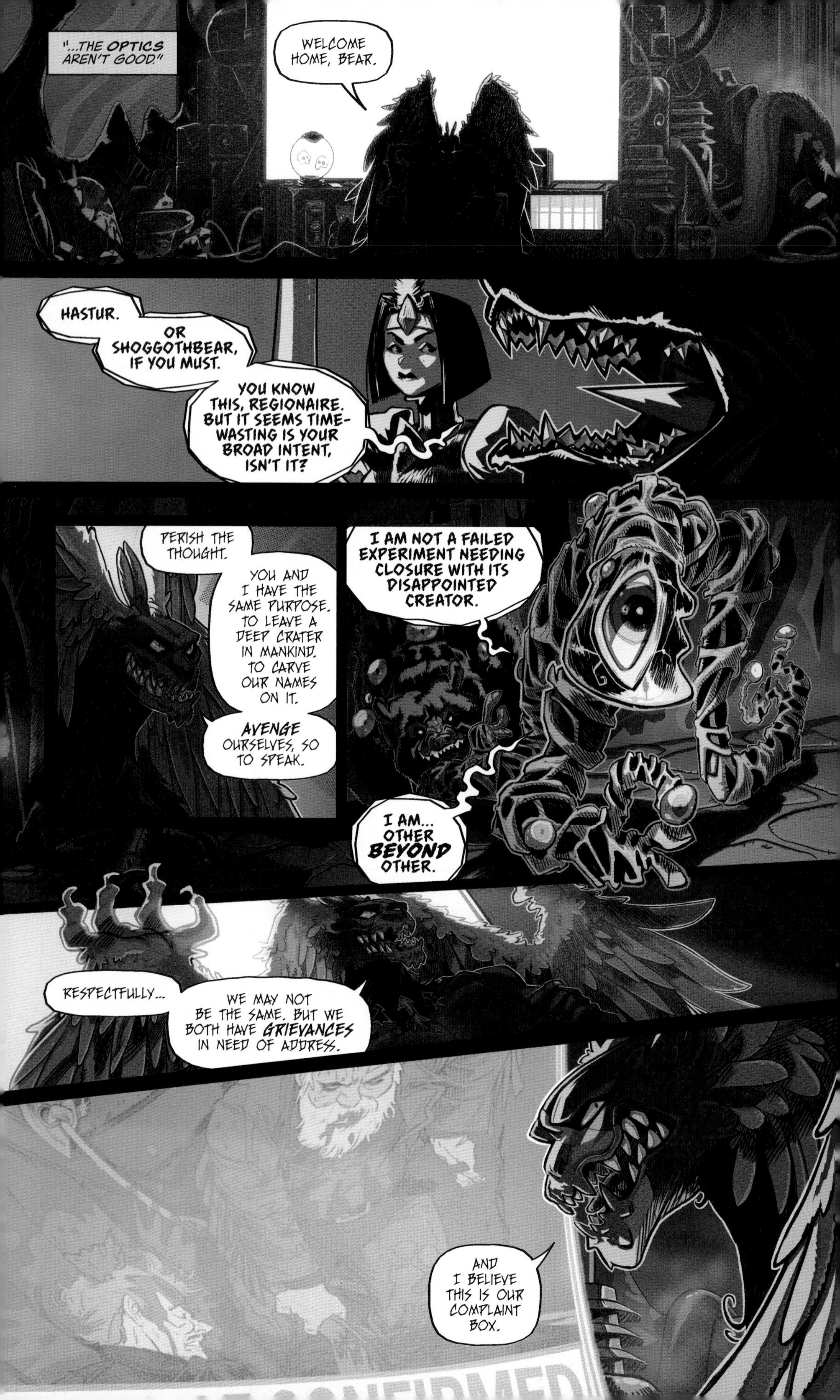

"...THE OPTICS AREN'T GOOD."
WELCOME HOME, BEAR.
HASTUR.
OR SHOGGOTHBEAR, IF YOU MUST.
YOU KNOW THIS, REGIONAIRE. BUT IT SEEMS TIME-WASTING IS YOUR BROAD INTENT, ISN'T IT?
PERISH THE THOUGHT.
YOU AND I HAVE THE SAME PURPOSE. TO LEAVE A DEEP CRATER IN MANKIND. TO CARVE OUR NAMES ON IT.
AVENGE OURSELVES, SO TO SPEAK.
I AM NOT A FAILED EXPERIMENT NEEDING CLOSURE WITH ITS DISAPPOINTED CREATOR.
I AM... OTHER BEYOND OTHER.
RESPECTFULLY...
WE MAY NOT BE THE SAME. BUT WE BOTH HAVE GRIEVANCES IN NEED OF ADDRESS.
AND I BELIEVE THIS IS OUR COMPLAINT BOX.

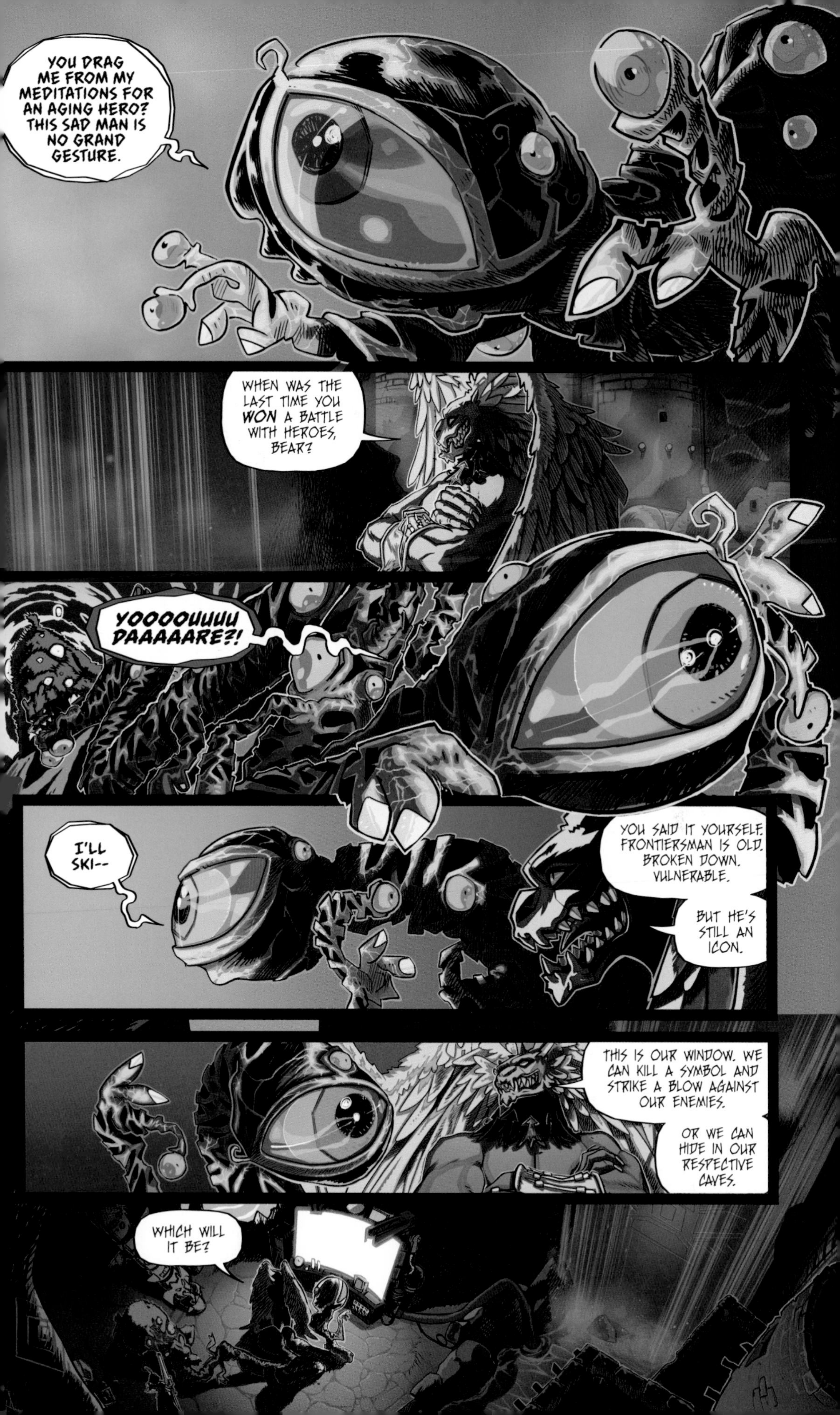
YOU DRAG ME FROM MY MEDITATIONS FOR AN AGING HERO? THIS SAD MAN IS NO GRAND GESTURE.
WHEN WAS THE LAST TIME YOU **WON** A BATTLE WITH HEROES, BEAR?
YOOOOUUUU DAAAAARE?!
I'LL SKI--
YOU SAID IT YOURSELF. FRONTIERSMAN IS OLD. BROKEN DOWN. VULNERABLE.
BUT HE'S STILL AN ICON.
THIS IS OUR WINDOW. WE CAN KILL A SYMBOL AND STRIKE A BLOW AGAINST OUR ENEMIES.
OR WE CAN HIDE IN OUR RESPECTIVE CAVES.
WHICH WILL IT BE?

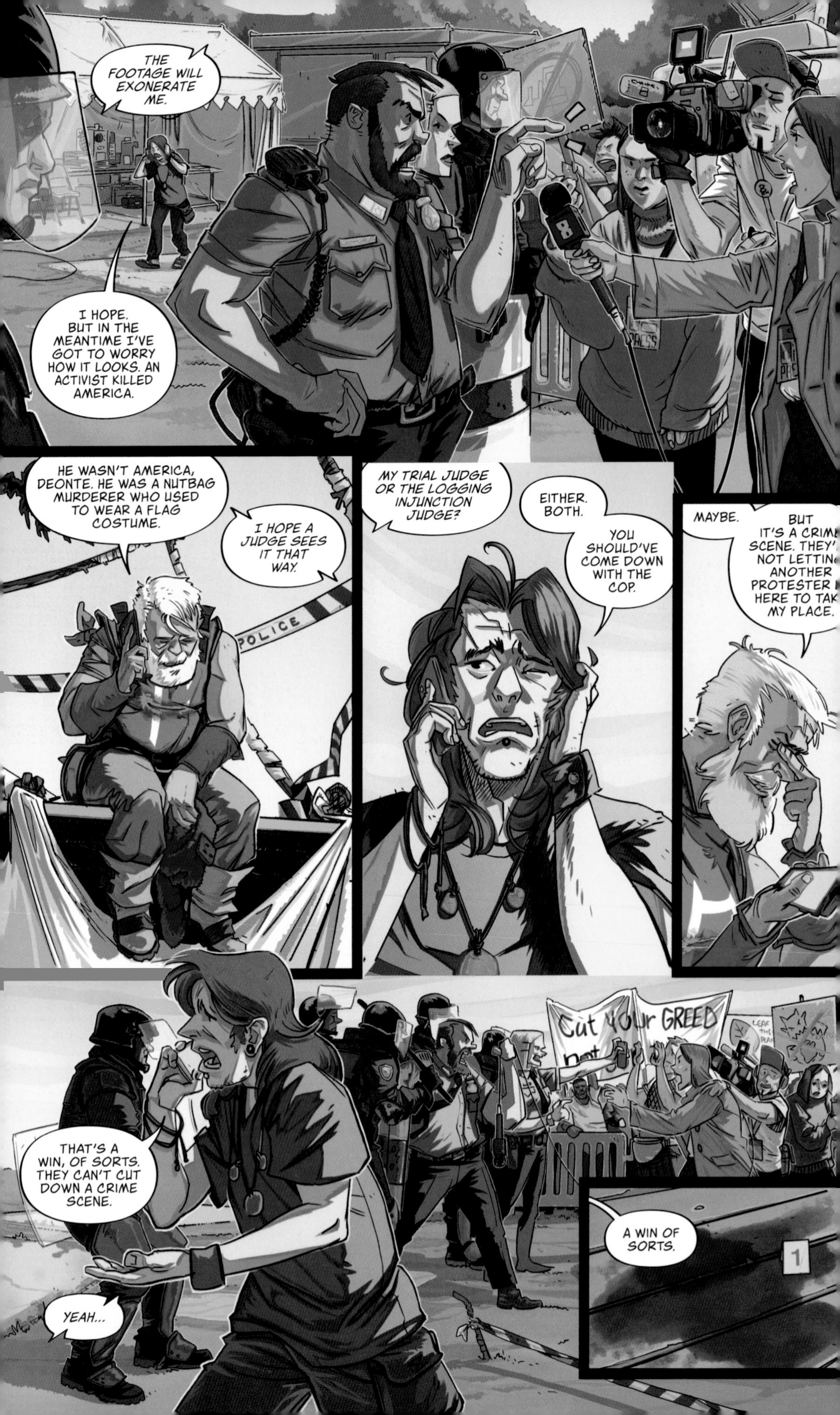
THE FOOTAGE WILL EXONERATE ME.
I HOPE. BUT IN THE MEANTIME I'VE GOT TO WORRY HOW IT LOOKS. AN ACTIVIST KILLED AMERICA.
PRESS
HE WASN'T AMERICA, DEONTE. HE WAS A NUTBAG MURDERER WHO USED TO WEAR A FLAG COSTUME.
I HOPE A JUDGE SEES IT THAT WAY.
POLICE
MY TRIAL JUDGE OR THE LOGGING INJUNCTION JUDGE?
EITHER. BOTH.
YOU SHOULD'VE COME DOWN WITH THE COP.
MAYBE.
BUT IT'S A CRIM SCENE. THEY' NOT LETTIN ANOTHER PROTESTER HERE TO TAK MY PLACE.
Cut Your GREED
THAT'S A WIN, OF SORTS. THEY CAN'T CUT DOWN A CRIME SCENE.
YEAH...
A WIN OF SORTS.
1

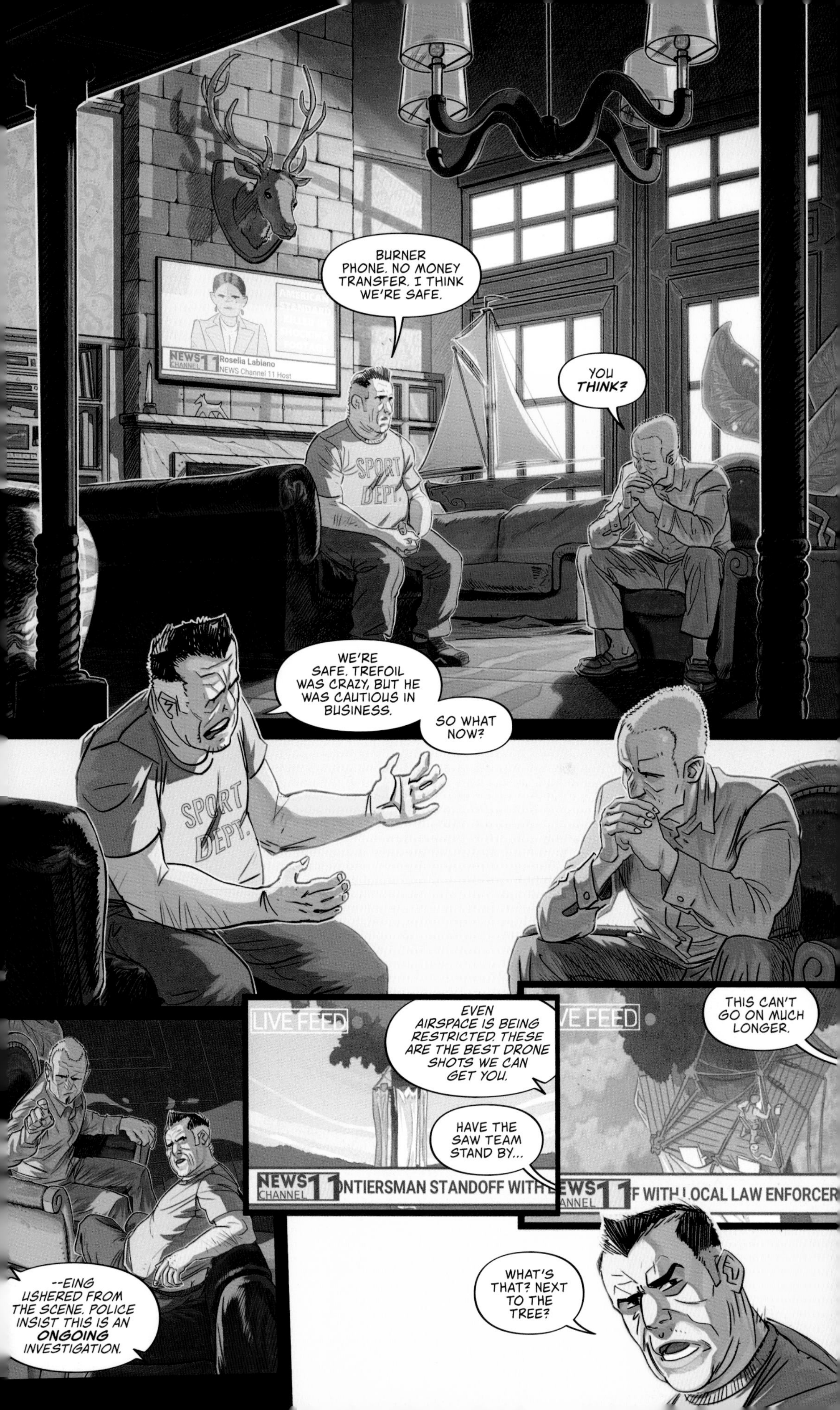
AMERICAN STANDARD
NEWS CHANNEL 11 Roselia Labiano
NEWS Channel 11 Host
BURNER PHONE. NO MONEY TRANSFER. I THINK WE'RE SAFE.
YOU *THINK?*
SPORT DEPT.
WE'RE SAFE. TREFOIL WAS CRAZY, BUT HE WAS CAUTIOUS IN BUSINESS.
SO WHAT NOW?
SPORT DEPT.
LIVE FEED
EVEN AIRSPACE IS BEING RESTRICTED. THESE ARE THE BEST DRONE SHOTS WE CAN GET YOU.
HAVE THE SAW TEAM STAND BY...
NEWS CHANNEL 11 ONTIERSMAN STANDOFF WITH
LIVE FEED
THIS CAN'T GO ON MUCH LONGER.
NEWS CHANNEL 11 F WITH LOCAL LAW ENFORCER
--EING USHERED FROM THE SCENE. POLICE INSIST THIS IS AN **ONGOING** INVESTIGATION.
WHAT'S THAT? NEXT TO THE TREE?

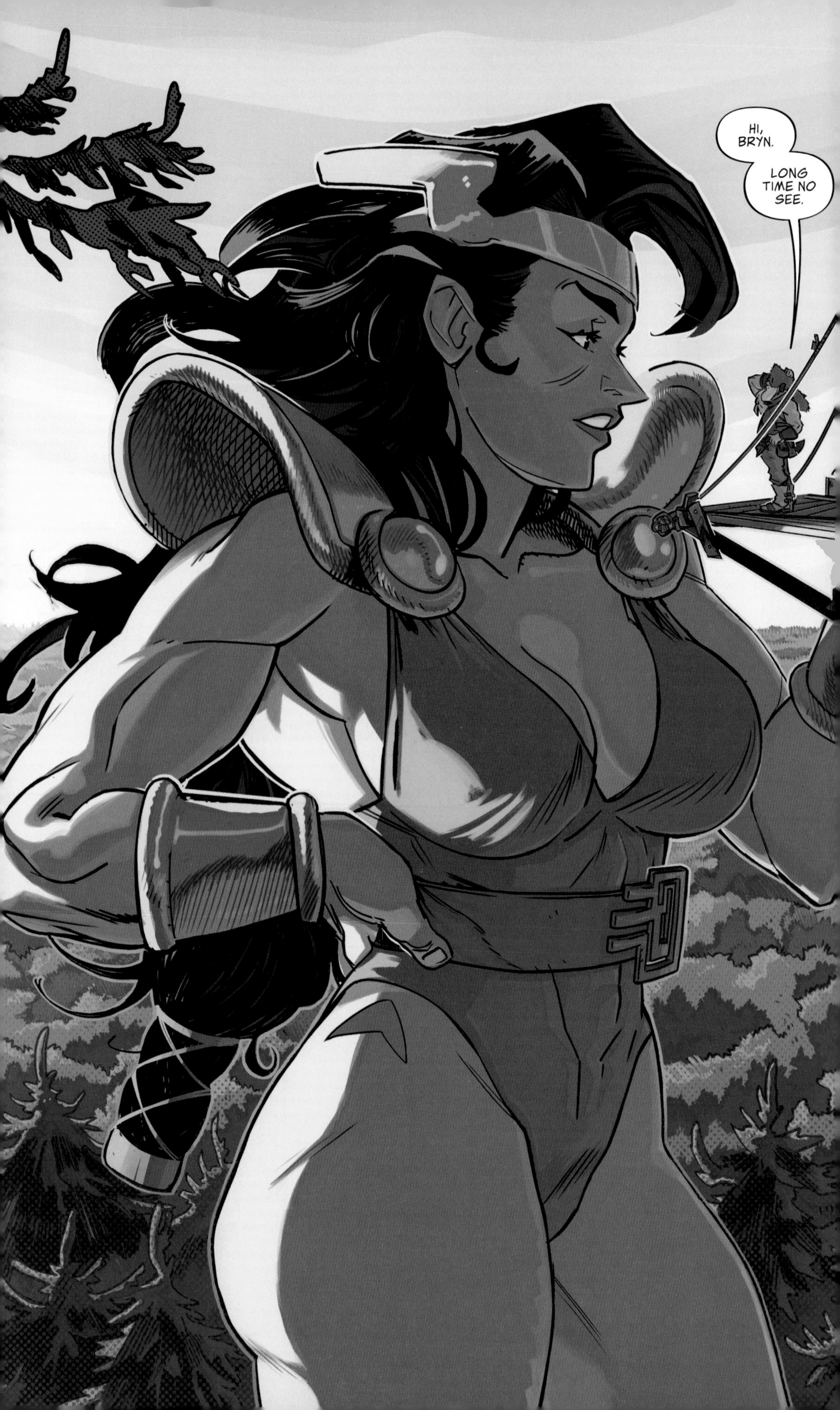
HI, BRYN.
LONG TIME NO SEE.

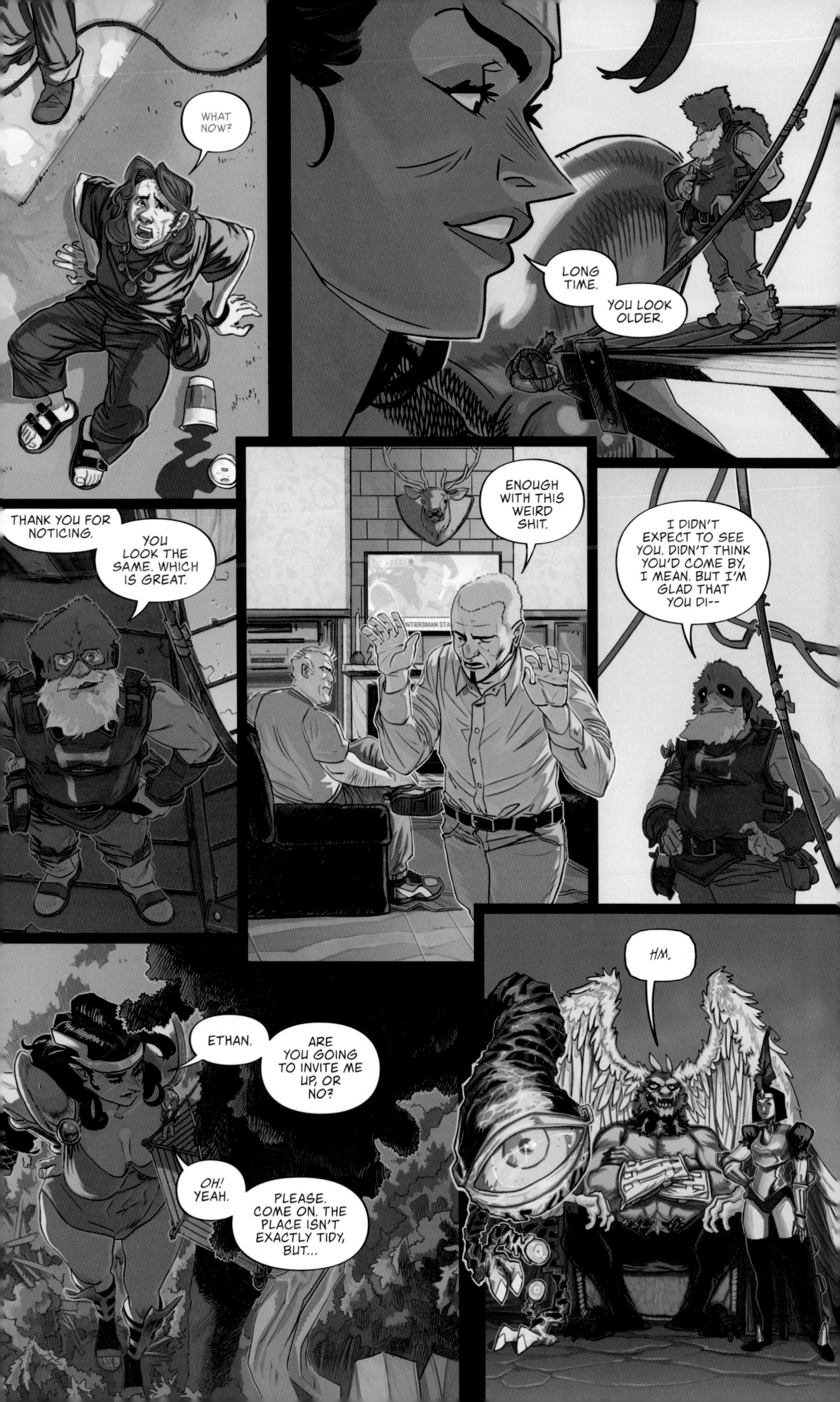
WHAT NOW?
LONG TIME.
YOU LOOK OLDER.
THANK YOU FOR NOTICING.
YOU LOOK THE SAME. WHICH IS GREAT.
ENOUGH WITH THIS WEIRD SHIT.
I DIDN'T EXPECT TO SEE YOU. DIDN'T THINK YOU'D COME BY, I MEAN. BUT I'M GLAD THAT YOU DI--
ETHAN.
ARE YOU GOING TO INVITE ME UP, OR NO?
OH! YEAH.
PLEASE. COME ON. THE PLACE ISN'T EXACTLY TIDY, BUT...
HM.

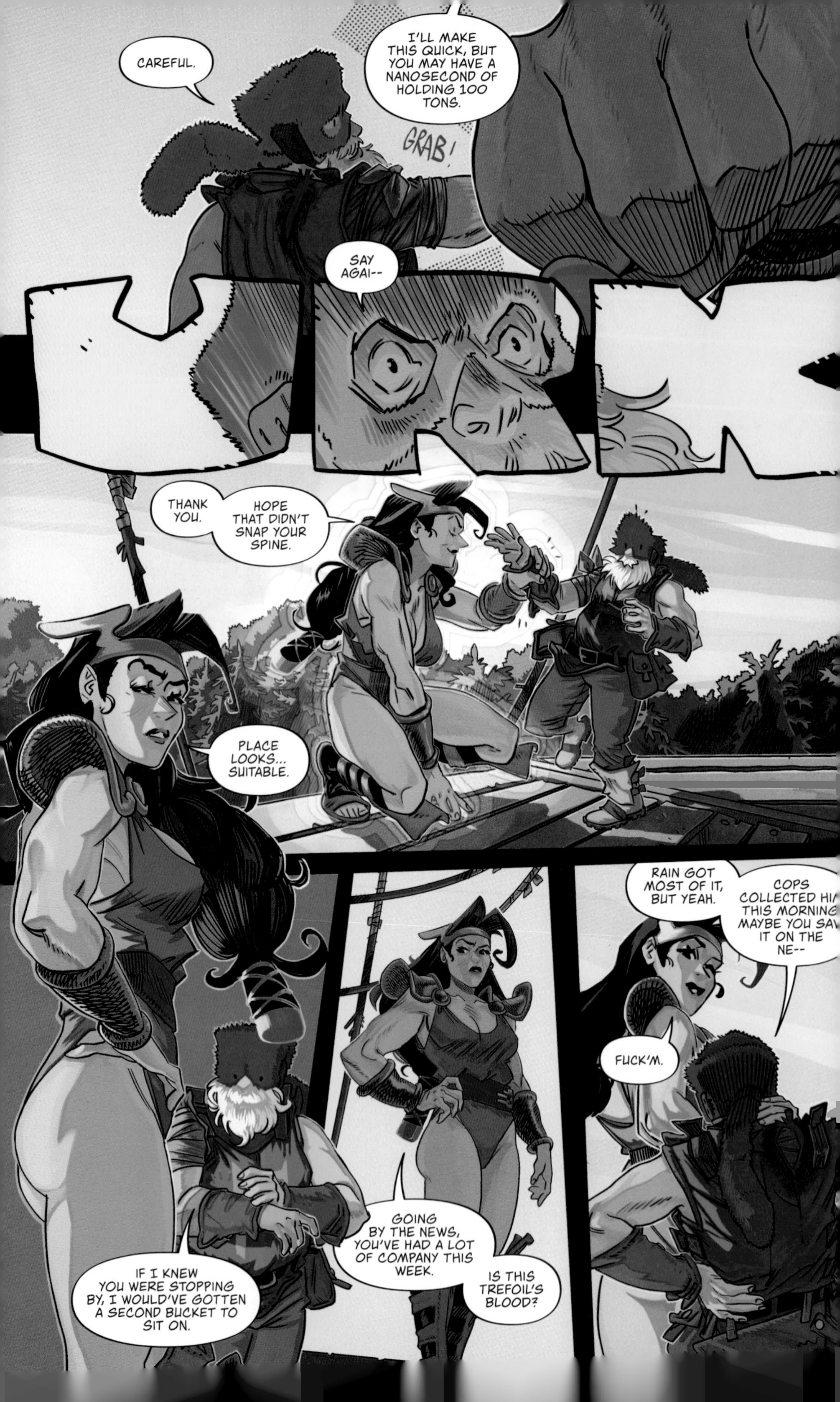
CAREFUL.
I'LL MAKE THIS QUICK, BUT YOU MAY HAVE A NANOSECOND OF HOLDING 100 TONS.
GRAB!
SAY AGAI--
THANK YOU.
HOPE THAT DIDN'T SNAP YOUR SPINE.
PLACE LOOKS... SUITABLE.
IF I KNEW YOU WERE STOPPING BY, I WOULD'VE GOTTEN A SECOND BUCKET TO SIT ON.
GOING BY THE NEWS, YOU'VE HAD A LOT OF COMPANY THIS WEEK.
IS THIS TREFOIL'S BLOOD?
RAIN GOT MOST OF IT, BUT YEAH.
FUCK'M.

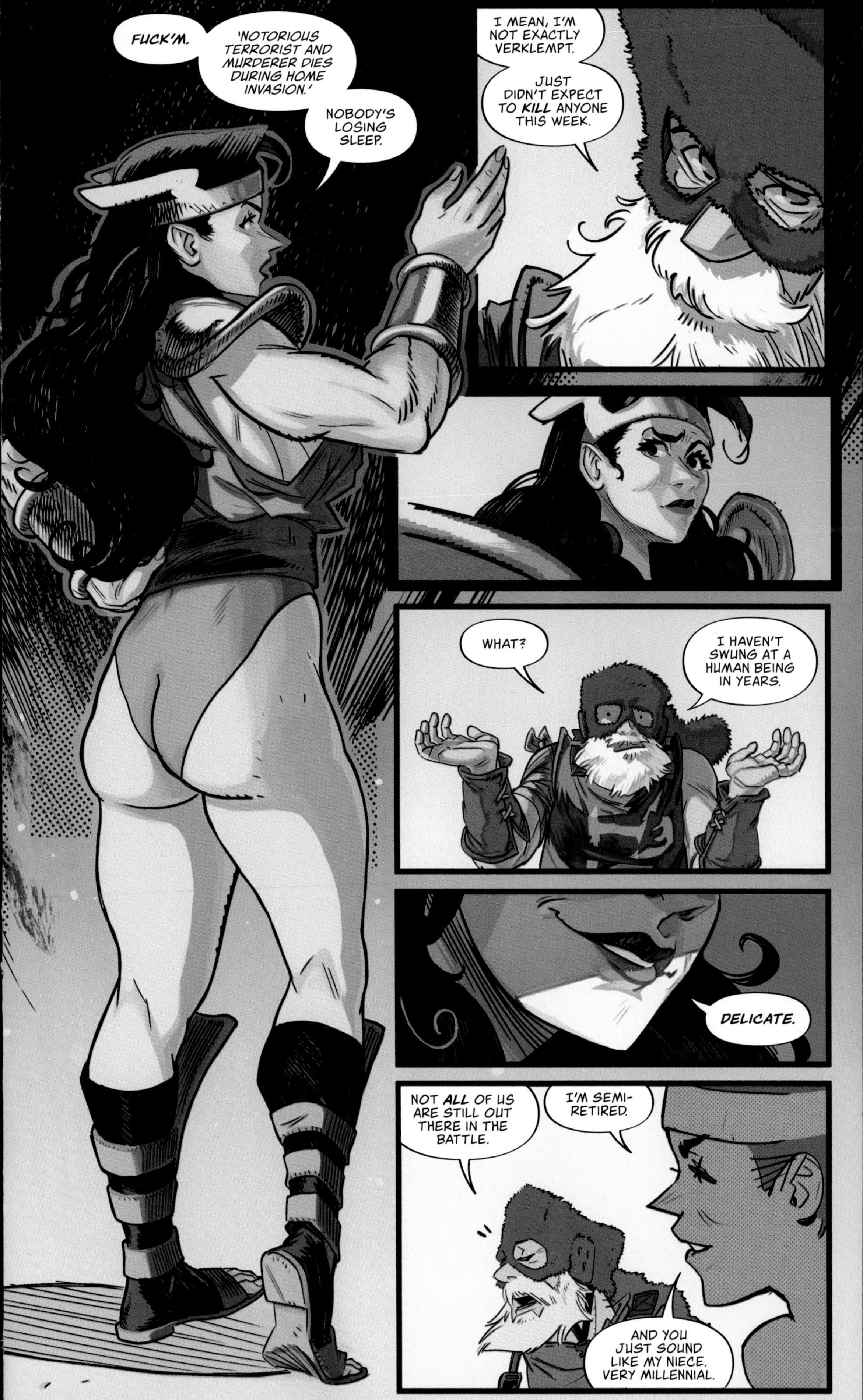
FUCK'M.
'NOTORIOUS TERRORIST AND MURDERER DIES DURING HOME INVASION.'
NOBODY'S LOSING SLEEP.
I MEAN, I'M NOT EXACTLY VERKLEMPT.
JUST DIDN'T EXPECT TO KILL ANYONE THIS WEEK.
WHAT?
I HAVEN'T SWUNG AT A HUMAN BEING IN YEARS.
DELICATE.
NOT ALL OF US ARE STILL OUT THERE IN THE BATTLE.
I'M SEMI-RETIRED.
AND YOU JUST SOUND LIKE MY NIECE. VERY MILLENNIAL.

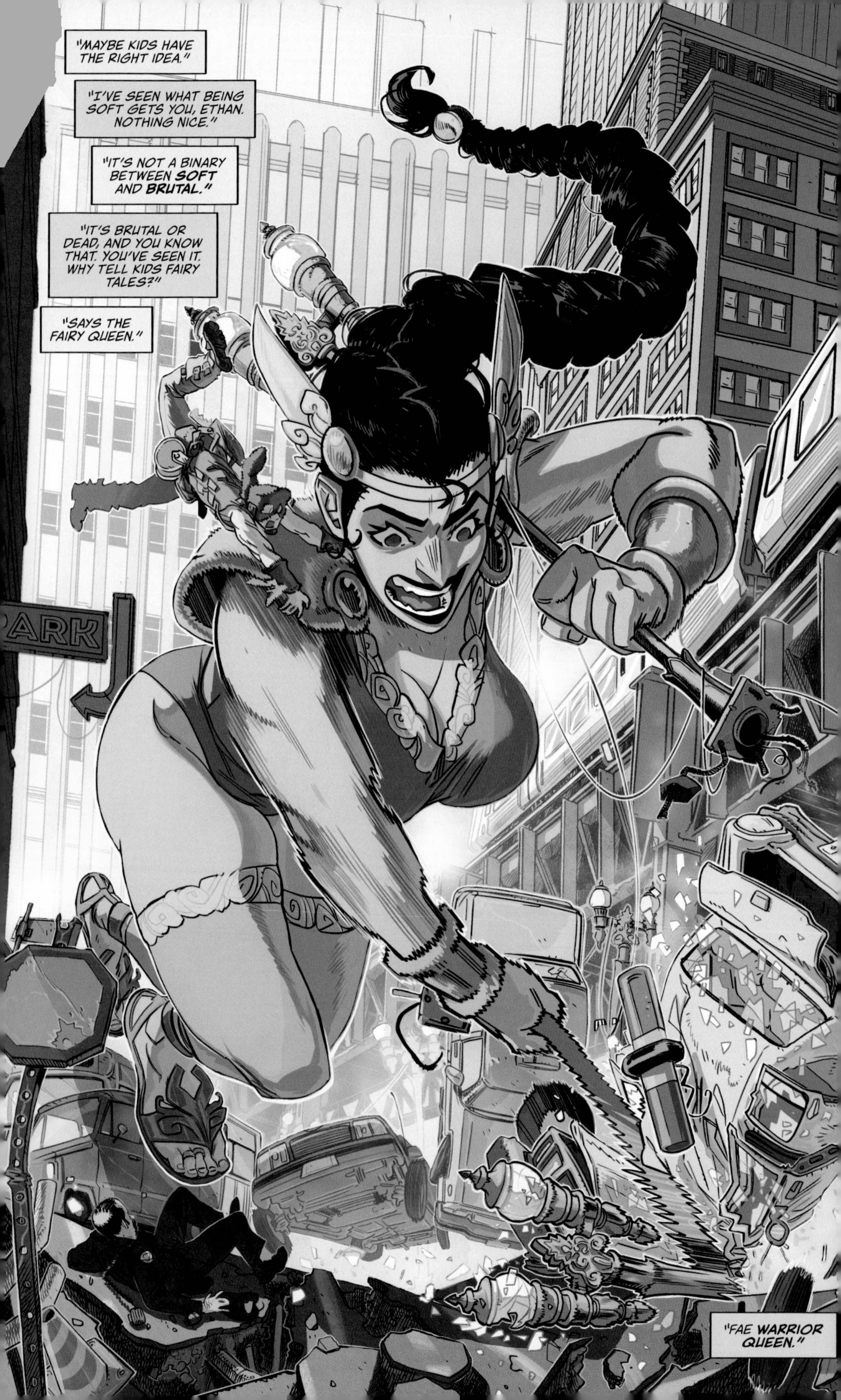
"MAYBE KIDS HAVE THE RIGHT IDEA."
"I'VE SEEN WHAT BEING SOFT GETS YOU, ETHAN. NOTHING NICE."
"IT'S NOT A BINARY BETWEEN SOFT AND BRUTAL."
"IT'S BRUTAL OR DEAD, AND YOU KNOW THAT. YOU'VE SEEN IT. WHY TELL KIDS FAIRY TALES?"
"SAYS THE FAIRY QUEEN."
PARK
"FAE WARRIOR QUEEN."

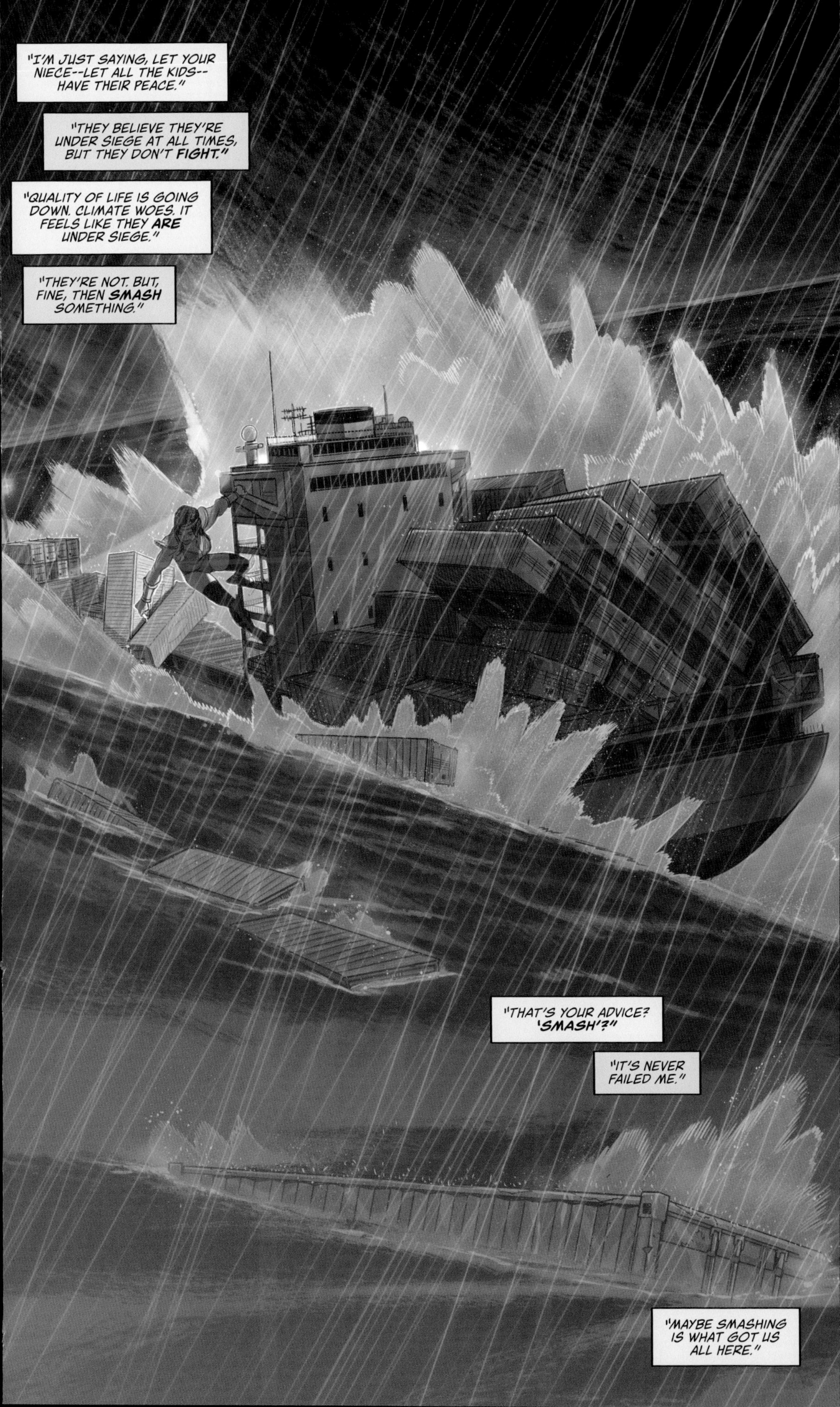
"I'M JUST SAYING, LET YOUR NIECE--LET ALL THE KIDS--HAVE THEIR PEACE."
"THEY BELIEVE THEY'RE UNDER SIEGE AT ALL TIMES, BUT THEY DON'T FIGHT."
"QUALITY OF LIFE IS GOING DOWN. CLIMATE WOES. IT FEELS LIKE THEY ARE UNDER SIEGE."
"THEY'RE NOT. BUT, FINE, THEN SMASH SOMETHING."
"THAT'S YOUR ADVICE? 'SMASH'?"
"IT'S NEVER FAILED ME."
"MAYBE SMASHING IS WHAT GOT US ALL HERE."

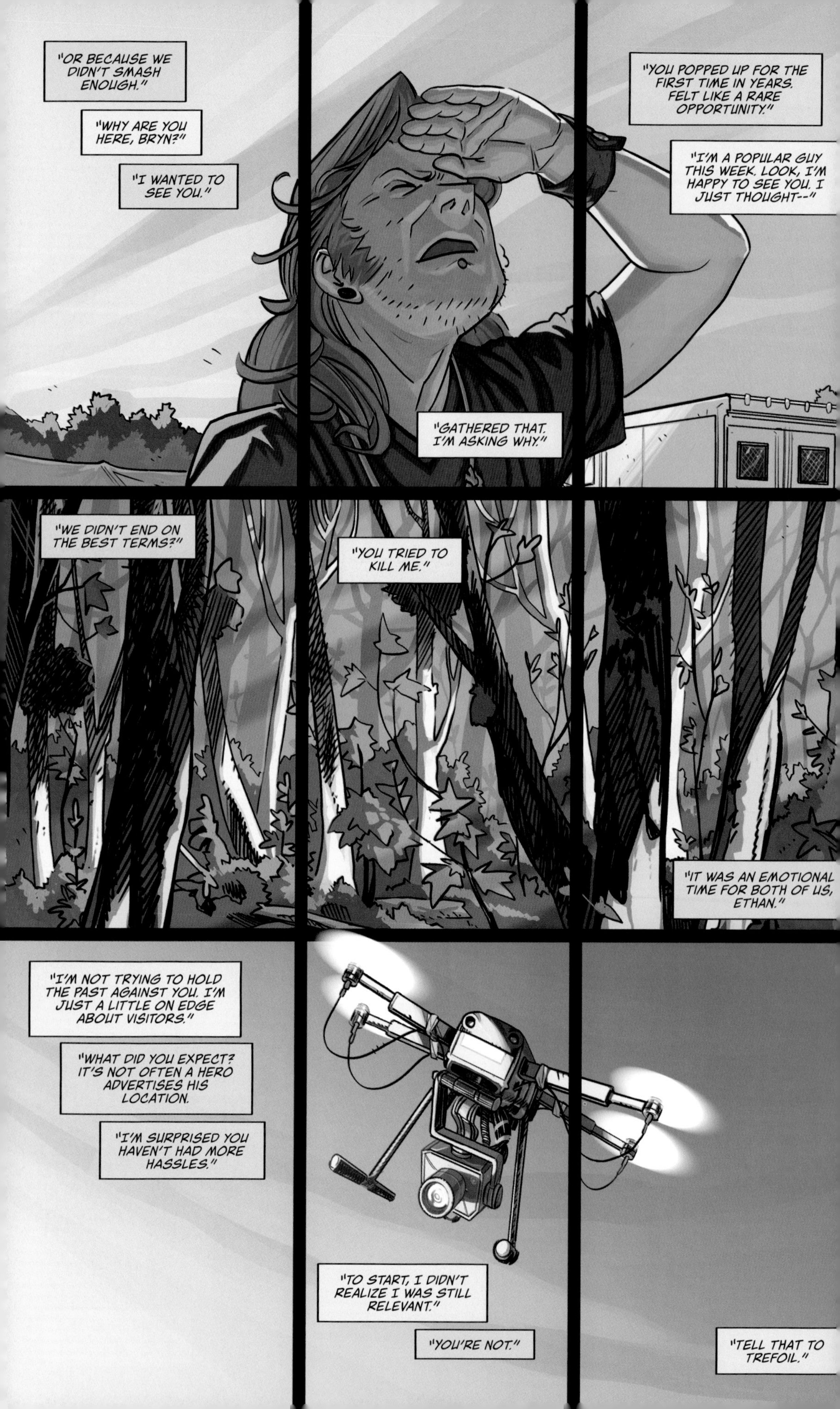
"OR BECAUSE WE DIDN'T SMASH ENOUGH."
"WHY ARE YOU HERE, BRYN?"
"I WANTED TO SEE YOU."
"GATHERED THAT. I'M ASKING WHY."
"YOU POPPED UP FOR THE FIRST TIME IN YEARS. FELT LIKE A RARE OPPORTUNITY."
"I'M A POPULAR GUY THIS WEEK. LOOK, I'M HAPPY TO SEE YOU. I JUST THOUGHT--"
"WE DIDN'T END ON THE BEST TERMS?"
"YOU TRIED TO KILL ME."
"IT WAS AN EMOTIONAL TIME FOR BOTH OF US, ETHAN."
"I'M NOT TRYING TO HOLD THE PAST AGAINST YOU. I'M JUST A LITTLE ON EDGE ABOUT VISITORS."
"WHAT DID YOU EXPECT? IT'S NOT OFTEN A HERO ADVERTISES HIS LOCATION.
"I'M SURPRISED YOU HAVEN'T HAD MORE HASSLES."
"TO START, I DIDN'T REALIZE I WAS STILL RELEVANT."
"YOU'RE NOT."
"TELL THAT TO TREFOIL."

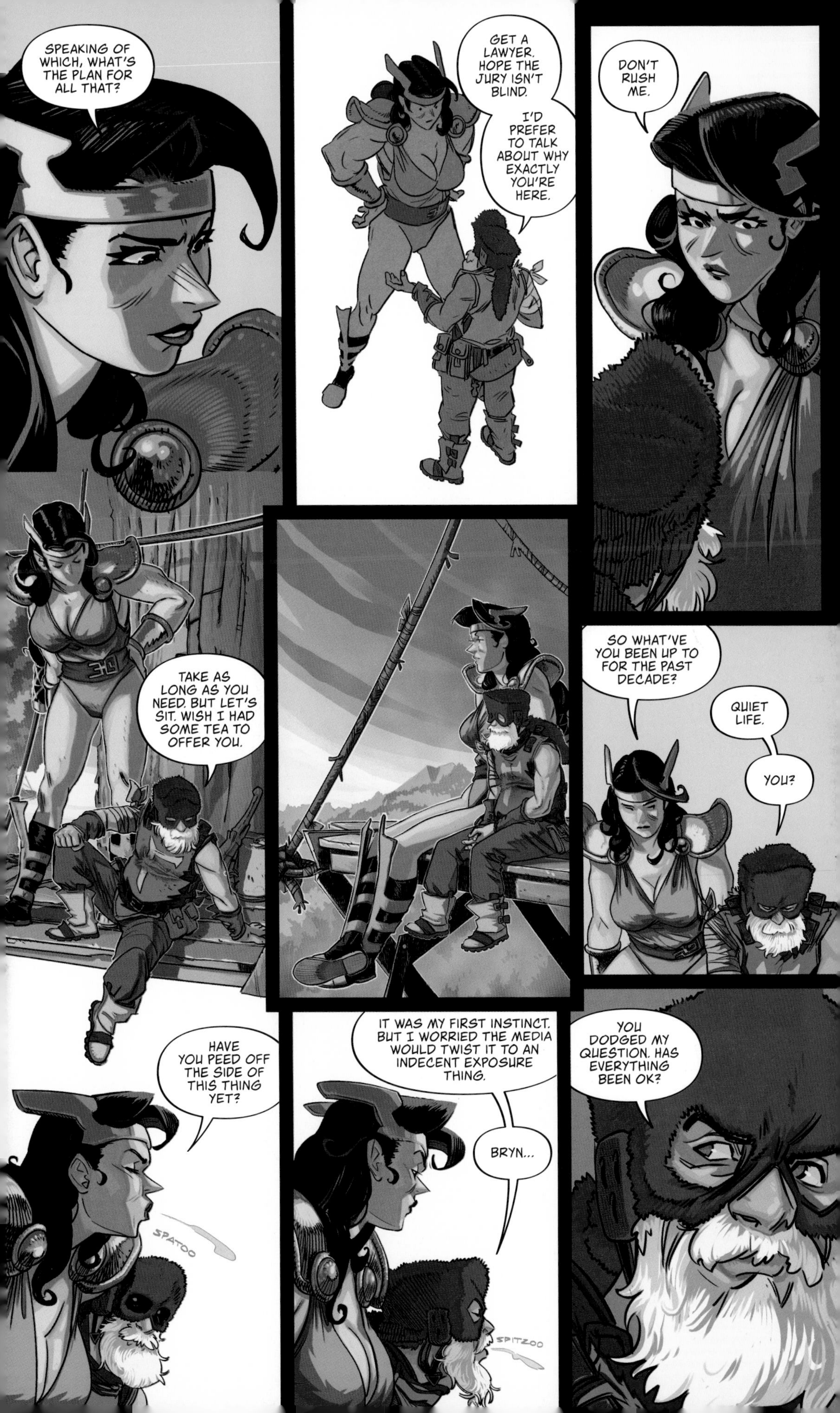
SPEAKING OF WHICH, WHAT'S THE PLAN FOR ALL THAT?
GET A LAWYER. HOPE THE JURY ISN'T BLIND.
I'D PREFER TO TALK ABOUT WHY EXACTLY YOU'RE HERE.
DON'T RUSH ME.
TAKE AS LONG AS YOU NEED. BUT LET'S SIT. WISH I HAD SOME TEA TO OFFER YOU.
SO WHAT'VE YOU BEEN UP TO FOR THE PAST DECADE?
QUIET LIFE.
YOU?
HAVE YOU PEED OFF THE SIDE OF THIS THING YET?
SPATOO
IT WAS MY FIRST INSTINCT. BUT I WORRIED THE MEDIA WOULD TWIST IT TO AN INDECENT EXPOSURE THING.
BRYN...
SPITZOO
YOU DODGED MY QUESTION. HAS EVERYTHING BEEN OK?

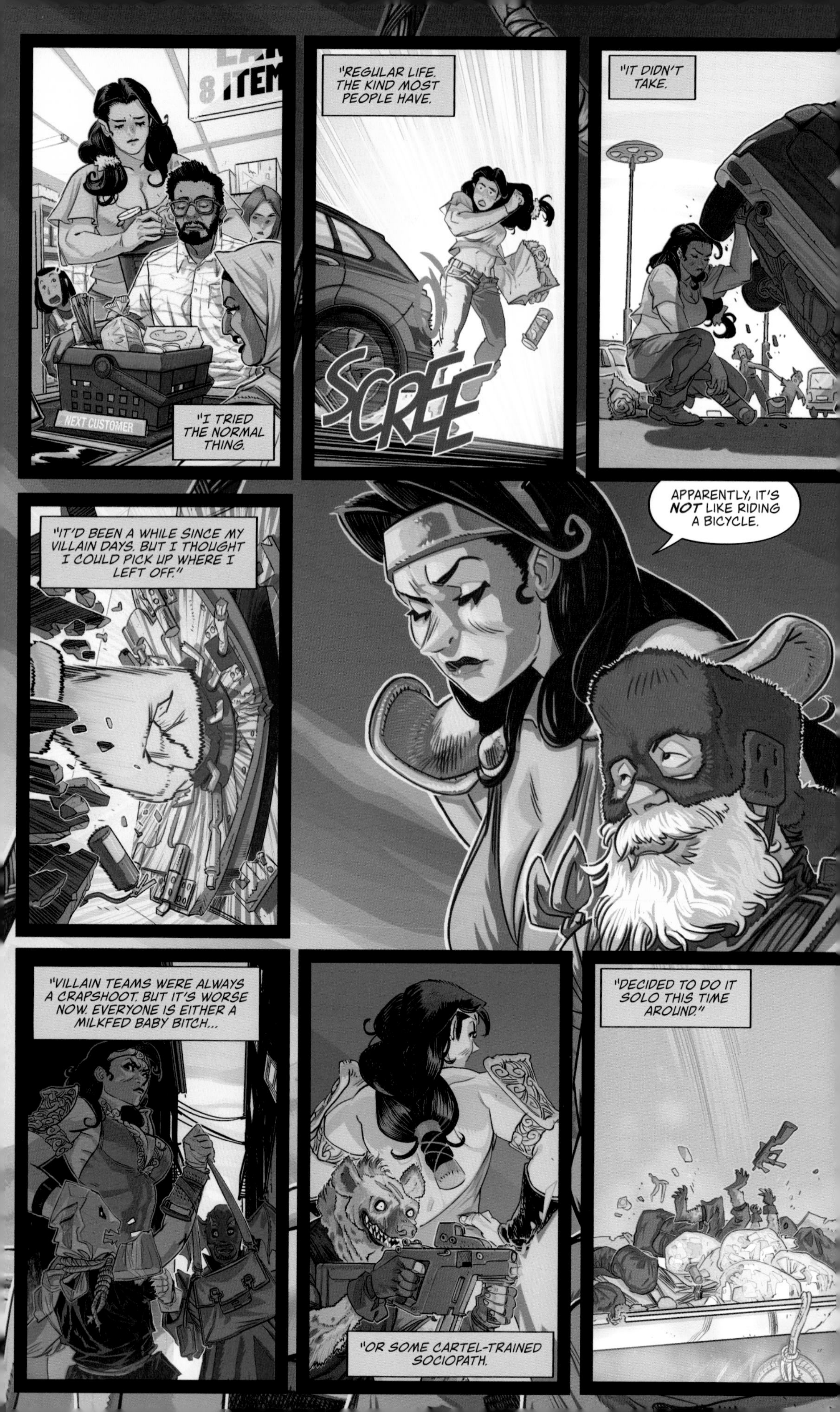

8 ITEM
NEXT CUSTOMER
"I TRIED THE NORMAL THING.
"REGULAR LIFE. THE KIND MOST PEOPLE HAVE.
SCREE
"IT DIDN'T TAKE.
"IT'D BEEN A WHILE SINCE MY VILLAIN DAYS. BUT I THOUGHT I COULD PICK UP WHERE I LEFT OFF."
APPARENTLY, IT'S **NOT** LIKE RIDING A BICYCLE.
"VILLAIN TEAMS WERE ALWAYS A CRAPSHOOT. BUT IT'S WORSE NOW. EVERYONE IS EITHER A MILKFED BABY BITCH...
"OR SOME CARTEL-TRAINED SOCIOPATH.
"DECIDED TO DO IT SOLO THIS TIME AROUND."

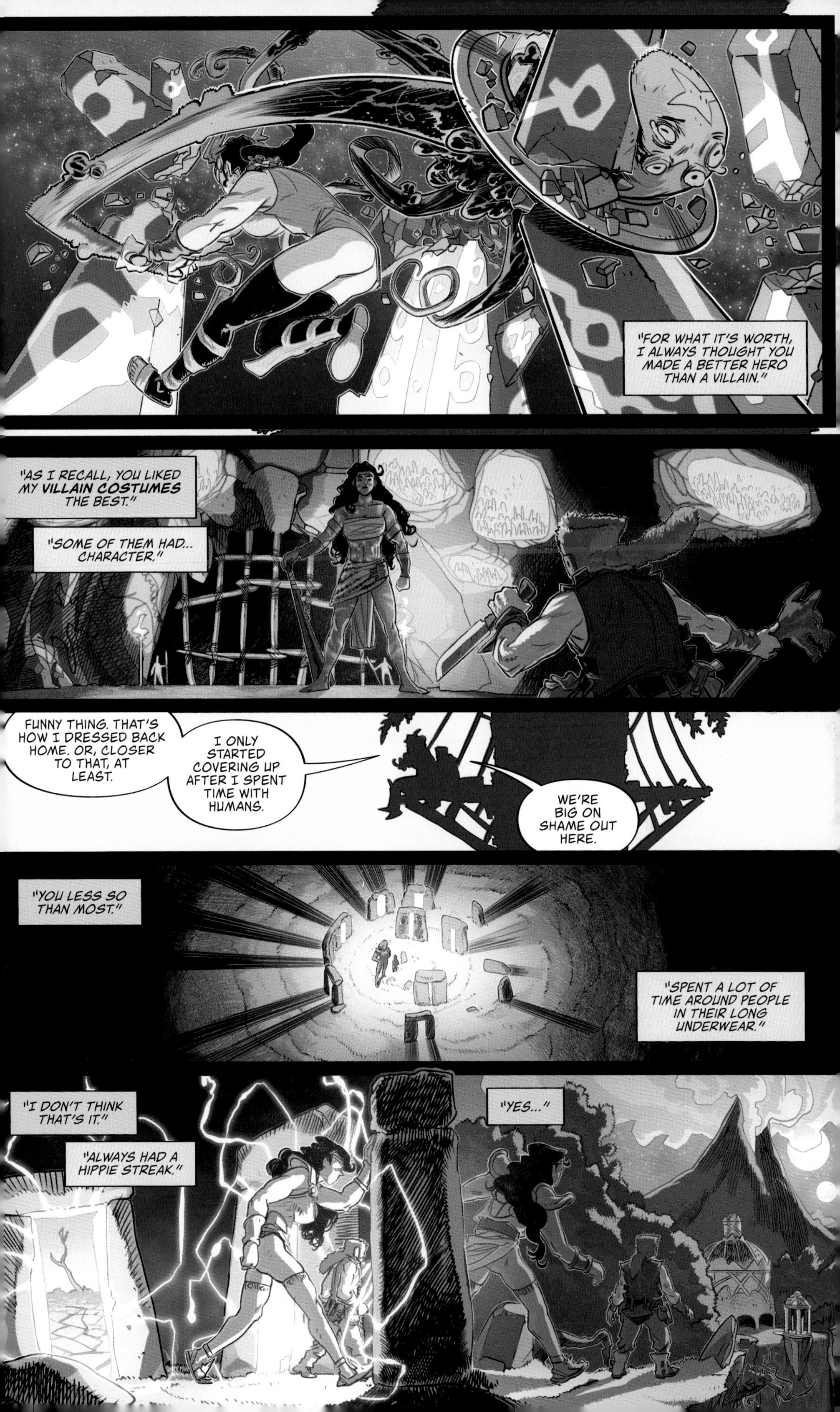
"FOR WHAT IT'S WORTH, I ALWAYS THOUGHT YOU MADE A BETTER HERO THAN A VILLAIN."
"AS I RECALL, YOU LIKED MY VILLAIN COSTUMES THE BEST."
"SOME OF THEM HAD... CHARACTER."
FUNNY THING. THAT'S HOW I DRESSED BACK HOME. OR, CLOSER TO THAT, AT LEAST.
I ONLY STARTED COVERING UP AFTER I SPENT TIME WITH HUMANS.
WE'RE BIG ON SHAME OUT HERE.
"YOU LESS SO THAN MOST."
"SPENT A LOT OF TIME AROUND PEOPLE IN THEIR LONG UNDERWEAR."
"I DON'T THINK THAT'S IT."
"ALWAYS HAD A HIPPIE STREAK."
"YES..."

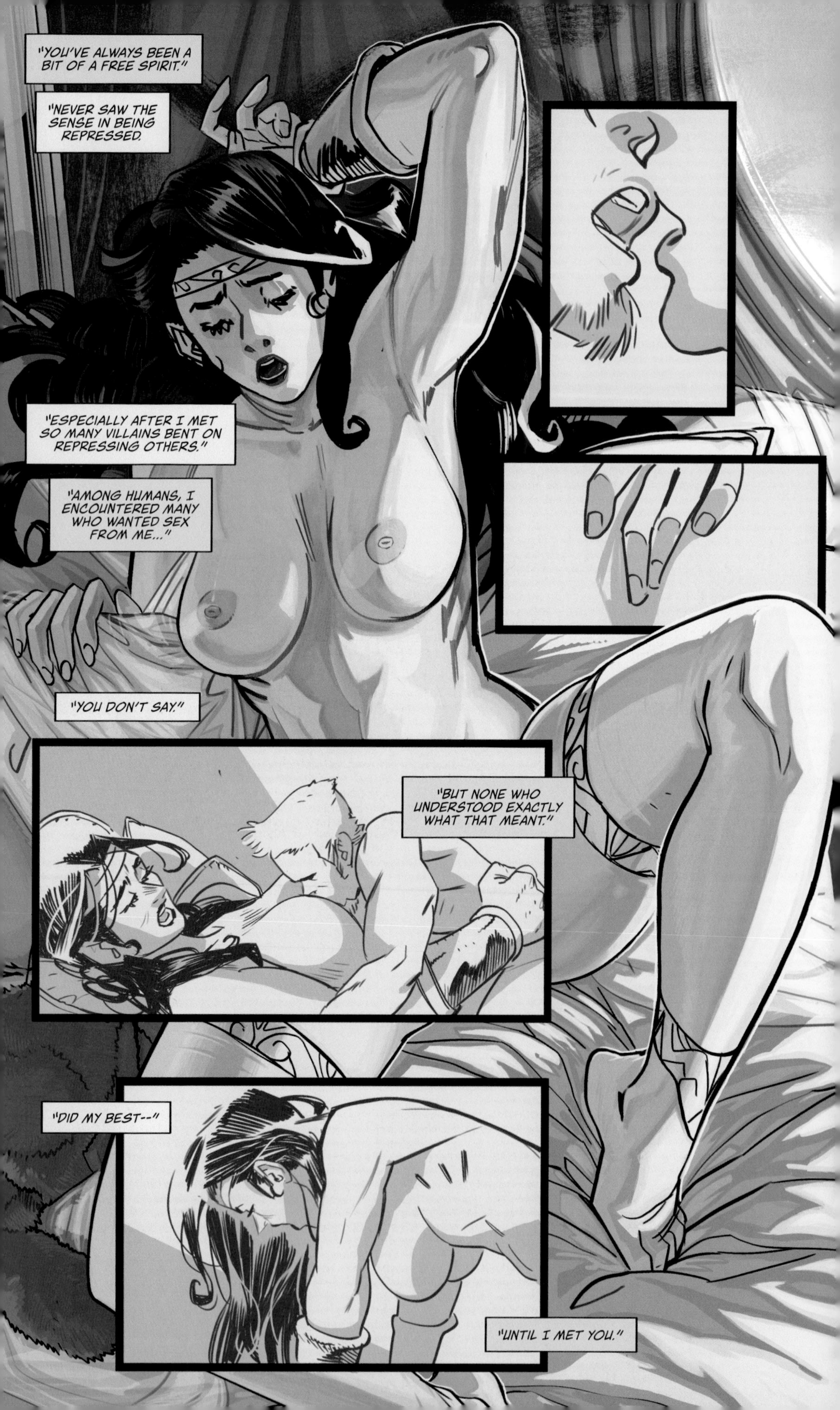
"YOU'VE ALWAYS BEEN A BIT OF A FREE SPIRIT."
"NEVER SAW THE SENSE IN BEING REPRESSED.
"ESPECIALLY AFTER I MET SO MANY VILLAINS BENT ON REPRESSING OTHERS."
"AMONG HUMANS, I ENCOUNTERED MANY WHO WANTED SEX FROM ME..."
"YOU DON'T SAY."
"BUT NONE WHO UNDERSTOOD EXACTLY WHAT THAT MEANT."
"DID MY BEST--"
"UNTIL I MET YOU."

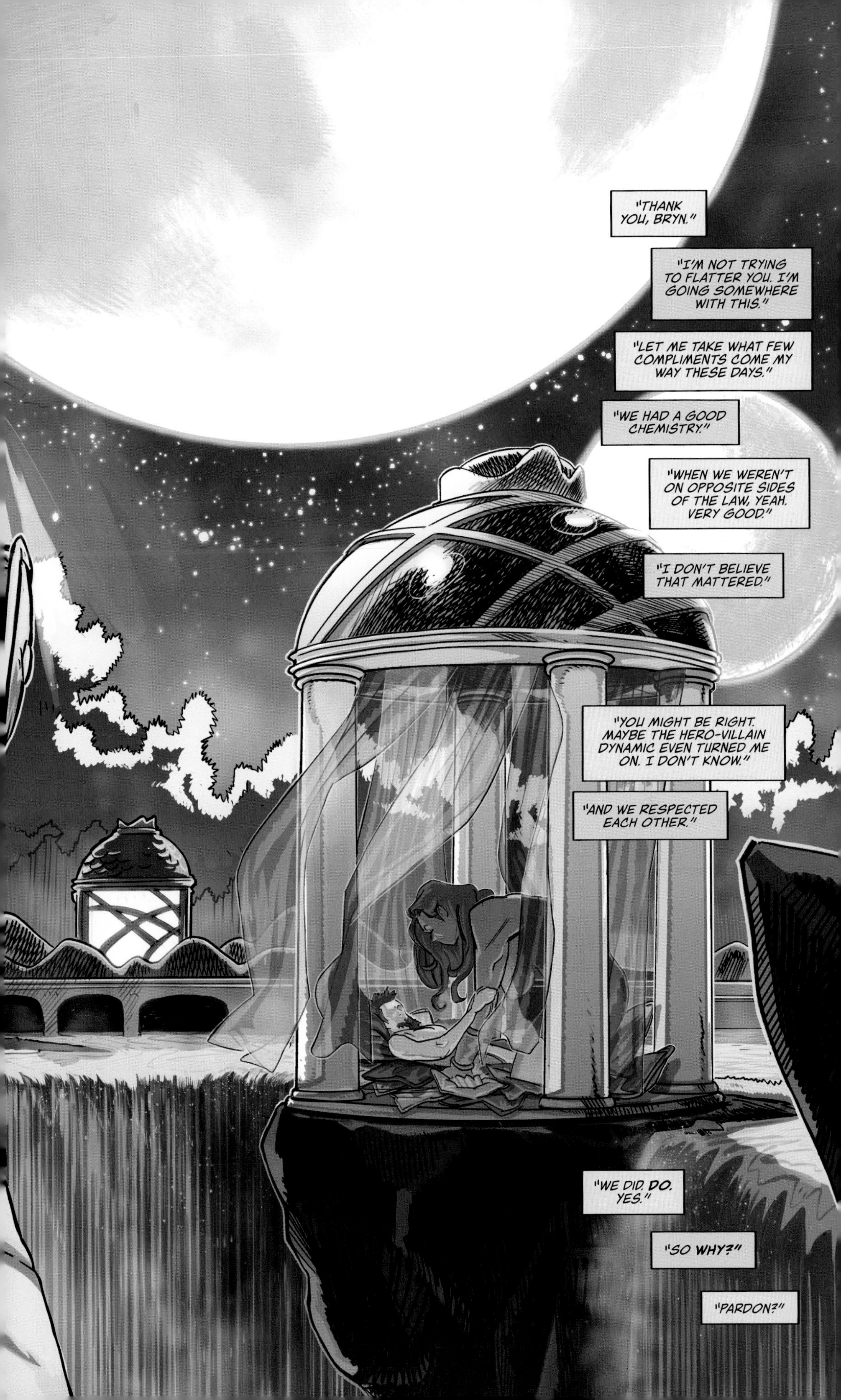
"THANK YOU, BRYN."
"I'M NOT TRYING TO FLATTER YOU. I'M GOING SOMEWHERE WITH THIS."
"LET ME TAKE WHAT FEW COMPLIMENTS COME MY WAY THESE DAYS."
"WE HAD A GOOD CHEMISTRY."
"WHEN WE WEREN'T ON OPPOSITE SIDES OF THE LAW, YEAH. VERY GOOD."
"I DON'T BELIEVE THAT MATTERED."
"YOU MIGHT BE RIGHT. MAYBE THE HERO-VILLAIN DYNAMIC EVEN TURNED ME ON. I DON'T KNOW."
"AND WE RESPECTED EACH OTHER."
"WE DID. DO. YES."
"SO WHY?"
"PARDON?"

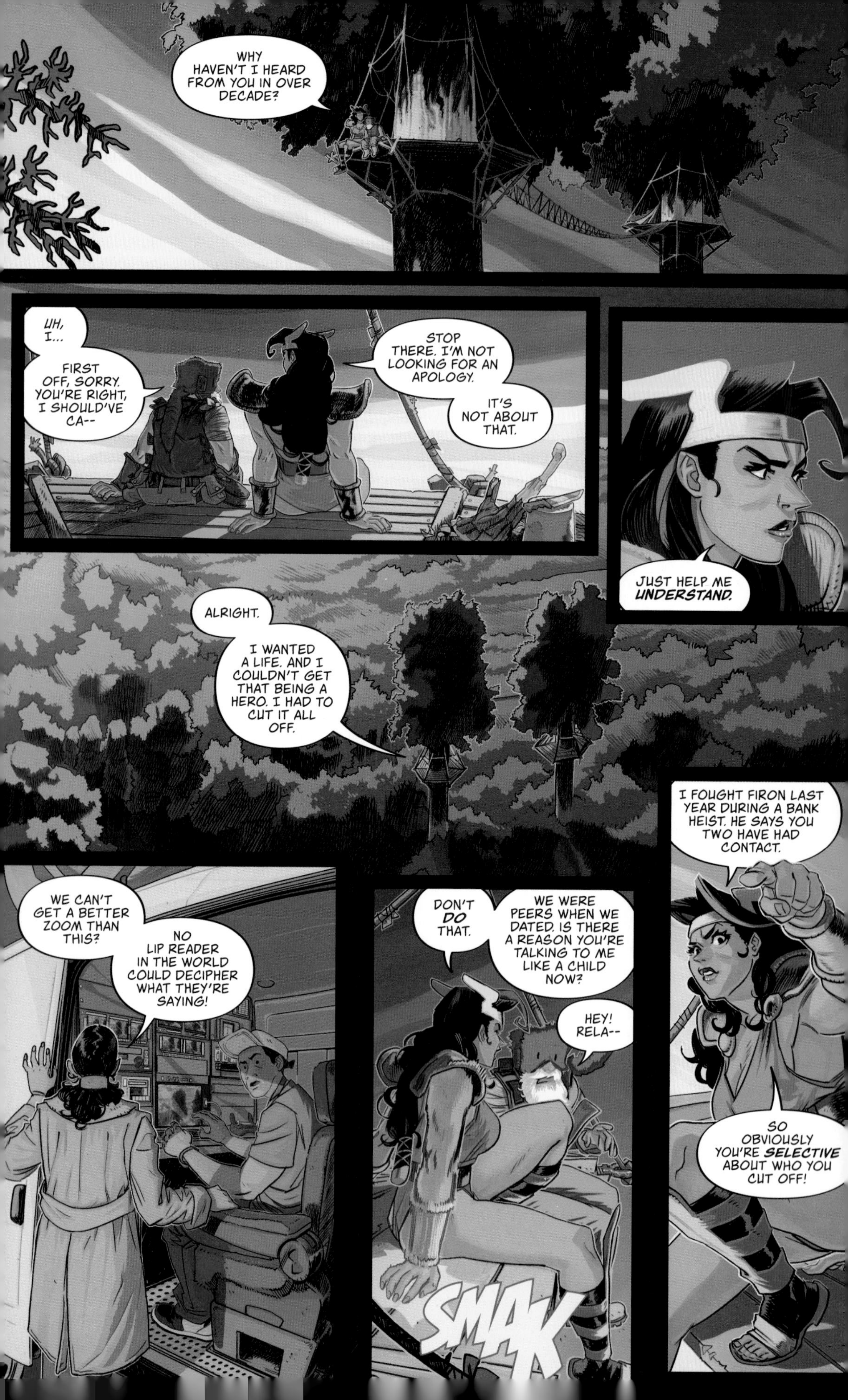
WHY HAVEN'T I HEARD FROM YOU IN OVER DECADE?
UH, I...
FIRST OFF, SORRY. YOU'RE RIGHT, I SHOULD'VE CA--
STOP THERE. I'M NOT LOOKING FOR AN APOLOGY.
IT'S NOT ABOUT THAT.
JUST HELP ME UNDERSTAND.
ALRIGHT.
I WANTED A LIFE. AND I COULDN'T GET THAT BEING A HERO. I HAD TO CUT IT ALL OFF.
I FOUGHT FIRON LAST YEAR DURING A BANK HEIST. HE SAYS YOU TWO HAVE HAD CONTACT.
WE CAN'T GET A BETTER ZOOM THAN THIS?
NO LIP READER IN THE WORLD COULD DECIPHER WHAT THEY'RE SAYING!
DON'T DO THAT.
WE WERE PEERS WHEN WE DATED. IS THERE A REASON YOU'RE TALKING TO ME LIKE A CHILD NOW?
HEY! RELA--
SMAK
SO OBVIOUSLY YOU'RE SELECTIVE ABOUT WHO YOU CUT OFF!

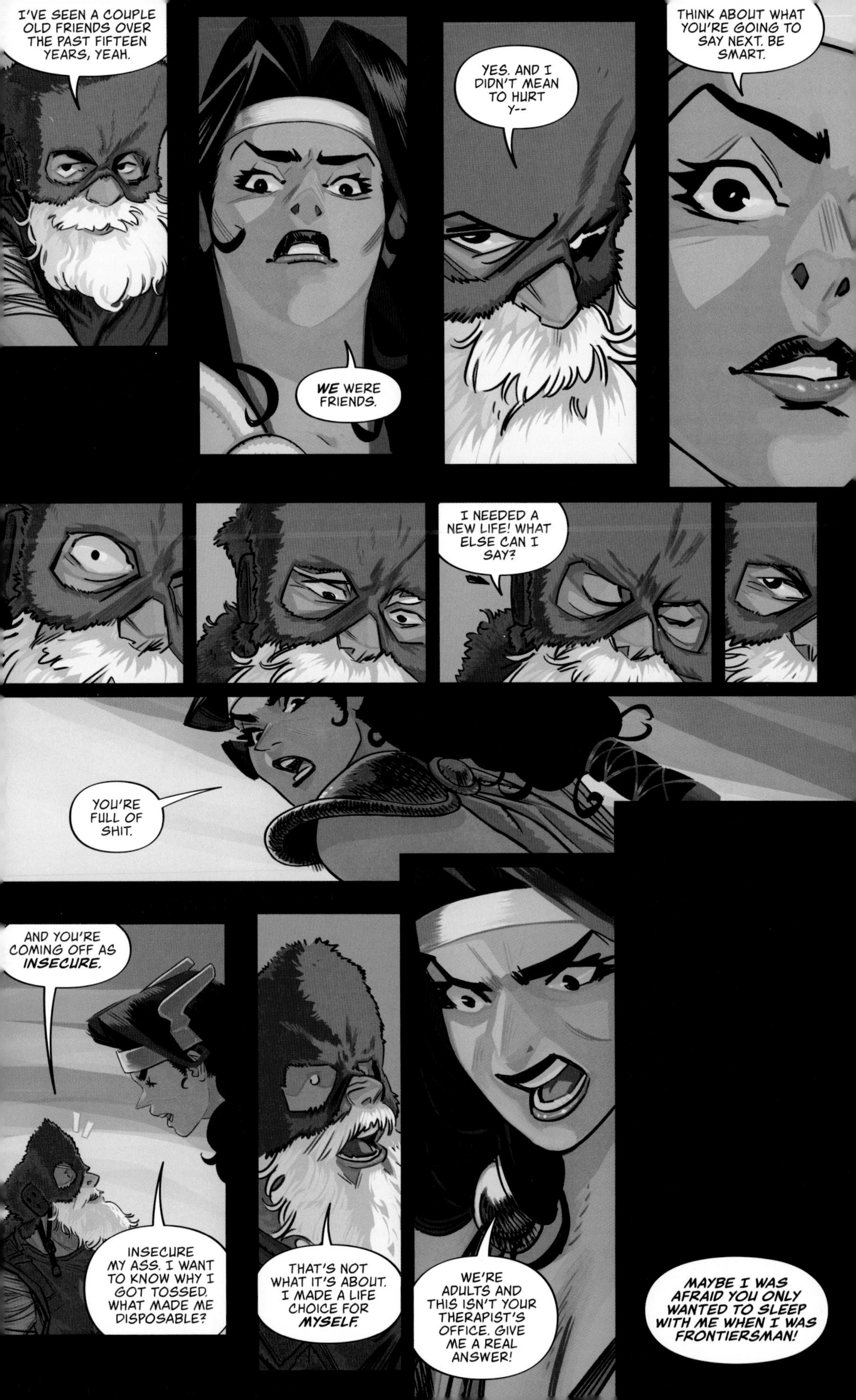
I'VE SEEN A COUPLE OLD FRIENDS OVER THE PAST FIFTEEN YEARS, YEAH.
WE WERE FRIENDS.
YES. AND I DIDN'T MEAN TO HURT Y--
THINK ABOUT WHAT YOU'RE GOING TO SAY NEXT. BE SMART.
I NEEDED A NEW LIFE! WHAT ELSE CAN I SAY?
YOU'RE FULL OF SHIT.
AND YOU'RE COMING OFF AS INSECURE.
INSECURE MY ASS. I WANT TO KNOW WHY I GOT TOSSED. WHAT MADE ME DISPOSABLE?
THAT'S NOT WHAT IT'S ABOUT. I MADE A LIFE CHOICE FOR MYSELF.
WE'RE ADULTS AND THIS ISN'T YOUR THERAPIST'S OFFICE. GIVE ME A REAL ANSWER!
MAYBE I WAS AFRAID YOU ONLY WANTED TO SLEEP WITH ME WHEN I WAS FRONTIERSMAN!

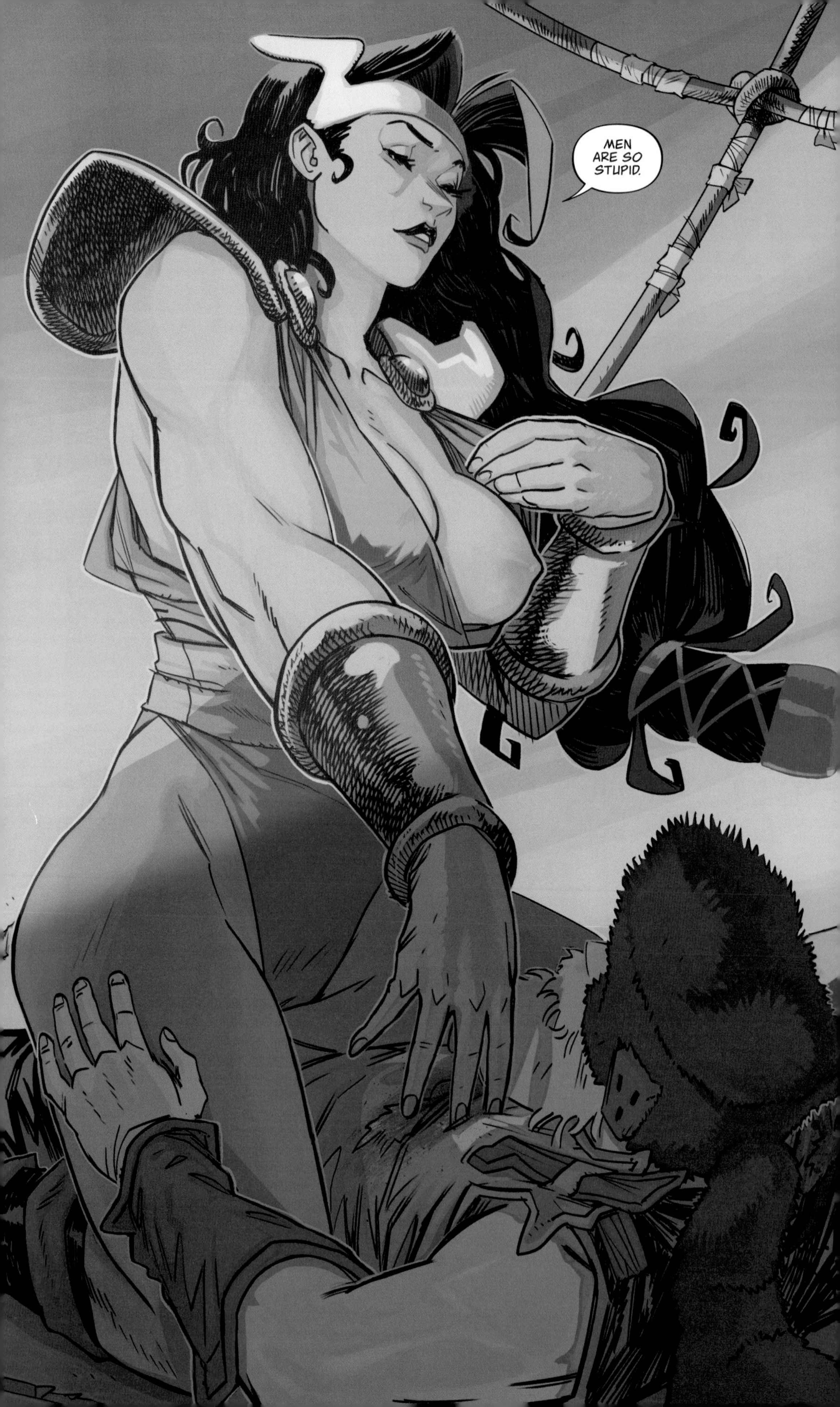
MEN ARE SO STUPID.

# BRYNHILDR

**Real name:** Brynhildr of Lanrhl
**Occupation:** Royalty; adventurer
**Identity:** Widely known
**Legal status:** Wanted criminal across several continents
**Known relatives:** Hulda (mother); Atil (brother)
**Group affiliation:** War Culture (former)
**Alias:** Brünnhilde; Brynhilde of the Shield
**History:** As the queen of a supernatural realm that exists just outside human perception, Brynhildr has a complex relationship with mankind. She's most often been a villain, battling with superheroes and occasionally joining superhuman criminal teams. But she's also spent time on the right side of the law, working alongside the Bold Travelers / Fellow Travelers and the Sacred Circle.

Like all fae royalty, Byrnhildr was born from the moss that covers the Living Shrine. She is the daughter of Hulda and an unnamed father. Some believe the females of the fae don't require a male for fertilization. In any case, Brunhildr became queen-in-waiting at the time of her birth. By fifteen her mother had fully stepped away from the throne, leaving Brunhildr as the leader of the realm. Under her rule, Lanrhl experienced prosperity and peace. And it was for that reason Brynhildr chose to leave.

Believing her role in life is to struggle and fight, the calm of Lanrhl was like a slow poison to her spirit. She entered the world of men when the stone portals of the British Isles were bombed in a still unsolved act of vandalism. Passing through the damaged doorway between realms, Brynhildr first encountered members of the UK's superhero team, Isle Walls. It was that battle that hooked her on the world of man. She found a worthy foe in the form of Earth's superhumans.

Shortly after her arrival, Byrnhildr was recruited to the supervillain guerrilla team War Culture. That group's leader, Verduner, attempted to mentor Byrnhildr but the relationship soon turned intimate. When the two split, it effectively ended War Culture and members went on to form smaller mercenary cells. Byrnhildr briefly aligned herself with the criminal organization the Oversight and worked on-and-off as an enforcer. This took her around the US and led to many encounters with superheroes.

While never a hero per se, she has aided the efforts of heroes during natural disasters and alien invasions. She has reluctantly recruited heroes to aid in the defense of Lanrhl. To those men and women, she has sworn an oath to repay that debt whenever they are in need.

**Height:** Variable; 8ft to 150ft
**Weight:** Variable
**Eyes:** Brown
**Hair:** Dark brown
**Strength level:** In her giant form Brynhildr has been observed lifting over 100 tons
**Known superhuman powers:** Size and density manipulation granted through fae magic. She can increase her size above that of her normal manifestation, but cannot decrease her size below it. She can slightly increase the density of any part of her body, and often employs this ability to deliver heavy blows in battle. Additionally, Brynhildr can travel between physics-bound realms (the world of the dead is prohibited to fae) without any type of pass or permission.

# REGIONAIRE

**Real name:** None
**Occupation:** Supervillain
**Identity:** N/A
**Legal status:** Wanted criminal across several continents
**Known relatives:** None
**Group affiliation:** The Lab
**Alias:** Beast Born; Voice of the Wild
**History:** [redacted]

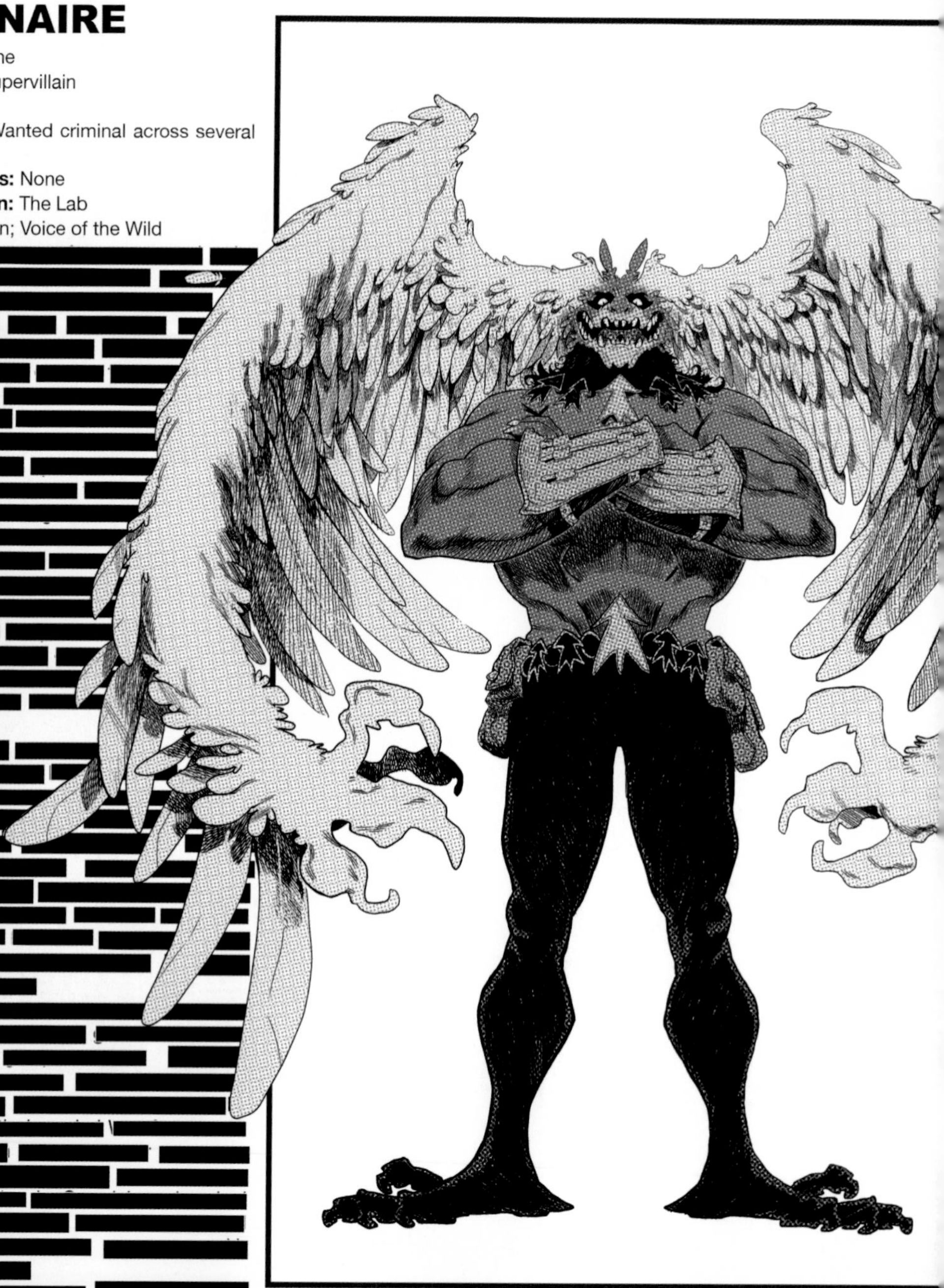

**Height:** 10ft
**Weight:** 400lbs
**Eyes:** Yellow
**Hair:** Black/red
**Strength level:** Enhanced, but below the one ton threshold
**Known superhuman powers:** Superanimal senses, including vision in near-total darkness. Enhanced strength and agility from increased muscle density and fast-twitch muscle fiber. Lightweight bone to assist in flight via feathered wings. Regionaire's jaw is capable of snapping bone and his claws able to tear Kevlar body armor.

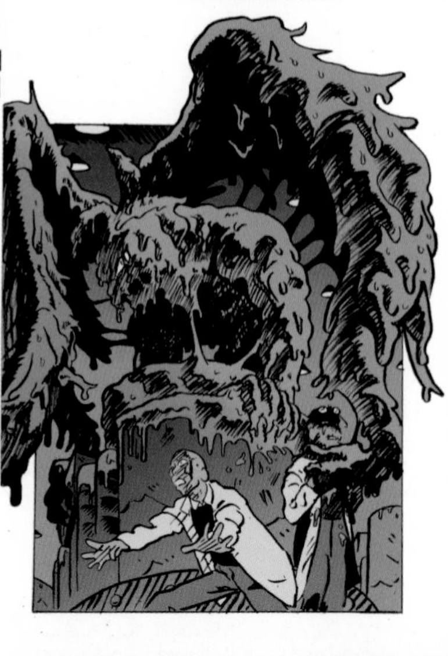

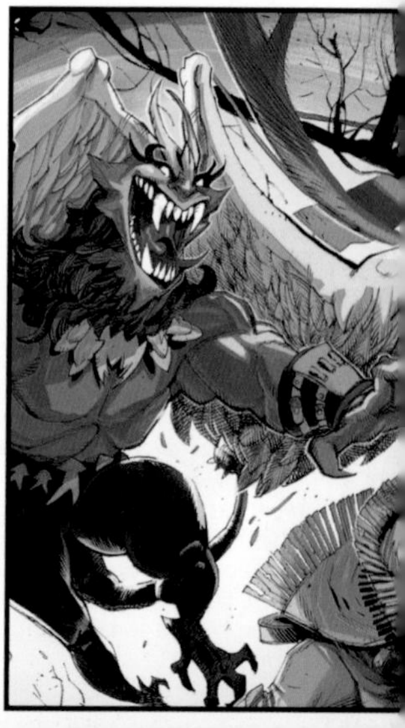

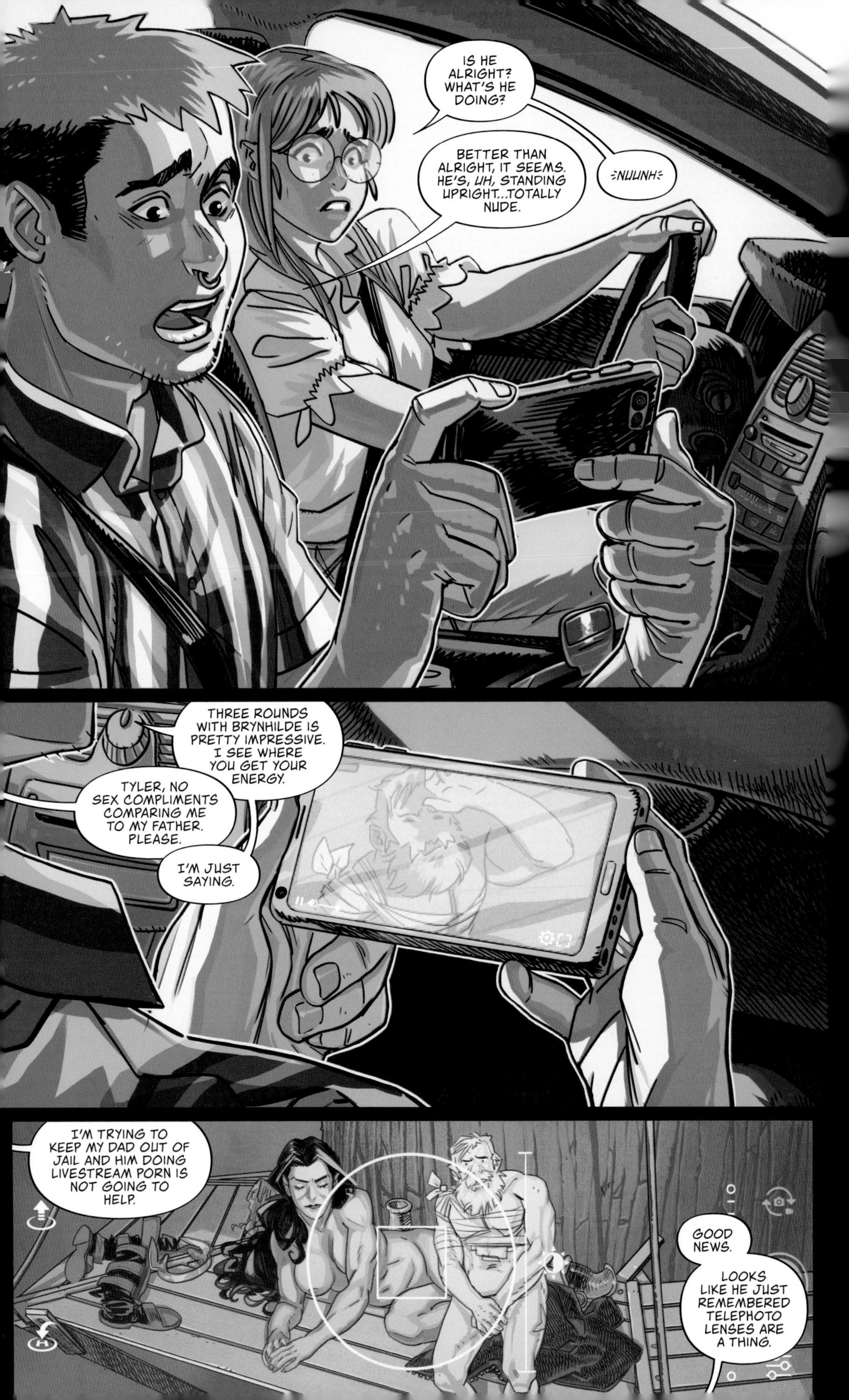
IS HE ALRIGHT? WHAT'S HE DOING?
BETTER THAN ALRIGHT, IT SEEMS. HE'S, *UH*, STANDING UPRIGHT...TOTALLY NUDE.
=NUUNH=
THREE ROUNDS WITH BRYNHILDE IS PRETTY IMPRESSIVE. I SEE WHERE YOU GET YOUR ENERGY.
TYLER, NO SEX COMPLIMENTS COMPARING ME TO MY FATHER. PLEASE.
I'M JUST SAYING.
I'M TRYING TO KEEP MY DAD OUT OF JAIL AND HIM DOING LIVESTREAM PORN IS NOT GOING TO HELP.
GOOD NEWS.
LOOKS LIKE HE JUST REMEMBERED TELEPHOTO LENSES ARE A THING.

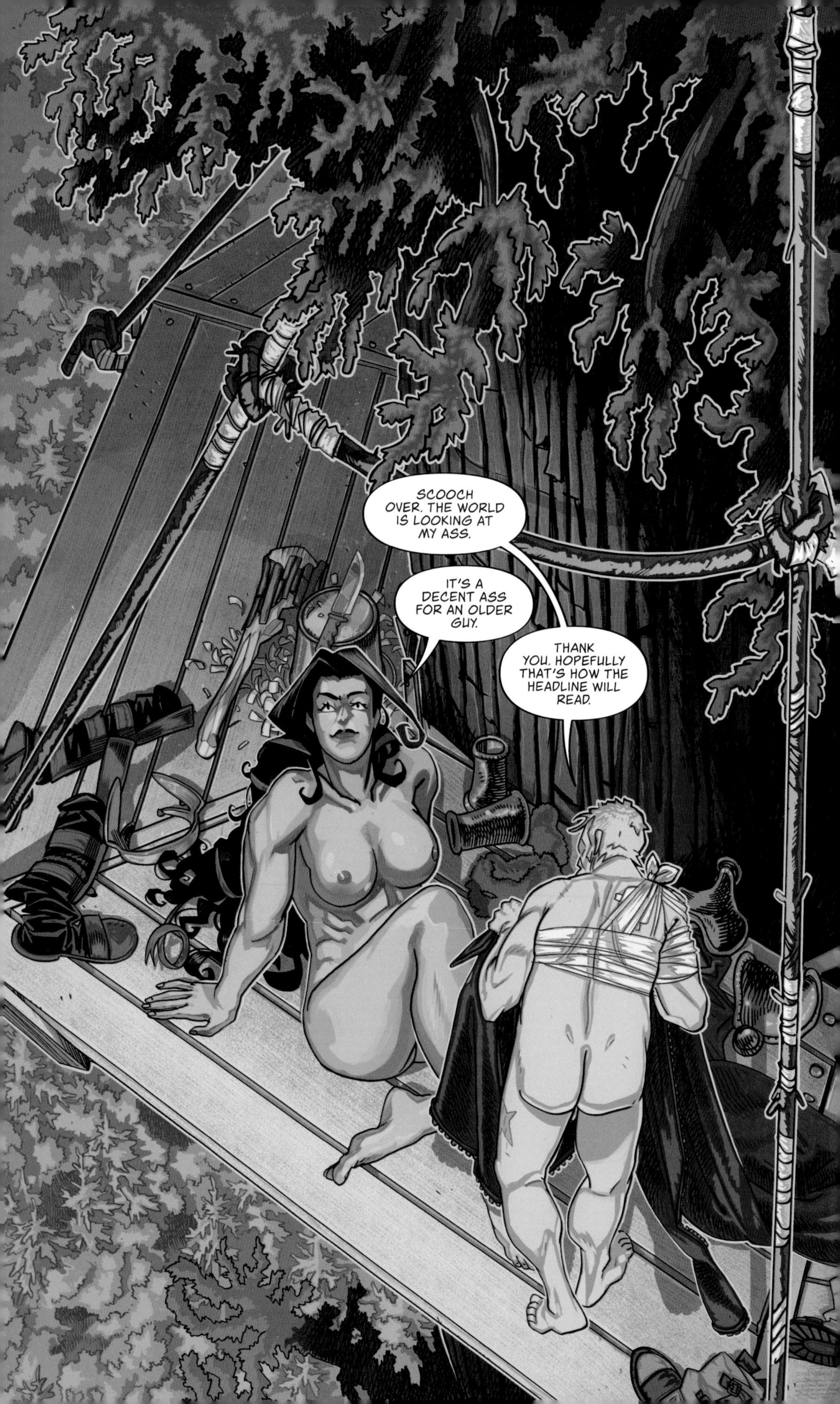
SCOOCH OVER. THE WORLD IS LOOKING AT MY ASS.
IT'S A DECENT ASS FOR AN OLDER GUY.
THANK YOU. HOPEFULLY THAT'S HOW THE HEADLINE WILL READ.

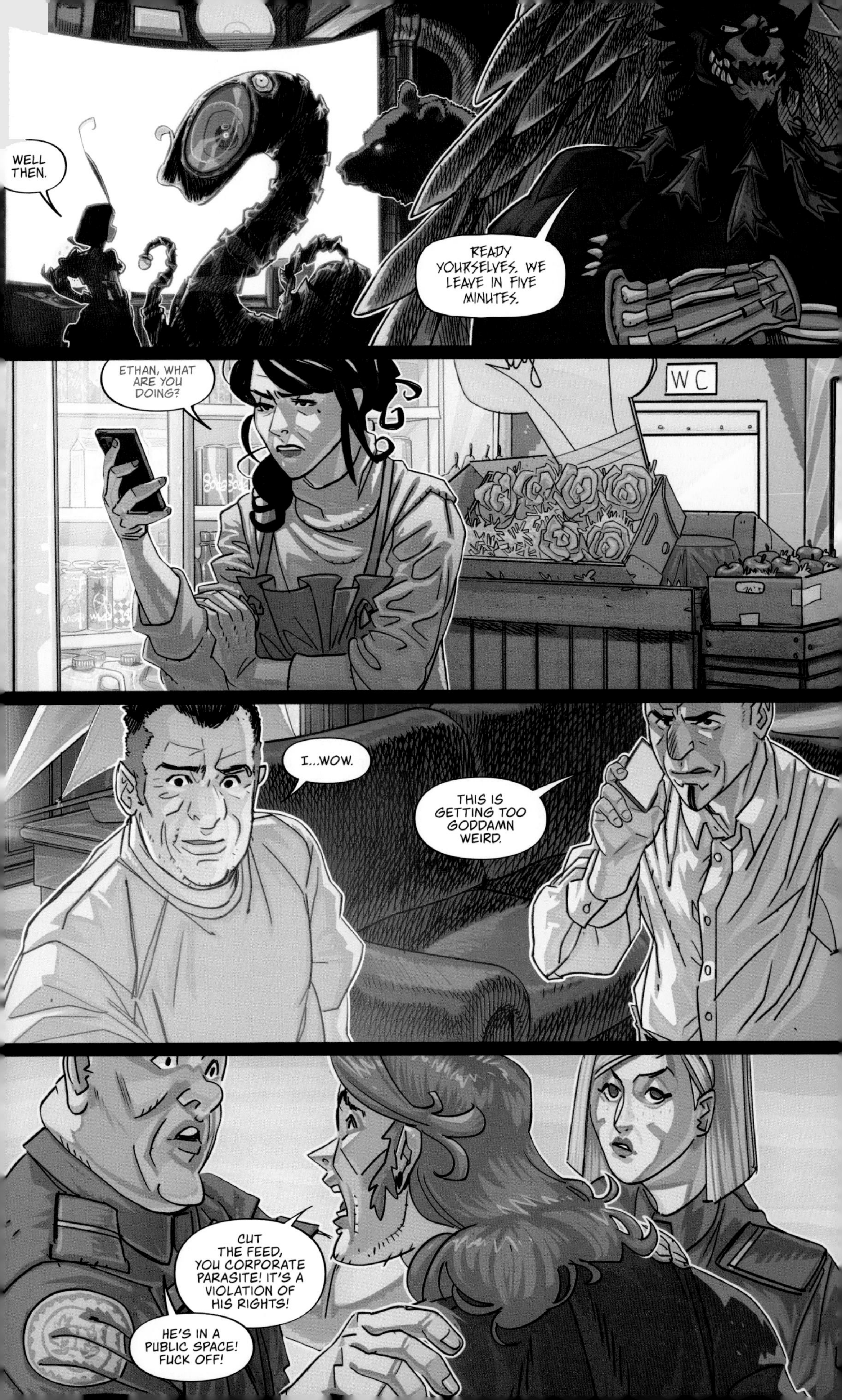
WELL THEN.
READY YOURSELVES. WE LEAVE IN FIVE MINUTES.
ETHAN, WHAT ARE YOU DOING?
WC
I...WOW.
THIS IS GETTING TOO GODDAMN WEIRD.
CUT THE FEED, YOU CORPORATE PARASITE! IT'S A VIOLATION OF HIS RIGHTS!
HE'S IN A PUBLIC SPACE! FUCK OFF!

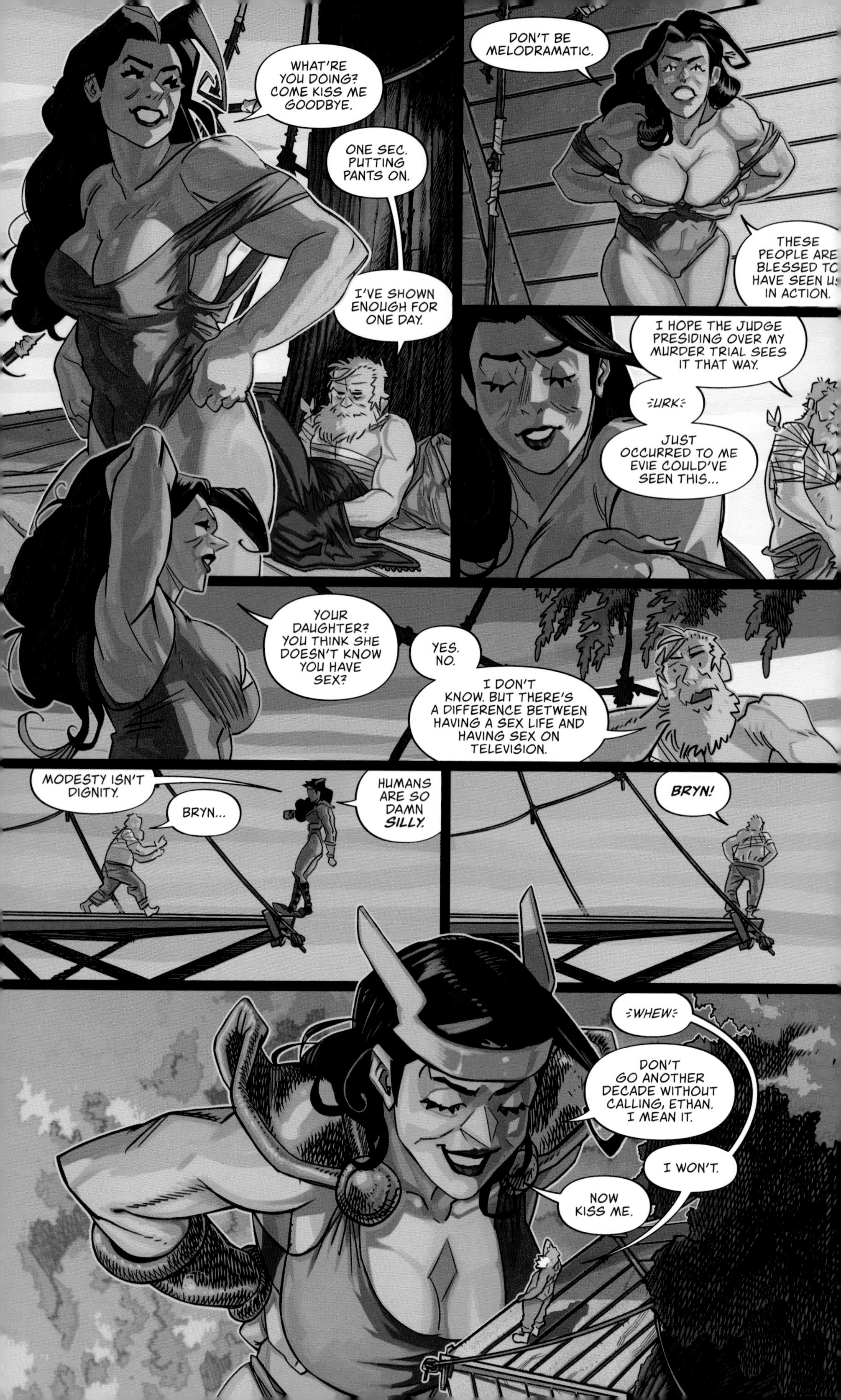
WHAT'RE YOU DOING? COME KISS ME GOODBYE.
ONE SEC. PUTTING PANTS ON.
I'VE SHOWN ENOUGH FOR ONE DAY.
DON'T BE MELODRAMATIC.
THESE PEOPLE ARE BLESSED TO HAVE SEEN US IN ACTION.
I HOPE THE JUDGE PRESIDING OVER MY MURDER TRIAL SEES IT THAT WAY.
URK
JUST OCCURRED TO ME EVIE COULD'VE SEEN THIS...
YOUR DAUGHTER? YOU THINK SHE DOESN'T KNOW YOU HAVE SEX?
YES. NO.
I DON'T KNOW. BUT THERE'S A DIFFERENCE BETWEEN HAVING A SEX LIFE AND HAVING SEX ON TELEVISION.
MODESTY ISN'T DIGNITY.
BRYN...
HUMANS ARE SO DAMN *SILLY.*
***BRYN!***
WHEW
DON'T GO ANOTHER DECADE WITHOUT CALLING, ETHAN. I MEAN IT.
I WON'T.
NOW KISS ME.

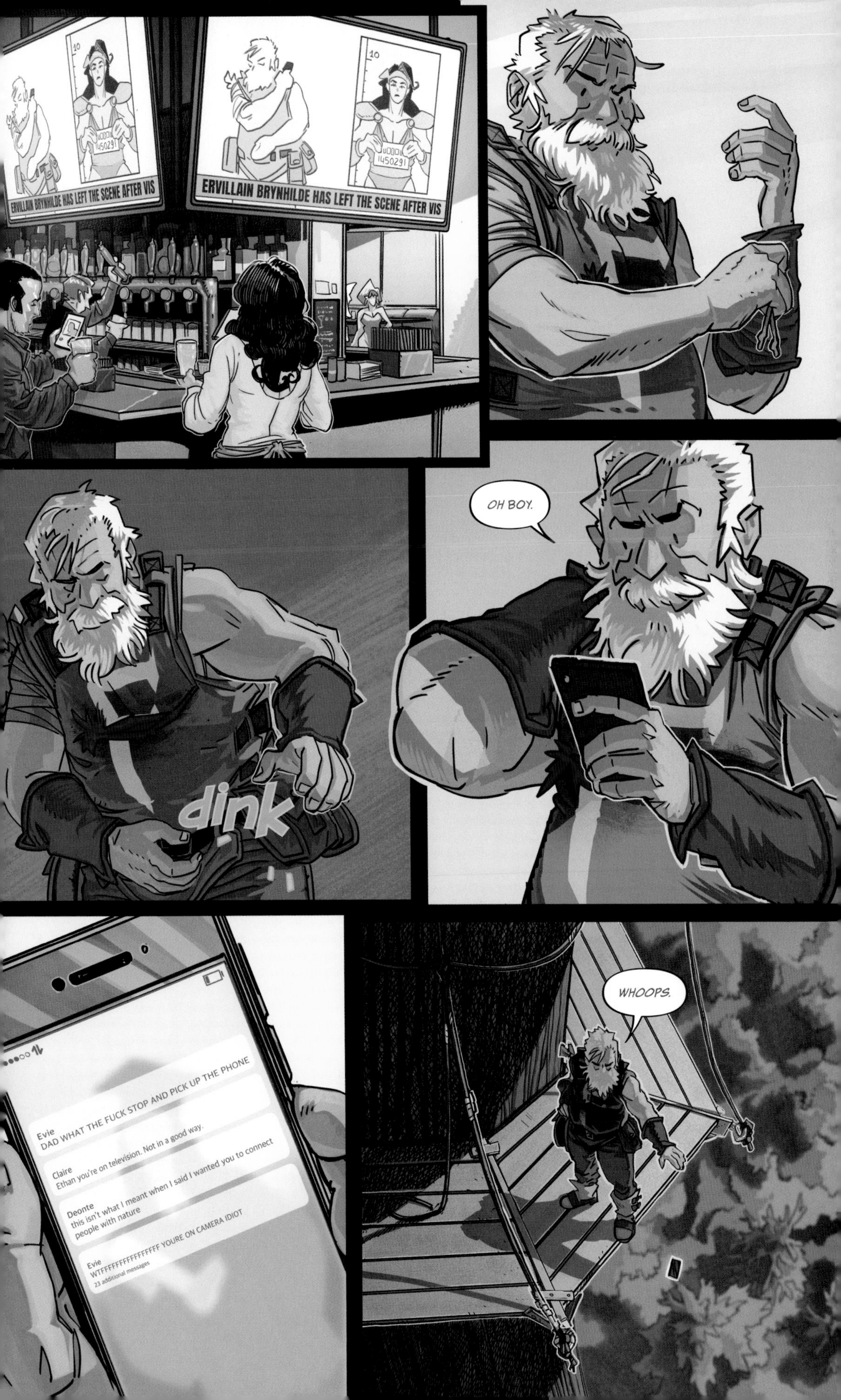
ERVILLAIN BRYNHILDE HAS LEFT THE SCENE AFTER VIS
ERVILLAIN BRYNHILDE HAS LEFT THE SCENE AFTER VIS
1450291
dink
OH BOY.
Evie
DAD WHAT THE FUCK STOP AND PICK UP THE PHONE
Claire
Ethan you're on television. Not in a good way.
Deonte
this isn't what I meant when I said I wanted you to connect people with nature
Evie
WTFFFFFFFFFFFFFFF YOURE ON CAMERA IDIOT
23 additional messages
WHOOPS.

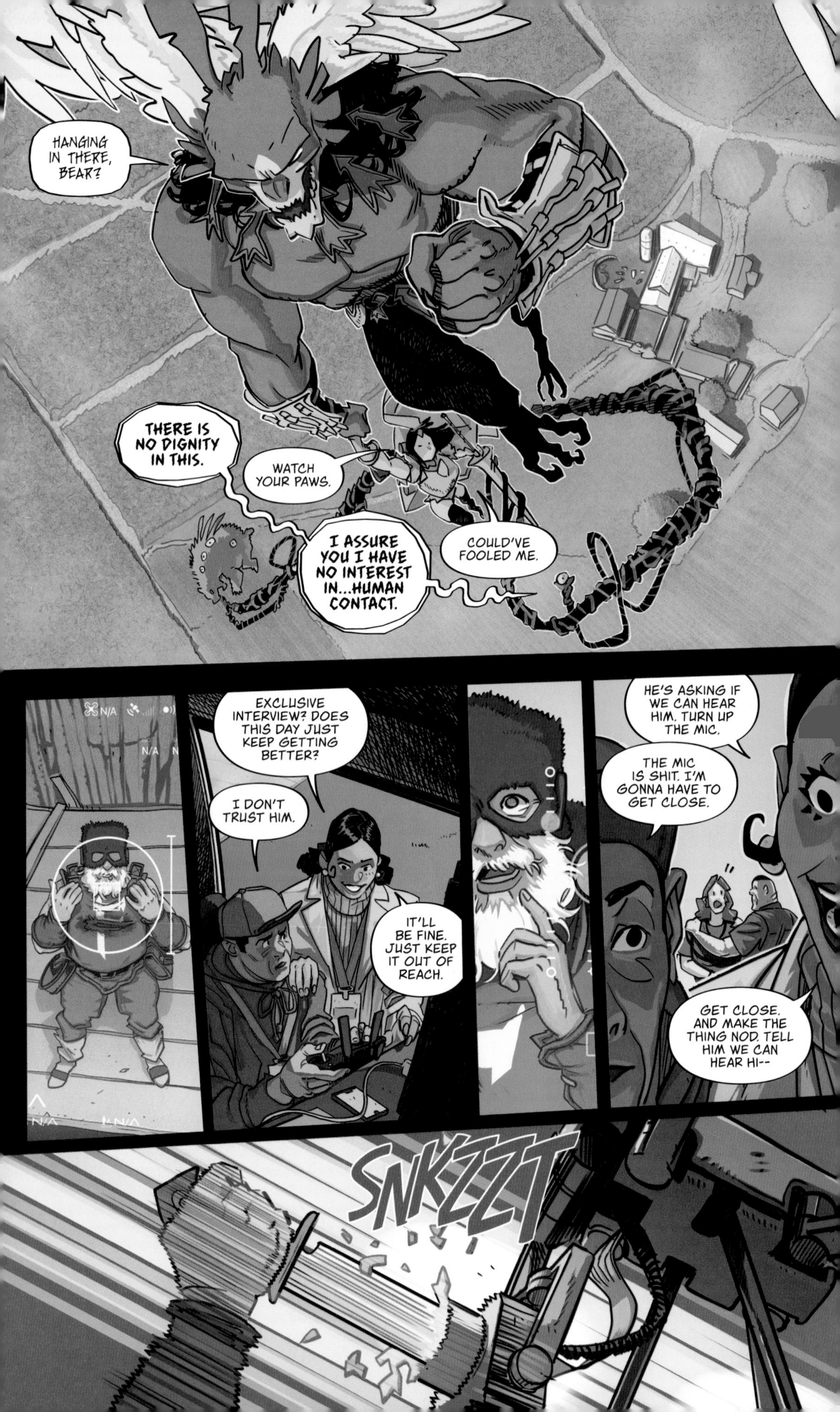
HANGING IN THERE, BEAR?
THERE IS NO DIGNITY IN THIS.
WATCH YOUR PAWS.
I ASSURE YOU I HAVE NO INTEREST IN...HUMAN CONTACT.
COULD'VE FOOLED ME.
N/A
N/A
N/A
EXCLUSIVE INTERVIEW? DOES THIS DAY JUST KEEP GETTING BETTER?
I DON'T TRUST HIM.
IT'LL BE FINE. JUST KEEP IT OUT OF REACH.
HE'S ASKING IF WE CAN HEAR HIM. TURN UP THE MIC.
THE MIC IS SHIT. I'M GONNA HAVE TO GET CLOSE.
GET CLOSE. AND MAKE THE THING NOD. TELL HIM WE CAN HEAR HI--
SNKZZT

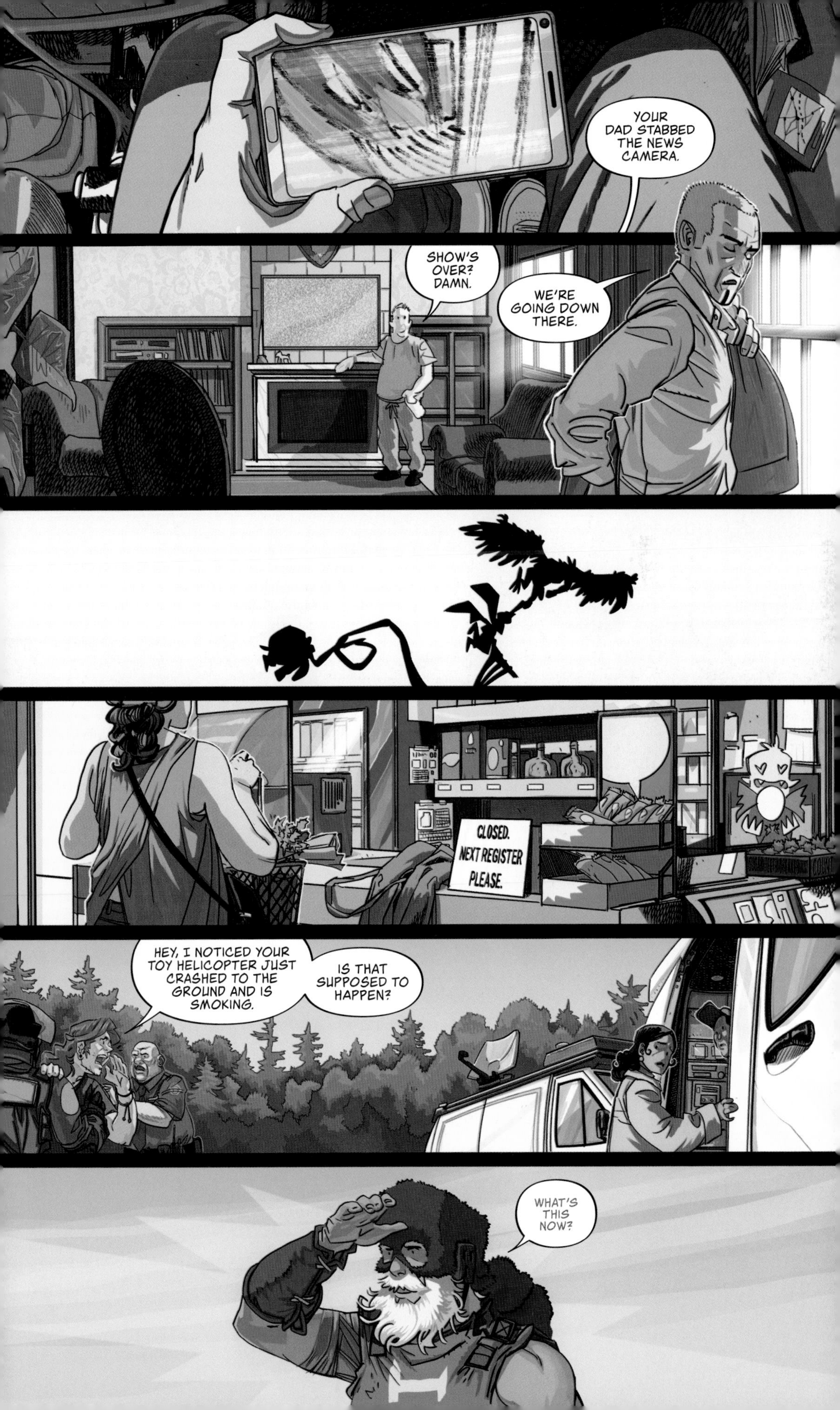
YOUR DAD STABBED THE NEWS CAMERA.
SHOW'S OVER? DAMN.
WE'RE GOING DOWN THERE.
CLOSED. NEXT REGISTER PLEASE.
HEY, I NOTICED YOUR TOY HELICOPTER JUST CRASHED TO THE GROUND AND IS SMOKING.
IS THAT SUPPOSED TO HAPPEN?
WHAT'S THIS NOW?

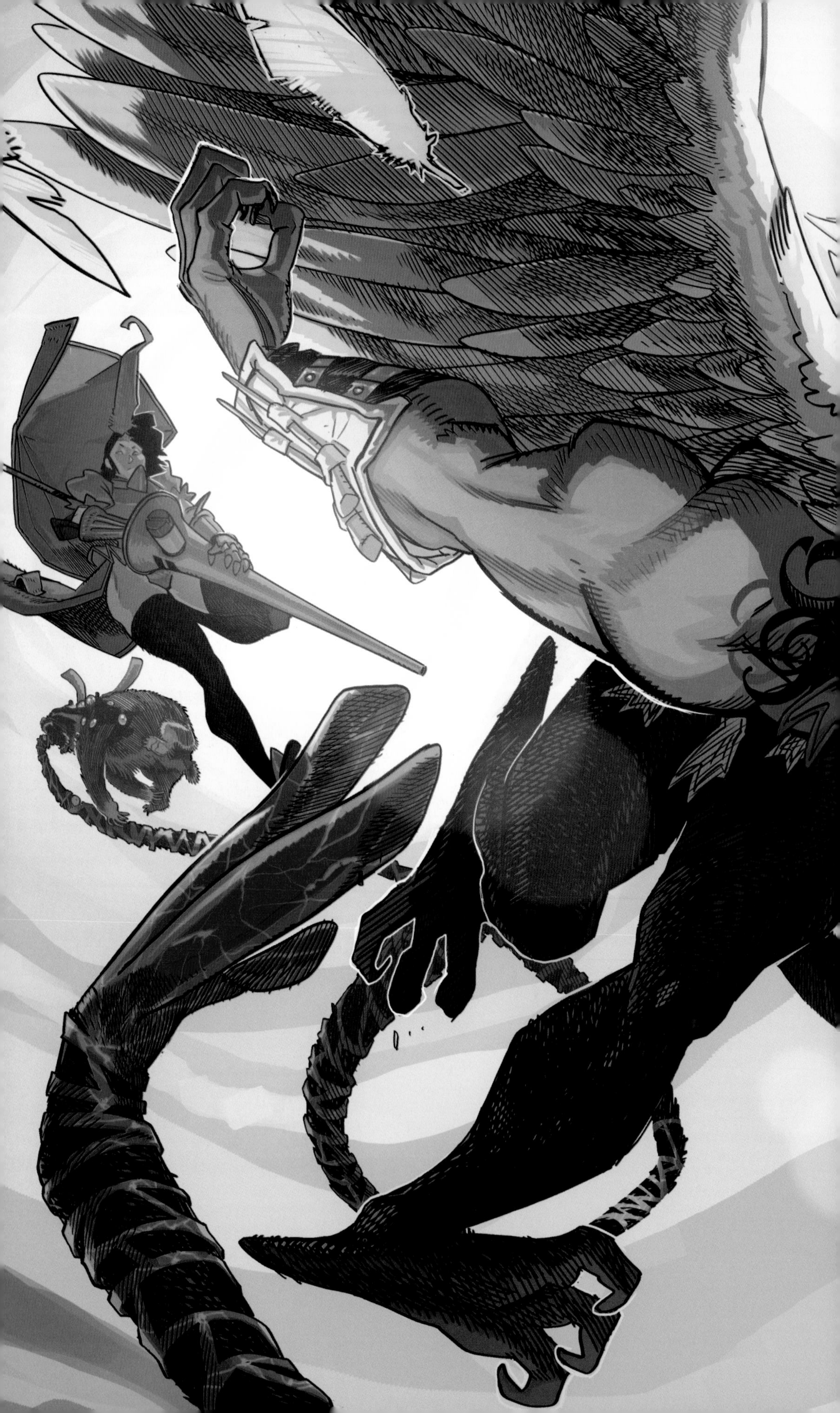

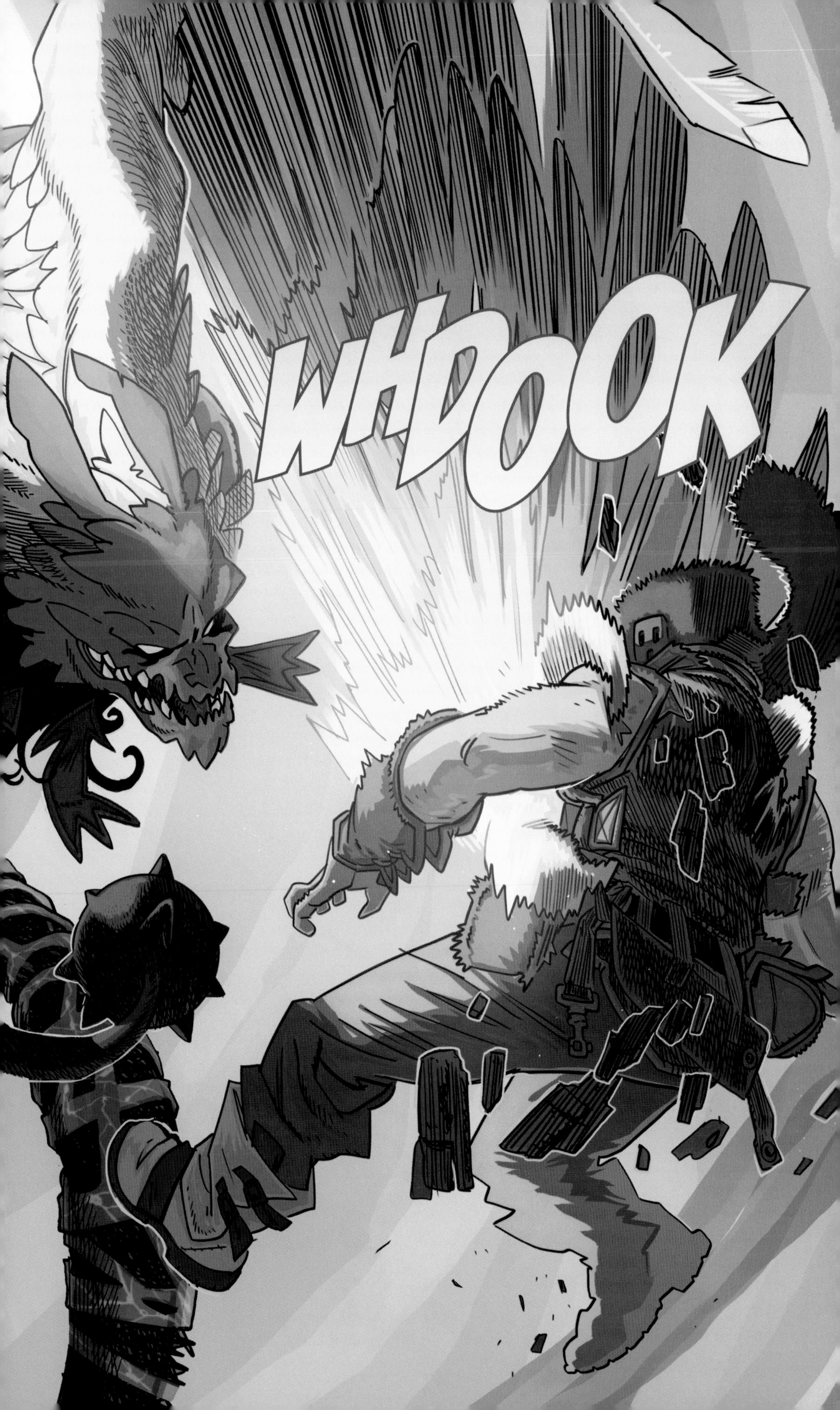
WHOOK

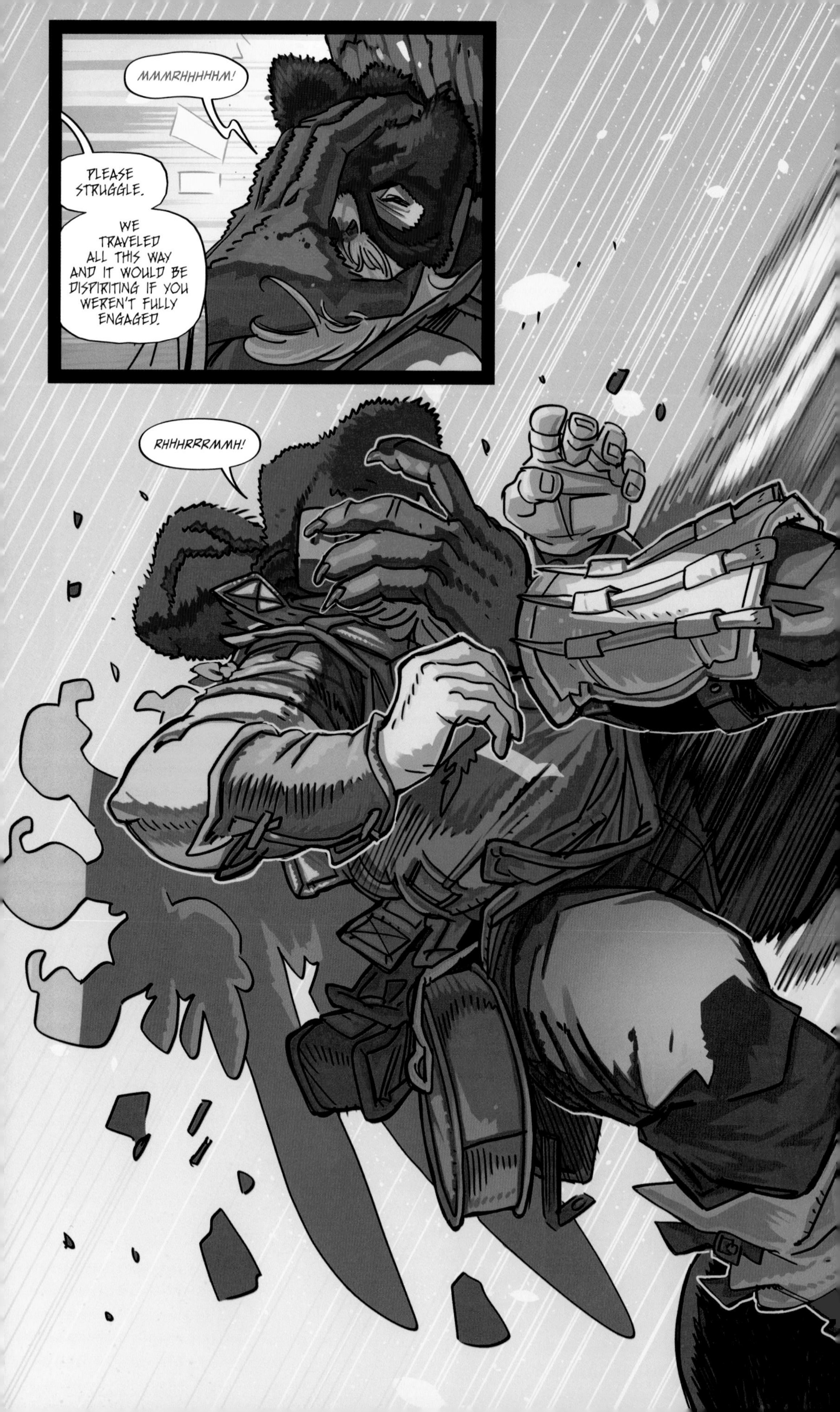
MMMRHHHHHM!
PLEASE STRUGGLE.
WE TRAVELED ALL THIS WAY AND IT WOULD BE DISPIRITING IF YOU WEREN'T FULLY ENGAGED.
RHHHRRRMMH!

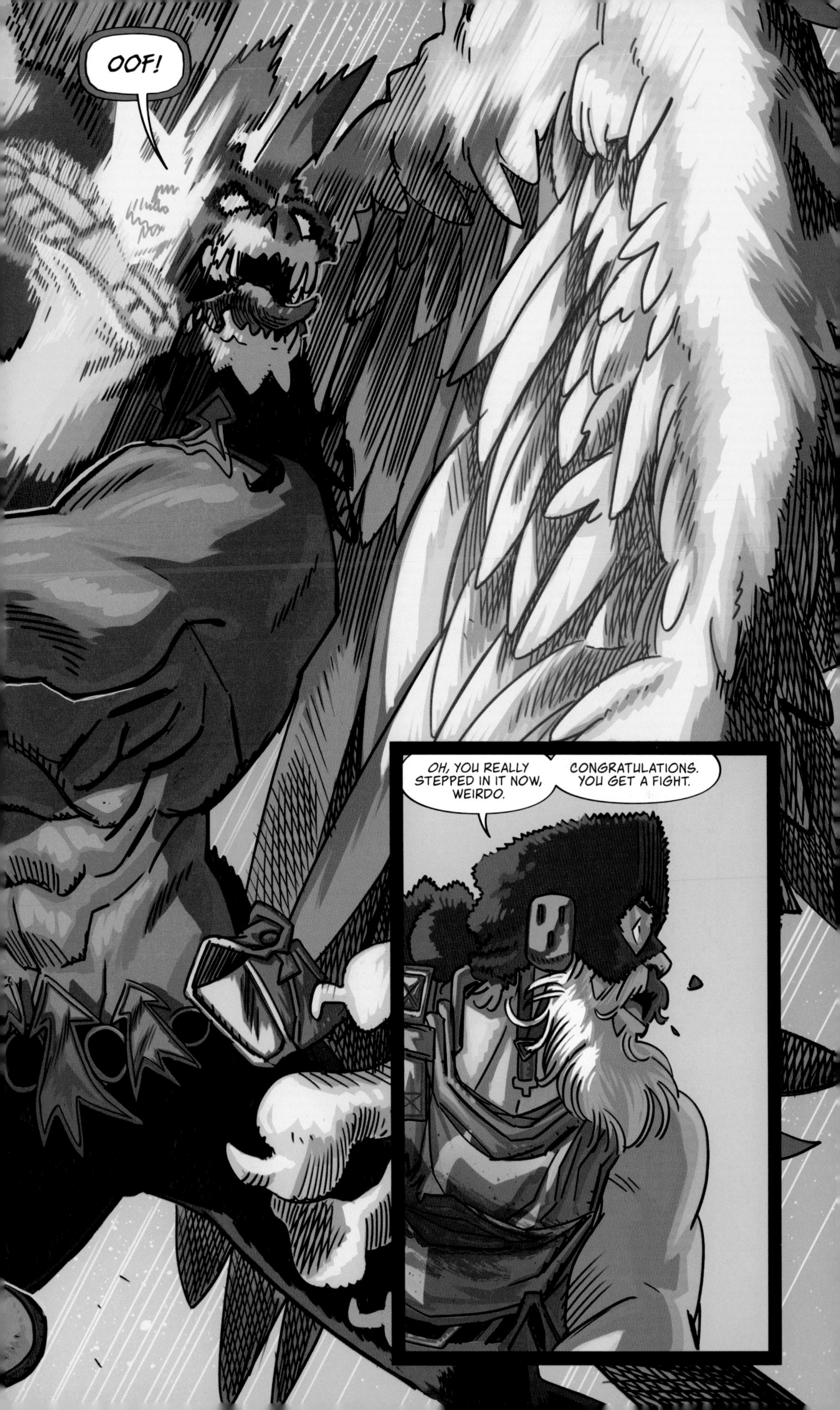
OOF!
OH, YOU REALLY STEPPED IN IT NOW, WEIRDO.
CONGRATULATIONS. YOU GET A FIGHT.

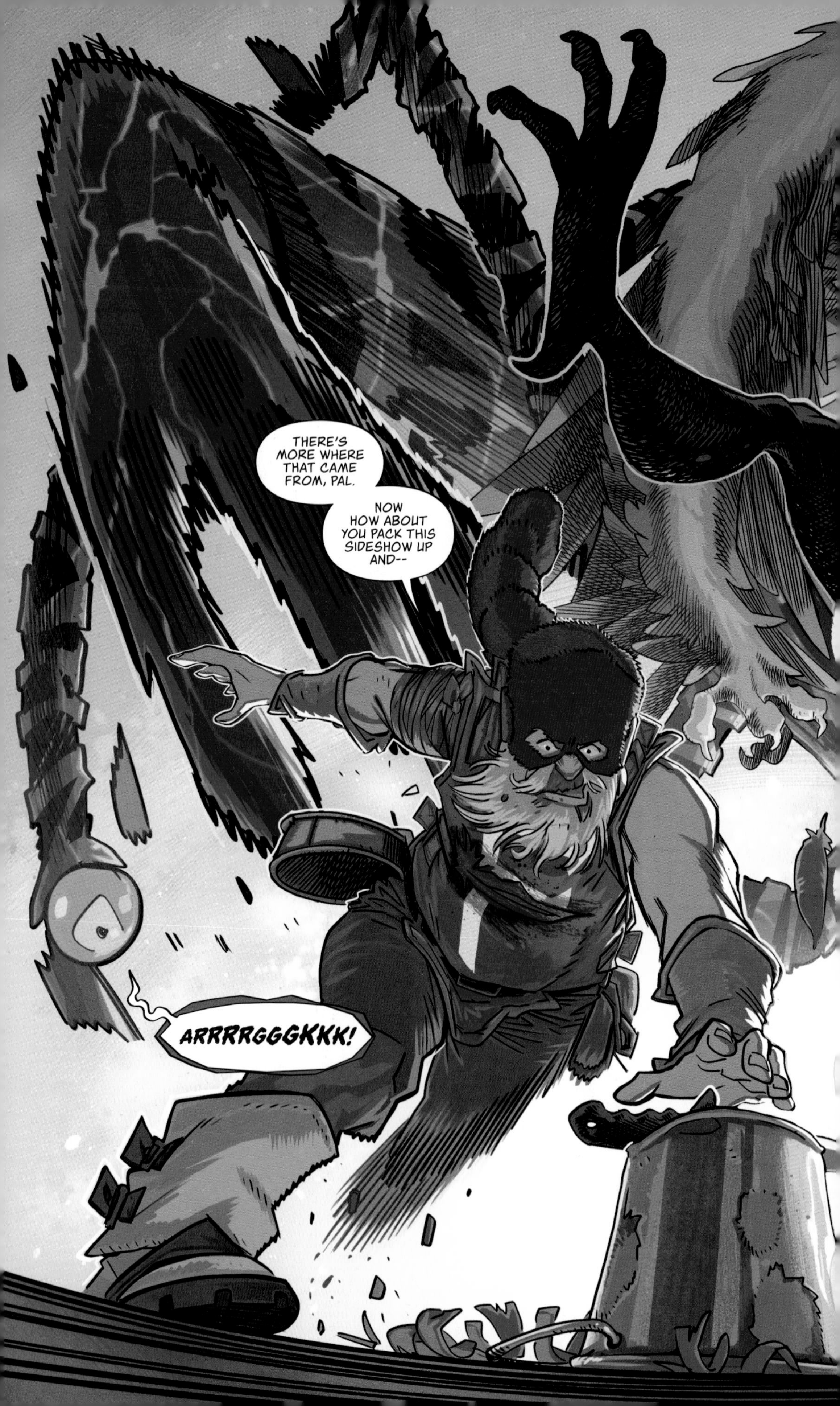

THERE'S MORE WHERE THAT CAME FROM, PAL.
NOW HOW ABOUT YOU PACK THIS SIDESHOW UP AND--
ARRRRGGGKKK!

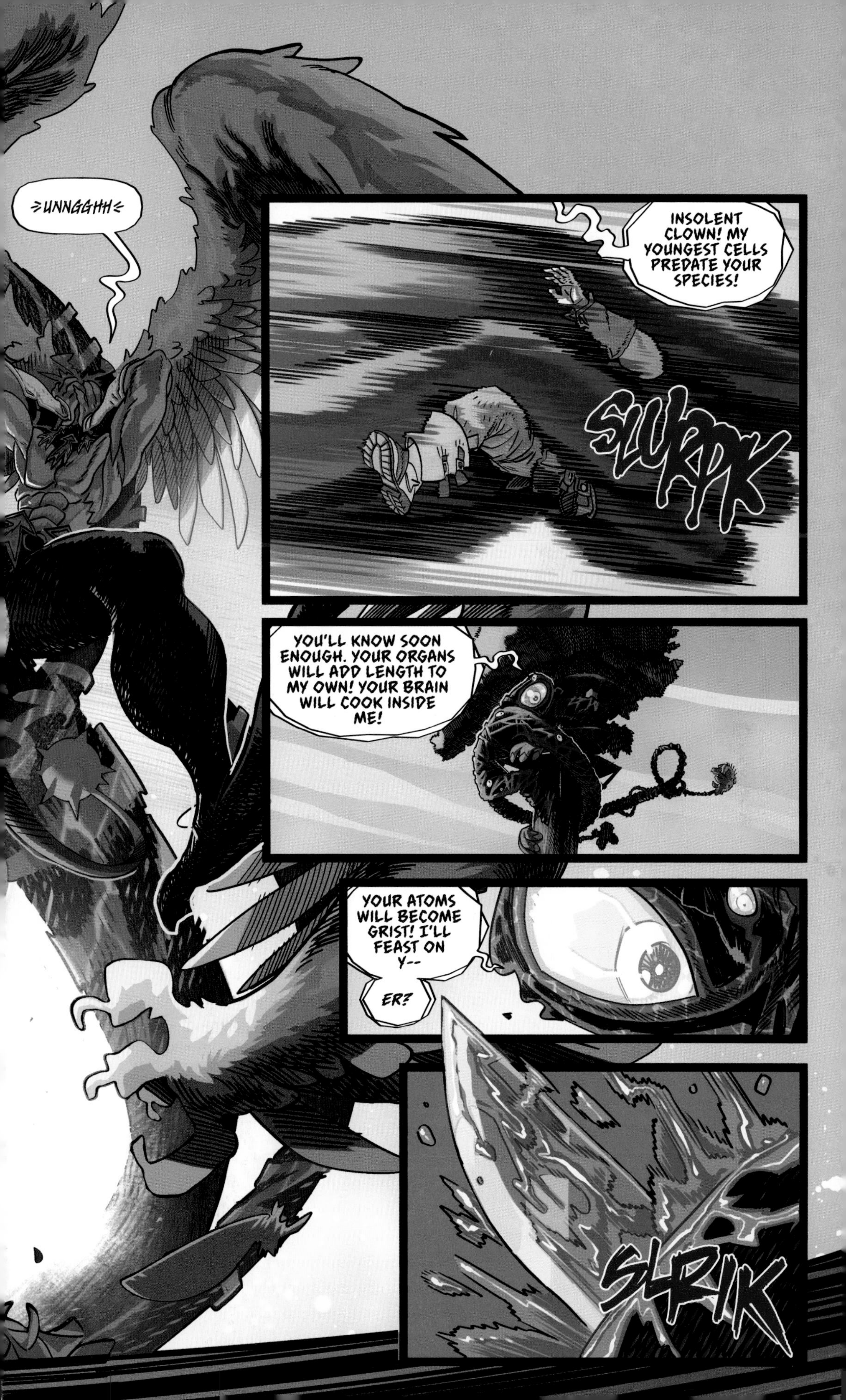

UNNGGHH
INSOLENT CLOWN! MY YOUNGEST CELLS PREDATE YOUR SPECIES!
SLURPK
YOU'LL KNOW SOON ENOUGH. YOUR ORGANS WILL ADD LENGTH TO MY OWN! YOUR BRAIN WILL COOK INSIDE ME!
YOUR ATOMS WILL BECOME GRIST! I'LL FEAST ON Y--
ER?
SLRIK

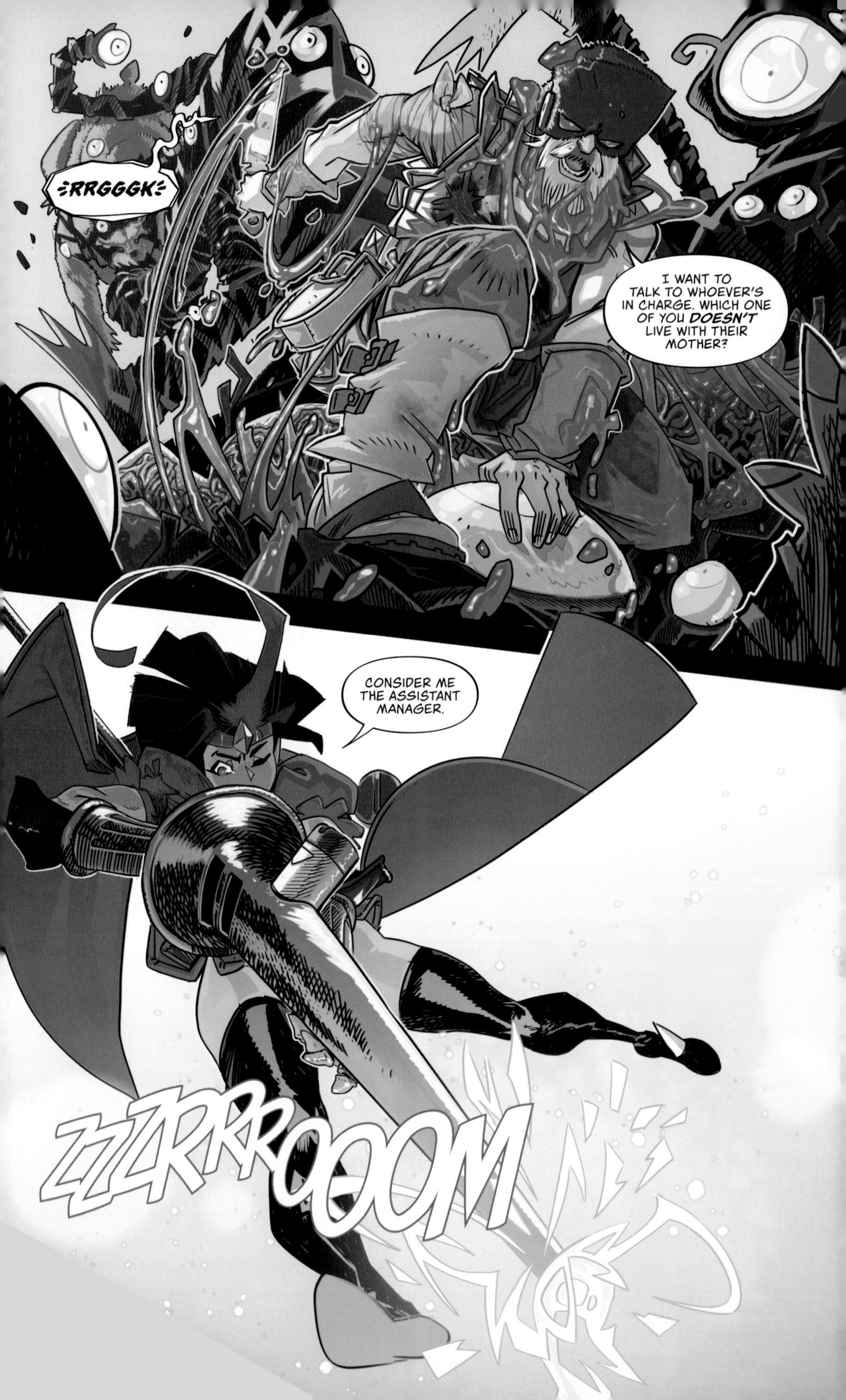
RRGGGK
I WANT TO TALK TO WHOEVER'S IN CHARGE. WHICH ONE OF YOU **DOESN'T** LIVE WITH THEIR MOTHER?
CONSIDER ME THE ASSISTANT MANAGER.
ZZZRRROOOM

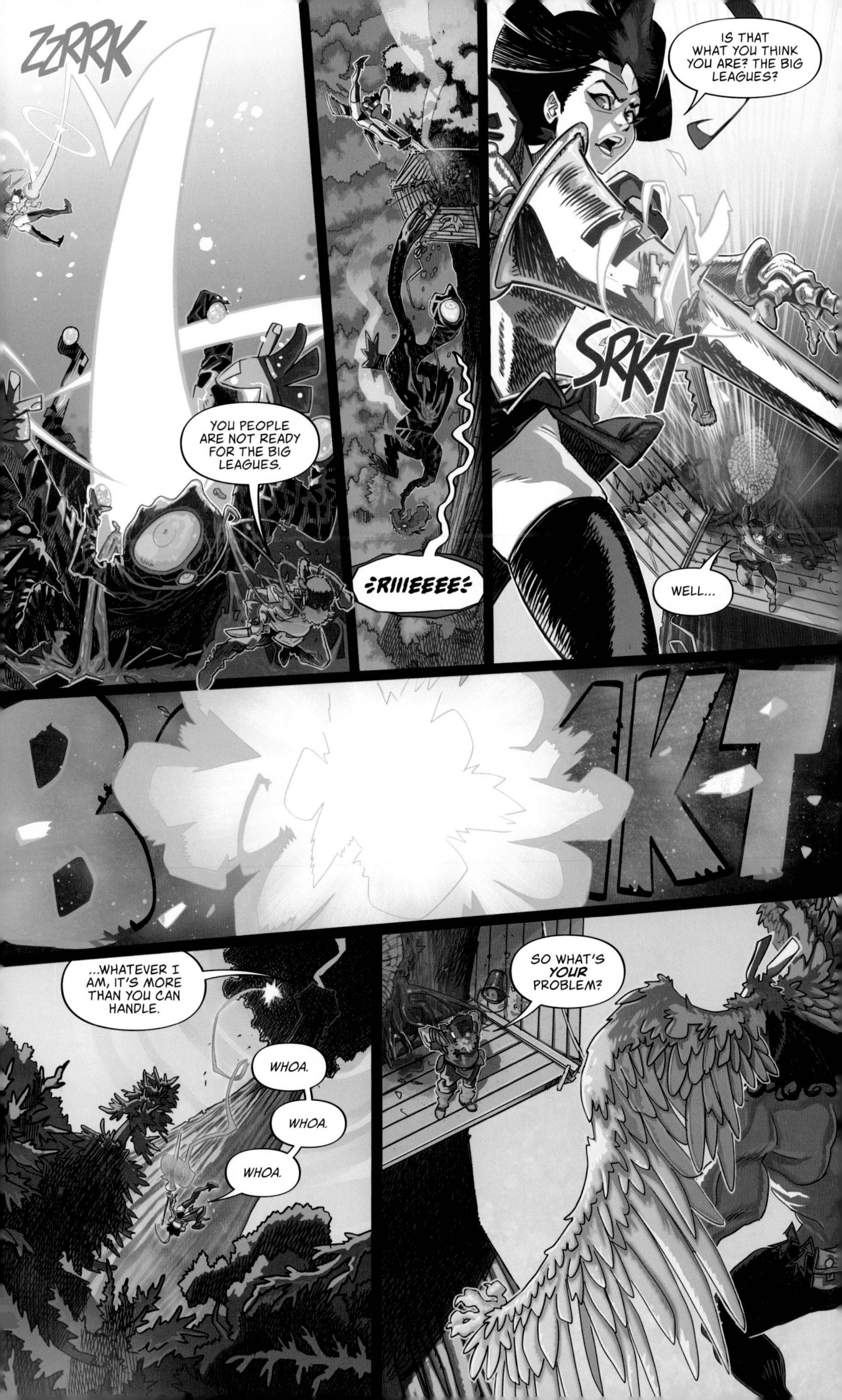
ZZRRK
YOU PEOPLE ARE NOT READY FOR THE BIG LEAGUES.
RIIIEEEE
IS THAT WHAT YOU THINK YOU ARE? THE BIG LEAGUES?
SRKT
WELL...
...WHATEVER I AM, IT'S MORE THAN YOU CAN HANDLE.
WHOA.
WHOA.
WHOA.
SO WHAT'S *YOUR* PROBLEM?

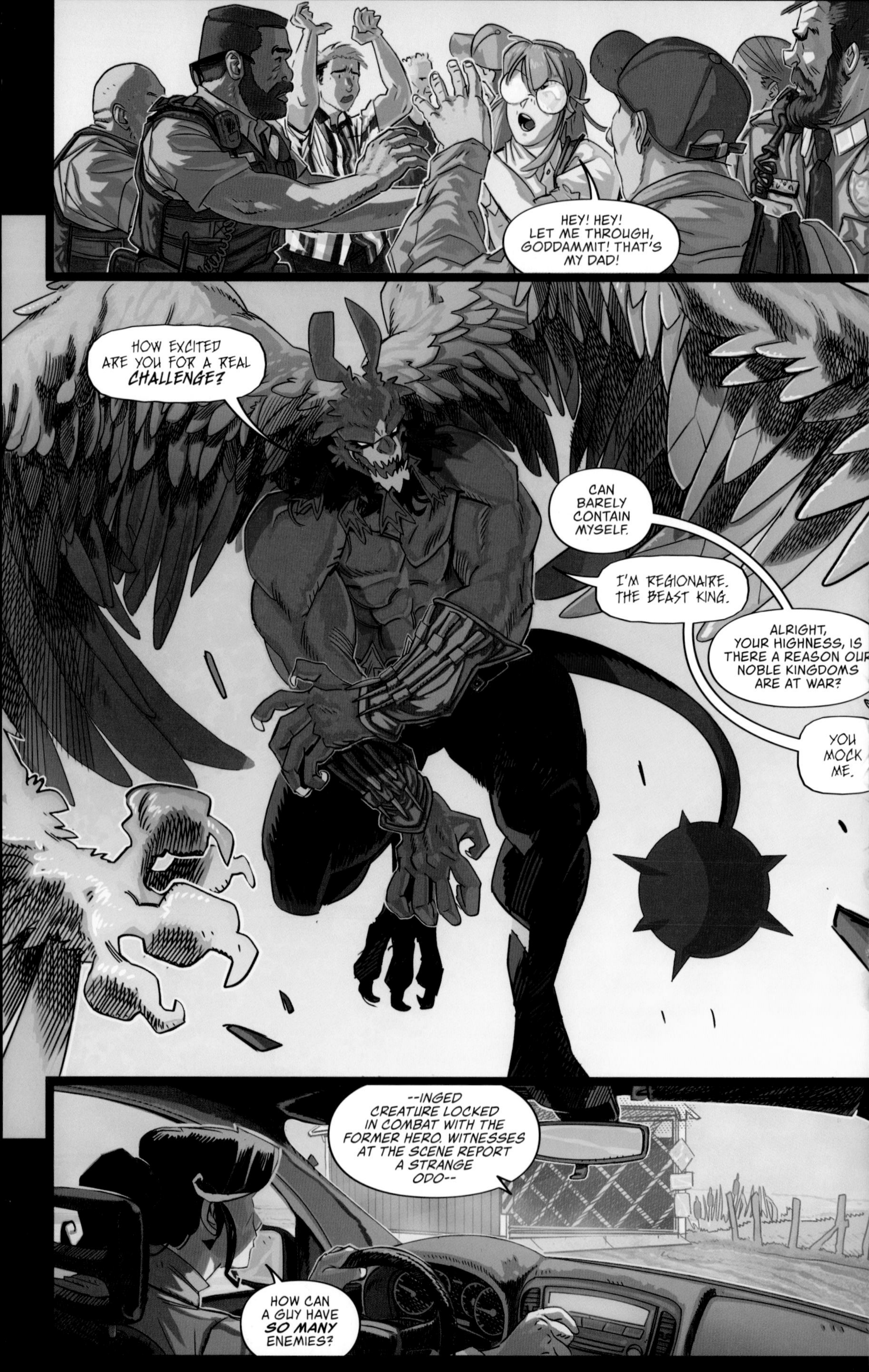
HEY! HEY! LET ME THROUGH, GODDAMMIT! THAT'S MY DAD!
HOW EXCITED ARE YOU FOR A REAL CHALLENGE?
CAN BARELY CONTAIN MYSELF.
I'M REGIONAIRE. THE BEAST KING.
ALRIGHT, YOUR HIGHNESS, IS THERE A REASON OUR NOBLE KINGDOMS ARE AT WAR?
YOU MOCK ME.
--INGED CREATURE LOCKED IN COMBAT WITH THE FORMER HERO. WITNESSES AT THE SCENE REPORT A STRANGE ODO--
HOW CAN A GUY HAVE SO MANY ENEMIES?

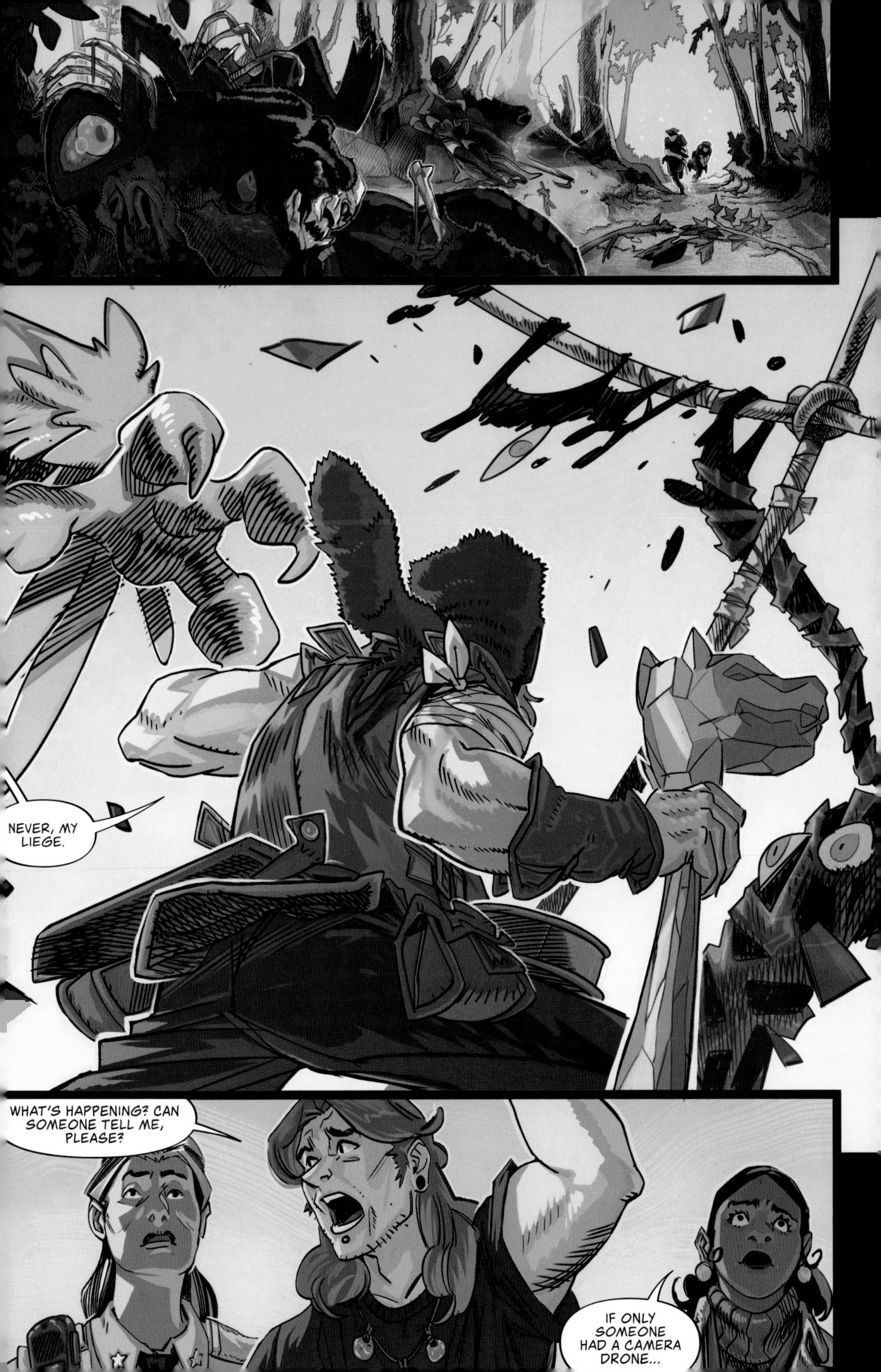
NEVER, MY LIEGE.
WHAT'S HAPPENING? CAN SOMEONE TELL ME, PLEASE?
IF ONLY SOMEONE HAD A CAMERA DRONE...

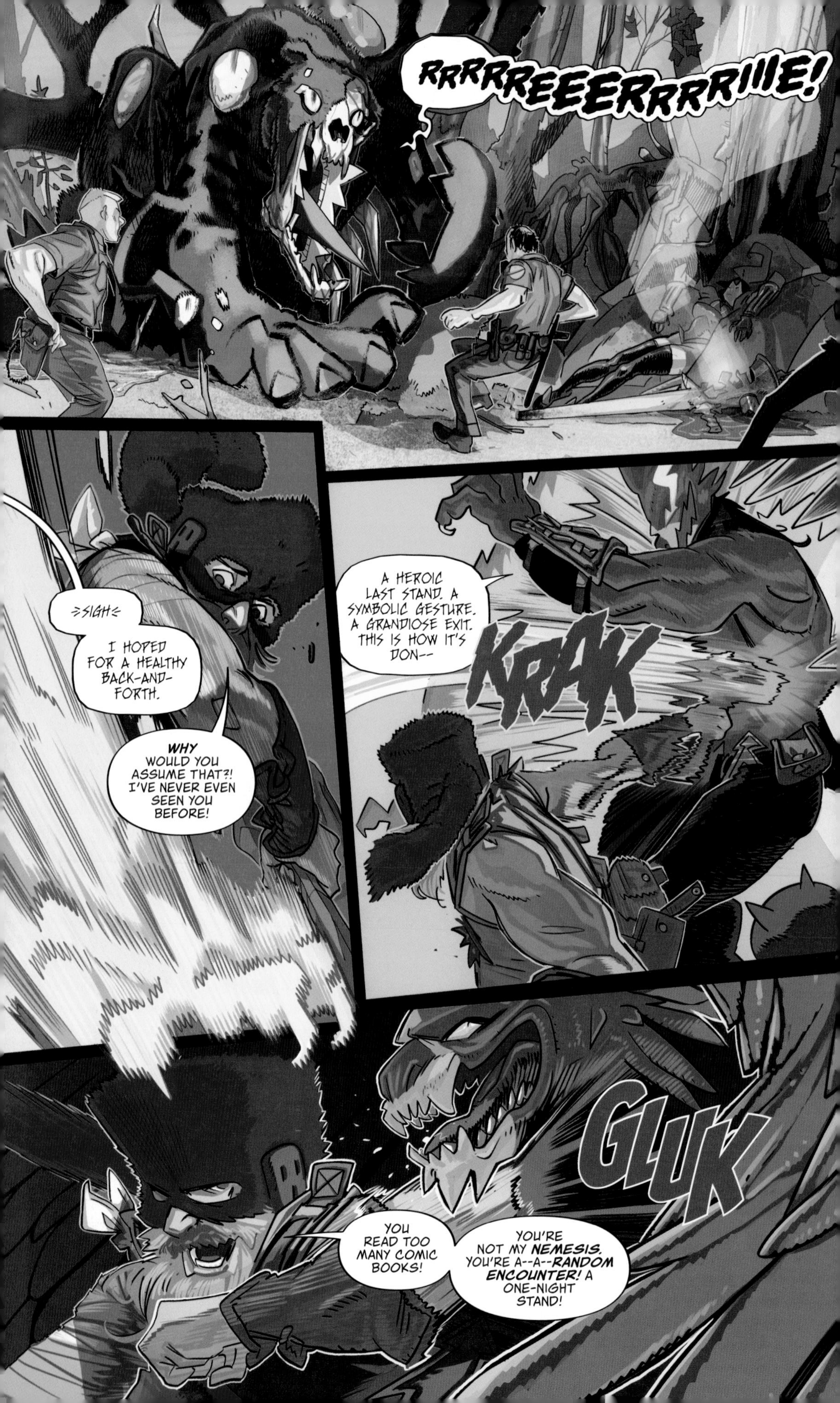
RRRRREEEERRRRRIIIE!
A HEROIC LAST STAND. A SYMBOLIC GESTURE. A GRANDIOSE EXIT. THIS IS HOW IT'S DON--
KRAK
>SIGH<
I HOPED FOR A HEALTHY BACK-AND-FORTH.
WHY WOULD YOU ASSUME THAT?! I'VE NEVER EVEN SEEN YOU BEFORE!
GLUK
YOU READ TOO MANY COMIC BOOKS!
YOU'RE NOT MY NEMESIS. YOU'RE A--A--RANDOM ENCOUNTER! A ONE-NIGHT STAND!

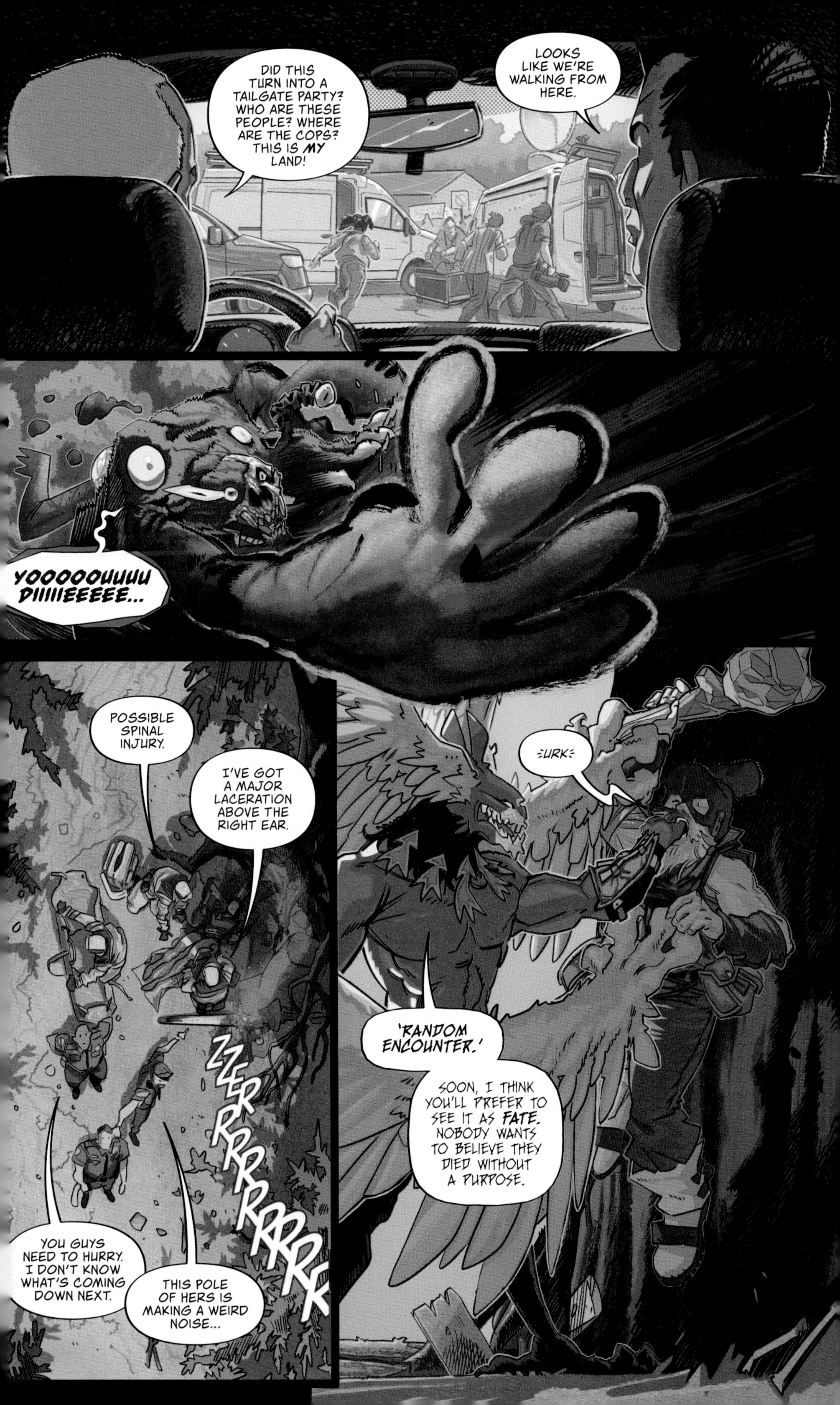
DID THIS TURN INTO A TAILGATE PARTY? WHO ARE THESE PEOPLE? WHERE ARE THE COPS? THIS IS *MY* LAND!
LOOKS LIKE WE'RE WALKING FROM HERE.
YOOOOOUUUU DIIIIEEEEE...
POSSIBLE SPINAL INJURY.
I'VE GOT A MAJOR LACERATION ABOVE THE RIGHT EAR.
ZZERRRRRRRRRRK
YOU GUYS NEED TO HURRY. I DON'T KNOW WHAT'S COMING DOWN NEXT.
THIS POLE OF HERS IS MAKING A WEIRD NOISE...
=URK=
'RANDOM ENCOUNTER.'
SOON, I THINK YOU'LL PREFER TO SEE IT AS *FATE*. NOBODY WANTS TO BELIEVE THEY DIED WITHOUT A PURPOSE.

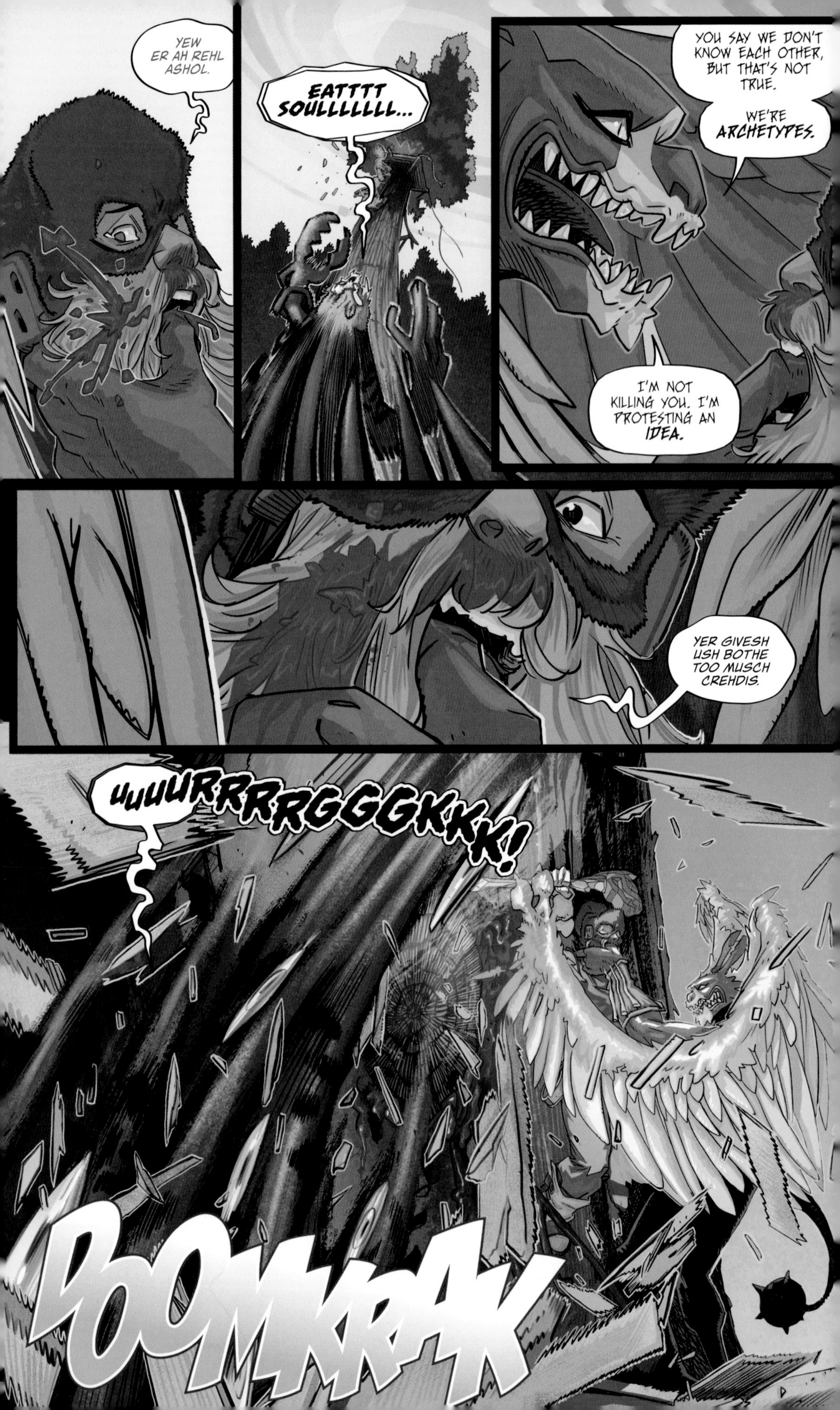

YEW ER AH REHL ASHOL.
EATTTT SOULLLLLLL...
YOU SAY WE DON'T KNOW EACH OTHER, BUT THAT'S NOT TRUE.
WE'RE ARCHETYPES.
I'M NOT KILLING YOU. I'M PROTESTING AN IDEA.
YER GIVESH USH BOTHE TOO MUSCH CREHDIS.
UUUURRRRGGGKKKK!
DOOMKRAK

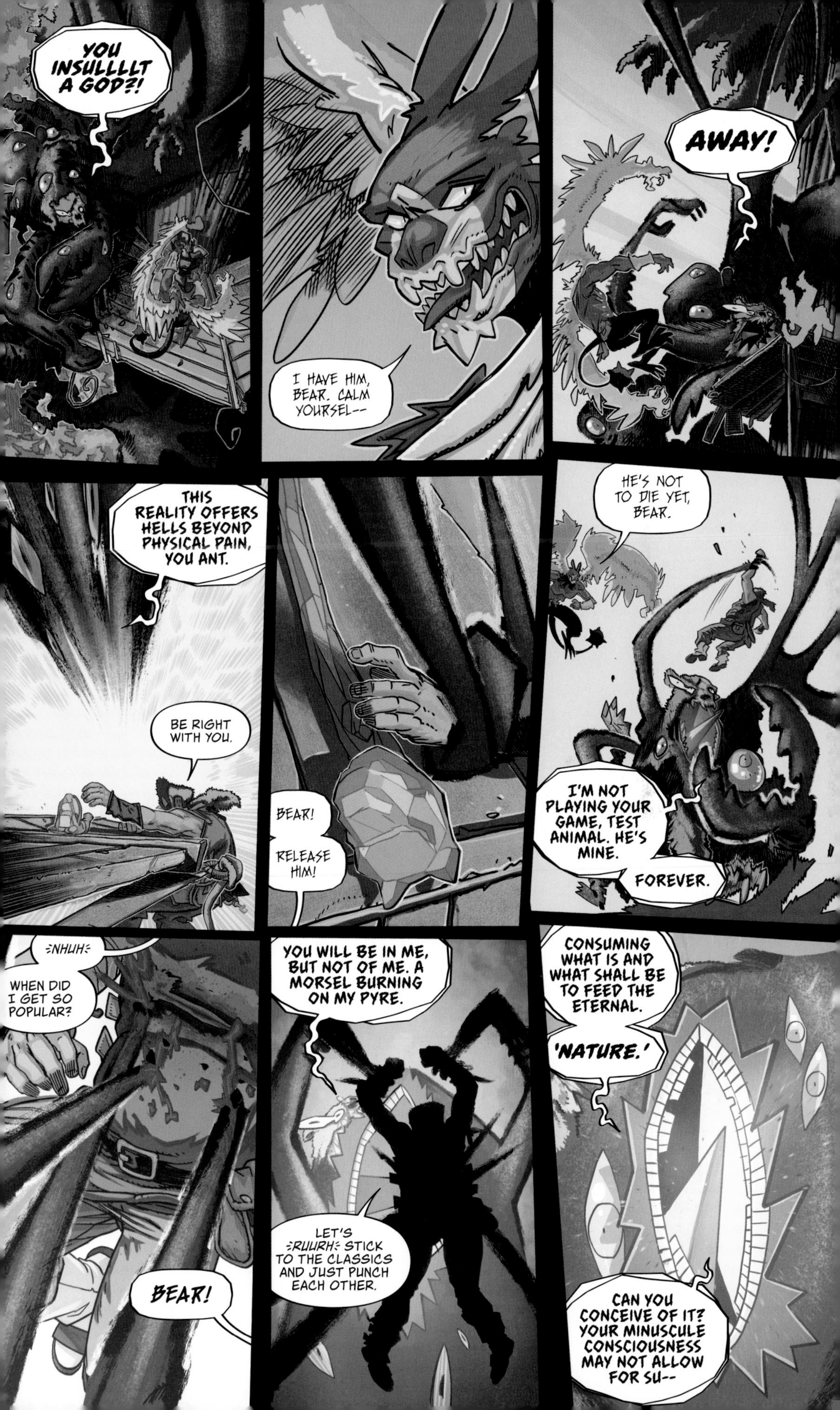
YOU INSULLLLT A GOD?!
I HAVE HIM, BEAR. CALM YOURSEL--
AWAY!
THIS REALITY OFFERS HELLS BEYOND PHYSICAL PAIN, YOU ANT.
BE RIGHT WITH YOU.
BEAR!
RELEASE HIM!
HE'S NOT TO DIE YET, BEAR.
I'M NOT PLAYING YOUR GAME, TEST ANIMAL. HE'S MINE.
FOREVER.
=NHUH=
WHEN DID I GET SO POPULAR?
BEAR!
YOU WILL BE IN ME, BUT NOT OF ME. A MORSEL BURNING ON MY PYRE.
LET'S =RUURH= STICK TO THE CLASSICS AND JUST PUNCH EACH OTHER.
CONSUMING WHAT IS AND WHAT SHALL BE TO FEED THE ETERNAL.
'NATURE.'
CAN YOU CONCEIVE OF IT? YOUR MINUSCULE CONSCIOUSNESS MAY NOT ALLOW FOR SU--

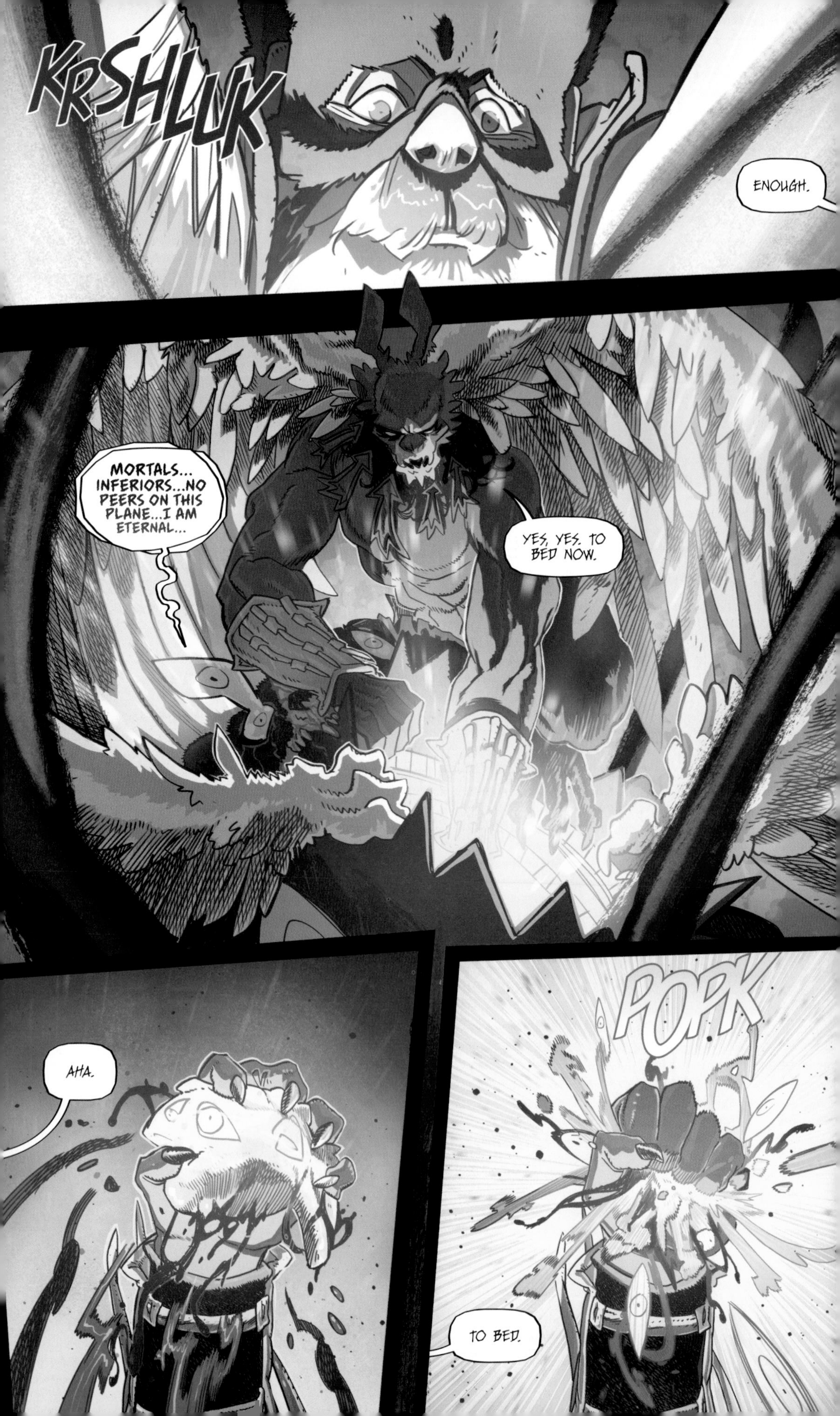
KRSHLUK
ENOUGH.
MORTALS... INFERIORS...NO PEERS ON THIS PLANE...I AM ETERNAL...
YES, YES. TO BED NOW.
AHA.
POPK
TO BED.

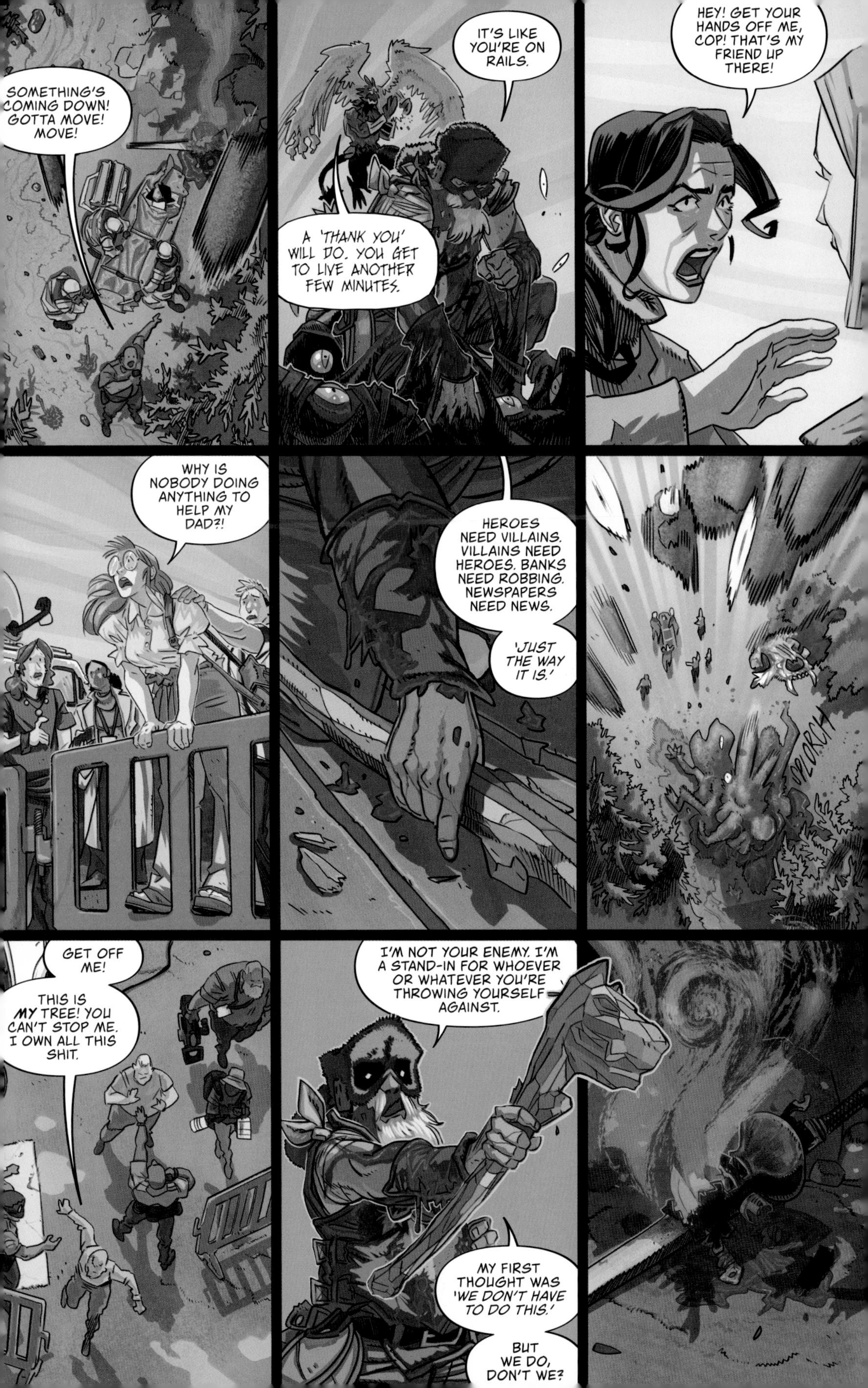
SOMETHING'S COMING DOWN! GOTTA MOVE! MOVE!
IT'S LIKE YOU'RE ON RAILS.
A 'THANK YOU' WILL DO. YOU GET TO LIVE ANOTHER FEW MINUTES.
HEY! GET YOUR HANDS OFF ME, COP! THAT'S MY FRIEND UP THERE!
WHY IS NOBODY DOING ANYTHING TO HELP MY DAD?!
HEROES NEED VILLAINS. VILLAINS NEED HEROES. BANKS NEED ROBBING. NEWSPAPERS NEED NEWS.
'JUST THE WAY IT IS.'
SPLORCH
GET OFF ME!
THIS IS MY TREE! YOU CAN'T STOP ME. I OWN ALL THIS SHIT.
I'M NOT YOUR ENEMY. I'M A STAND-IN FOR WHOEVER OR WHATEVER YOU'RE THROWING YOURSELF AGAINST.
MY FIRST THOUGHT WAS 'WE DON'T HAVE TO DO THIS.'
BUT WE DO, DON'T WE?

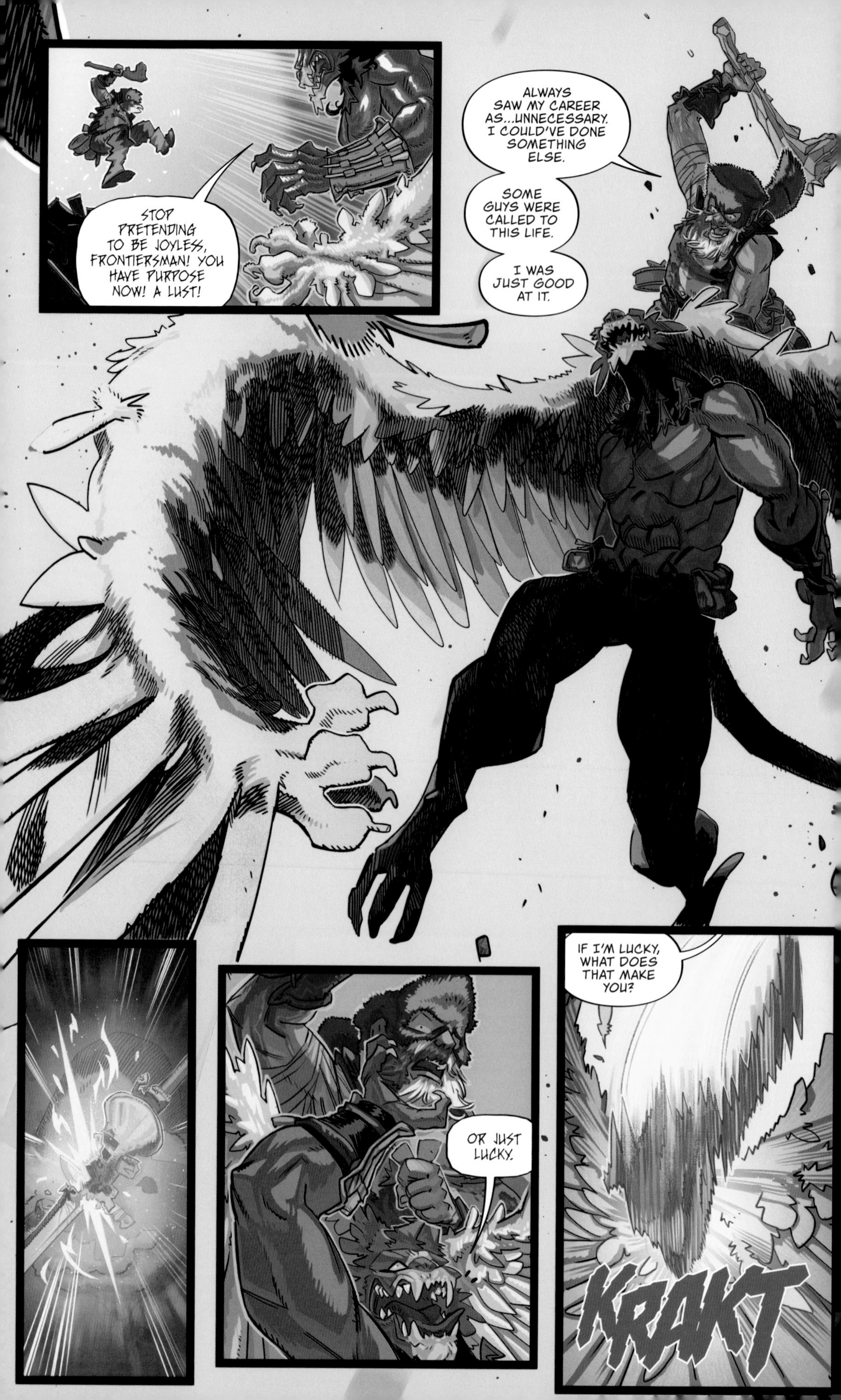
STOP PRETENDING TO BE JOYLESS, FRONTIERSMAN! YOU HAVE PURPOSE NOW! A LUST!
ALWAYS SAW MY CAREER AS...UNNECESSARY. I COULD'VE DONE SOMETHING ELSE.
SOME GUYS WERE CALLED TO THIS LIFE.
I WAS JUST GOOD AT IT.
OR JUST LUCKY.
IF I'M LUCKY, WHAT DOES THAT MAKE YOU?
KRAKT

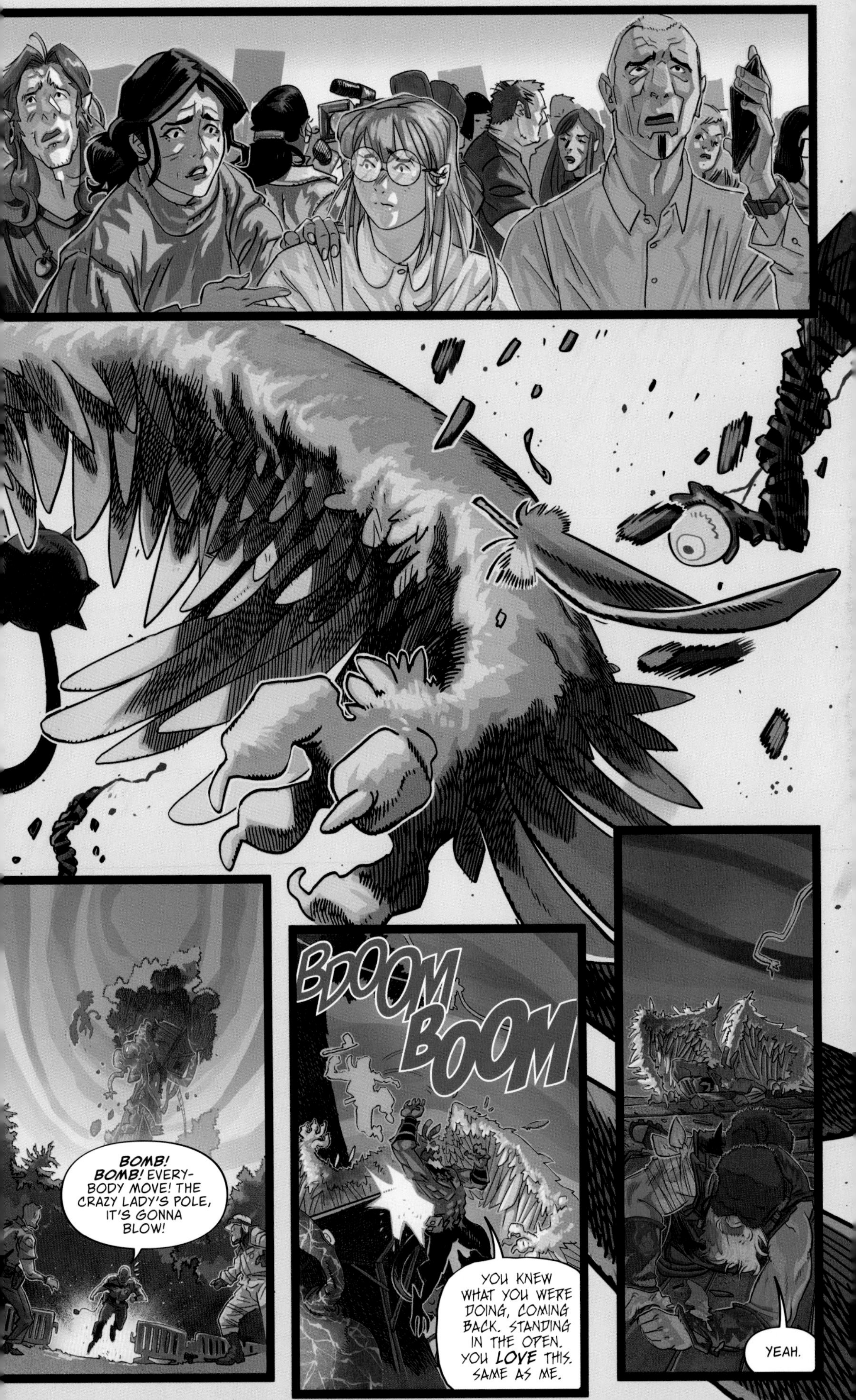
BOMB! BOMB! EVERY-BODY MOVE! THE CRAZY LADY'S POLE, IT'S GONNA BLOW!
BDOOM
BOOM
YOU KNEW WHAT YOU WERE DOING, COMING BACK. STANDING IN THE OPEN. YOU **LOVE** THIS. SAME AS ME.
YEAH.

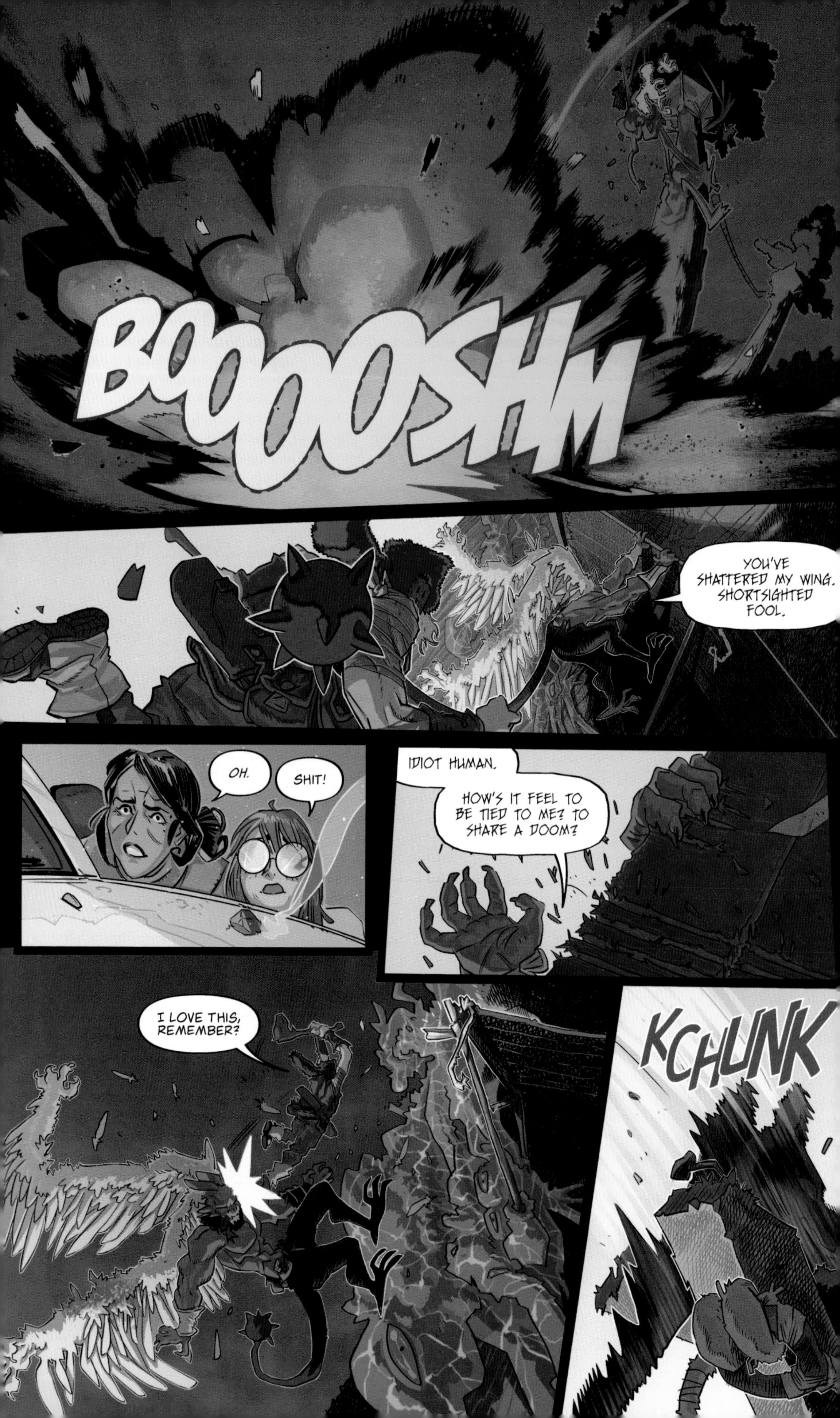
BOOOOSHM
YOU'VE SHATTERED MY WING. SHORTSIGHTED FOOL.
OH.
SHIT!
IDIOT HUMAN.
HOW'S IT FEEL TO BE TIED TO ME? TO SHARE A DOOM?
I LOVE THIS, REMEMBER?
KCHUNK

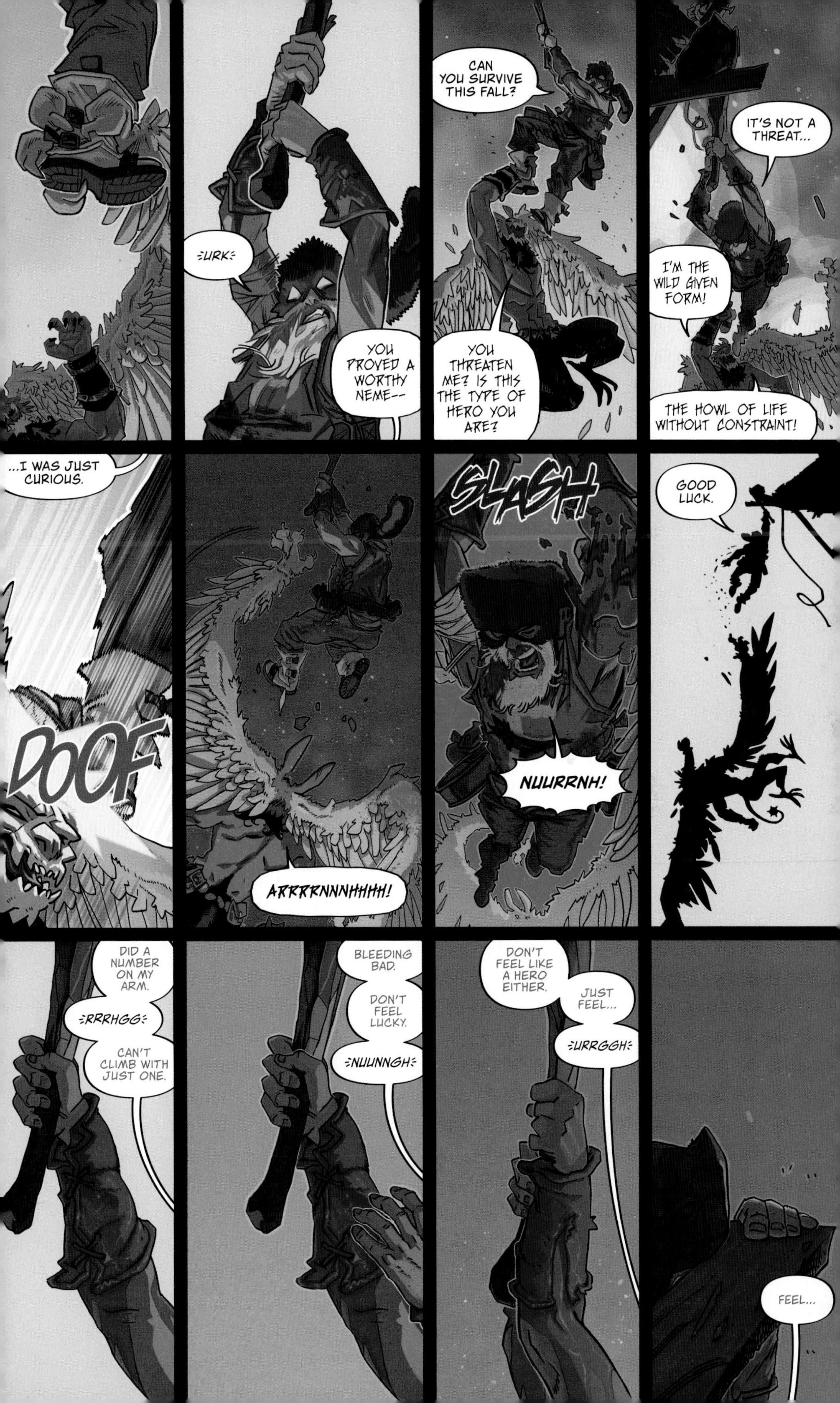

=URK=
YOU PROVED A WORTHY NEME--
CAN YOU SURVIVE THIS FALL?
YOU THREATEN ME? IS THIS THE TYPE OF HERO YOU ARE?
IT'S NOT A THREAT...
I'M THE WILD GIVEN FORM!
THE HOWL OF LIFE WITHOUT CONSTRAINT!
...I WAS JUST CURIOUS.
DOOF
ARRRRNNNHHHH!
SLASH
NUURRNH!
GOOD LUCK.
DID A NUMBER ON MY ARM.
=RRRHGG=
CAN'T CLIMB WITH JUST ONE.
BLEEDING BAD.
DON'T FEEL LUCKY.
=NUUNNGH=
DON'T FEEL LIKE A HERO EITHER.
JUST FEEL...
=URRGGH=
FEEL...

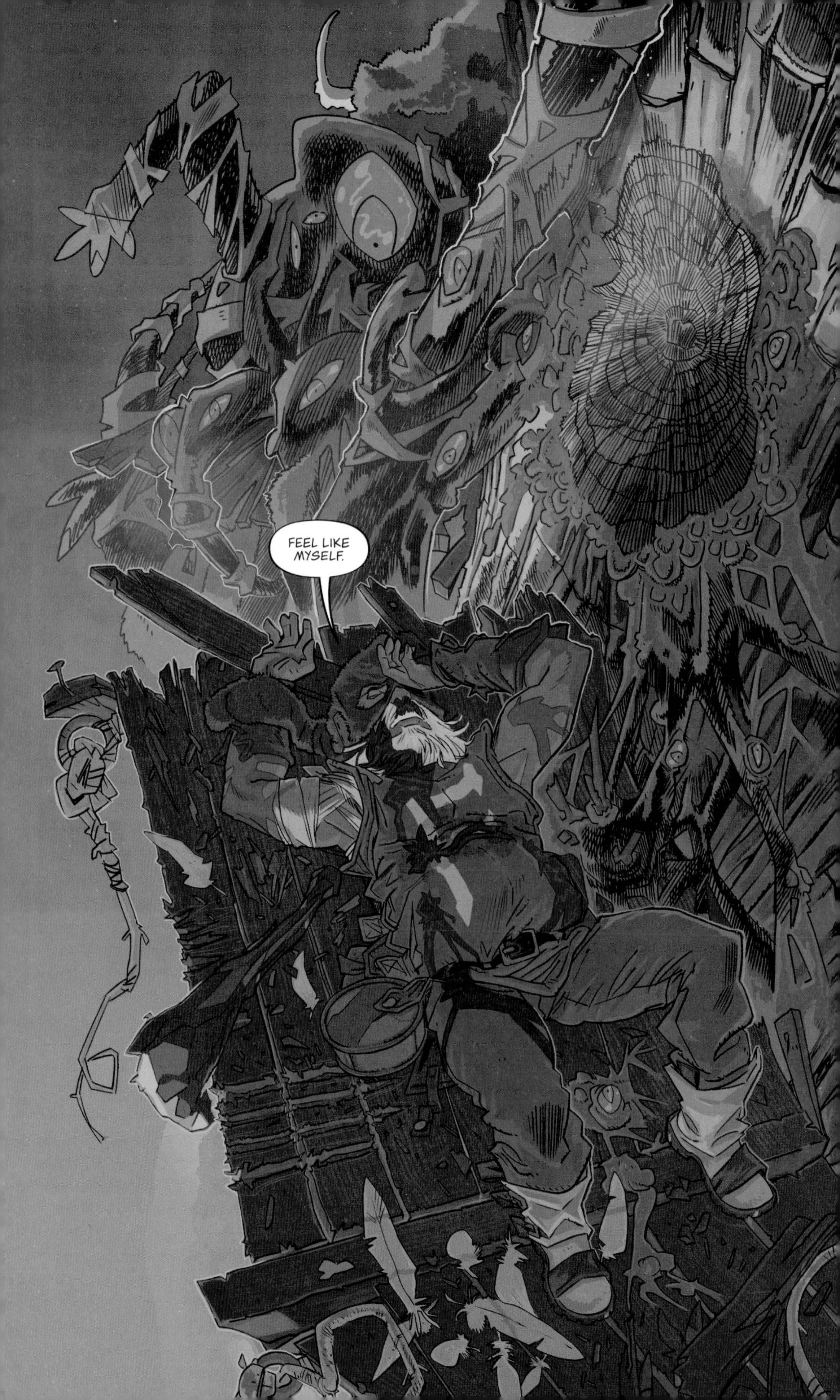
FEEL LIKE MYSELF.

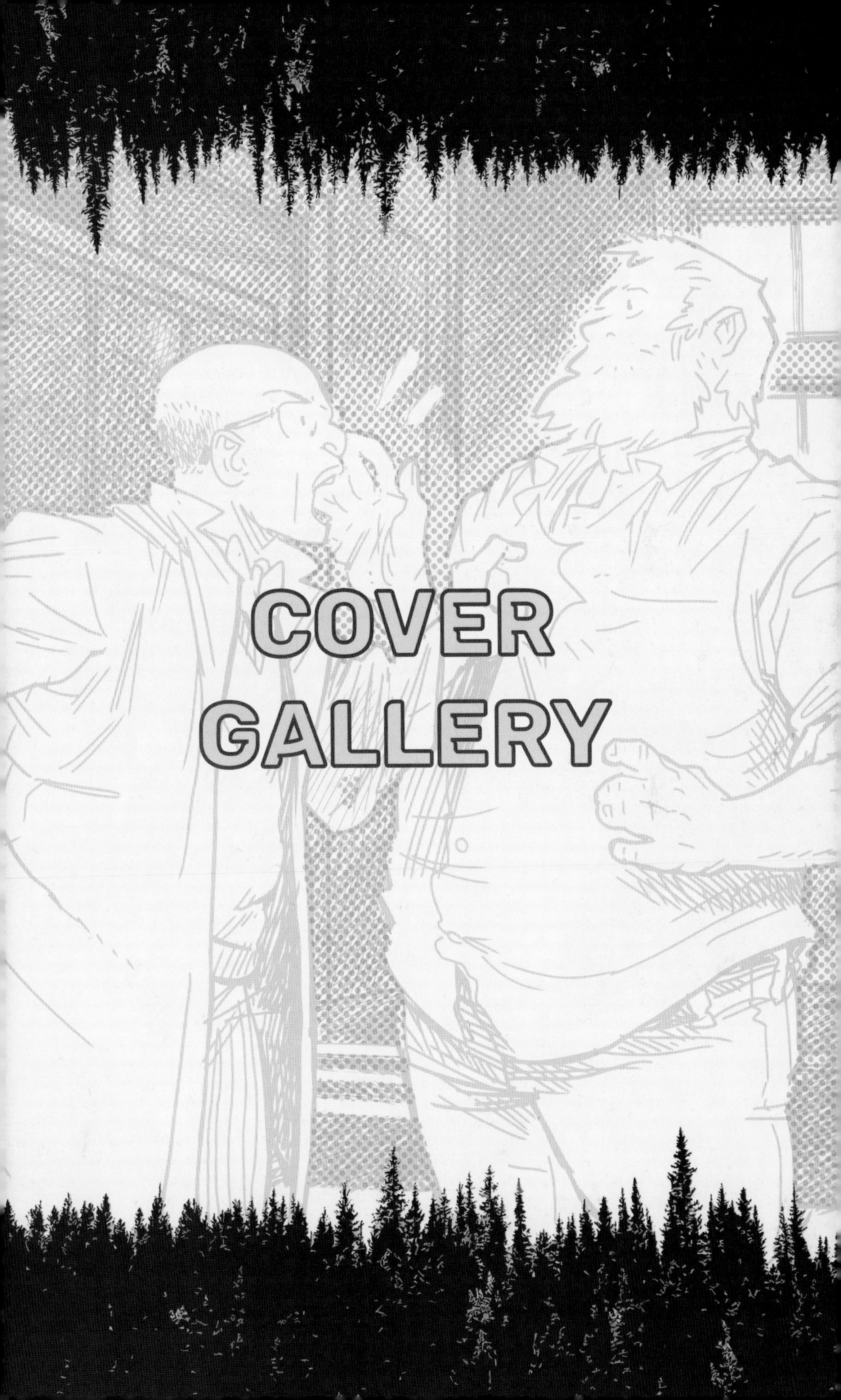

# COVER GALLERY

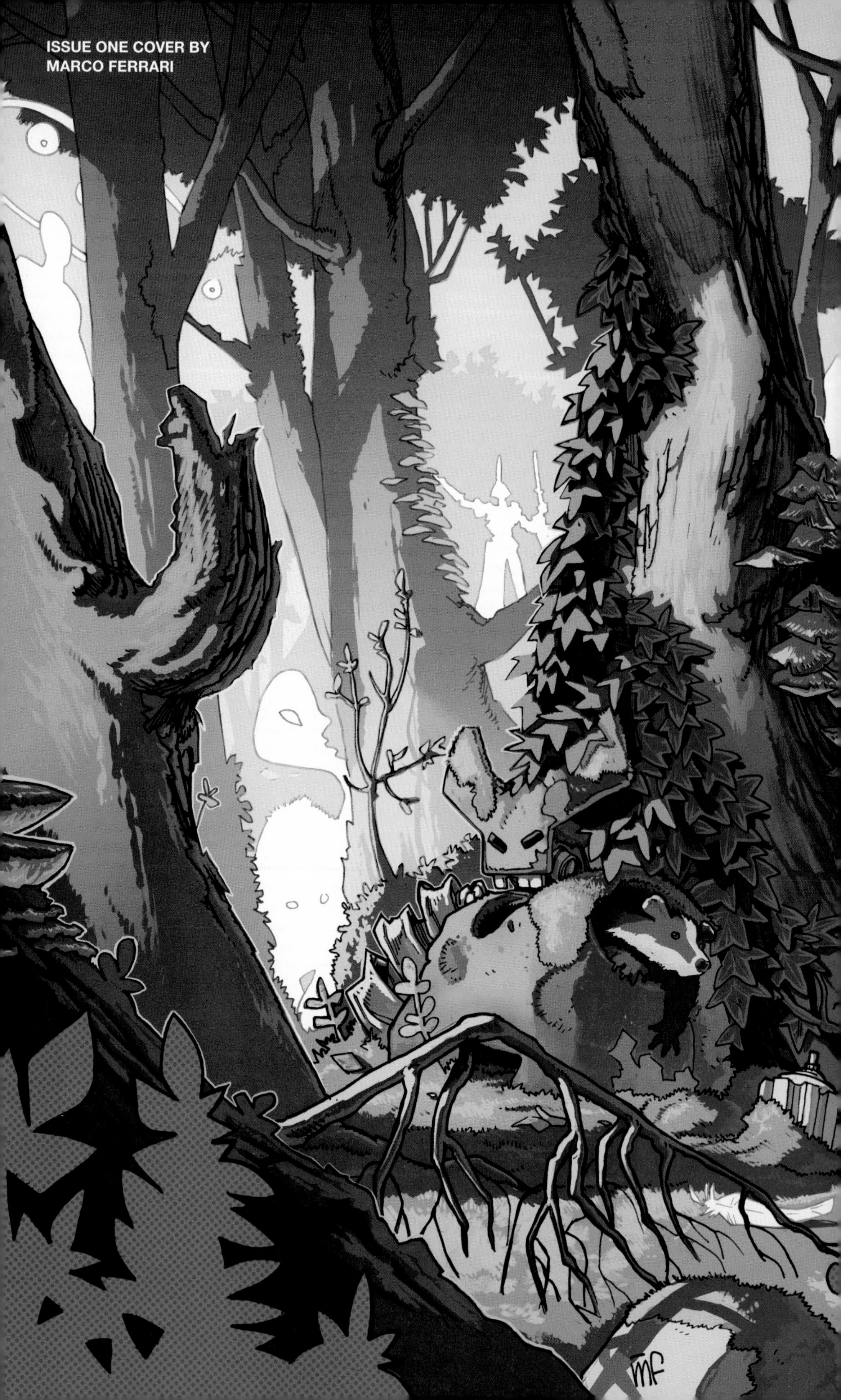

ISSUE ONE COVER BY
MARCO FERRARI

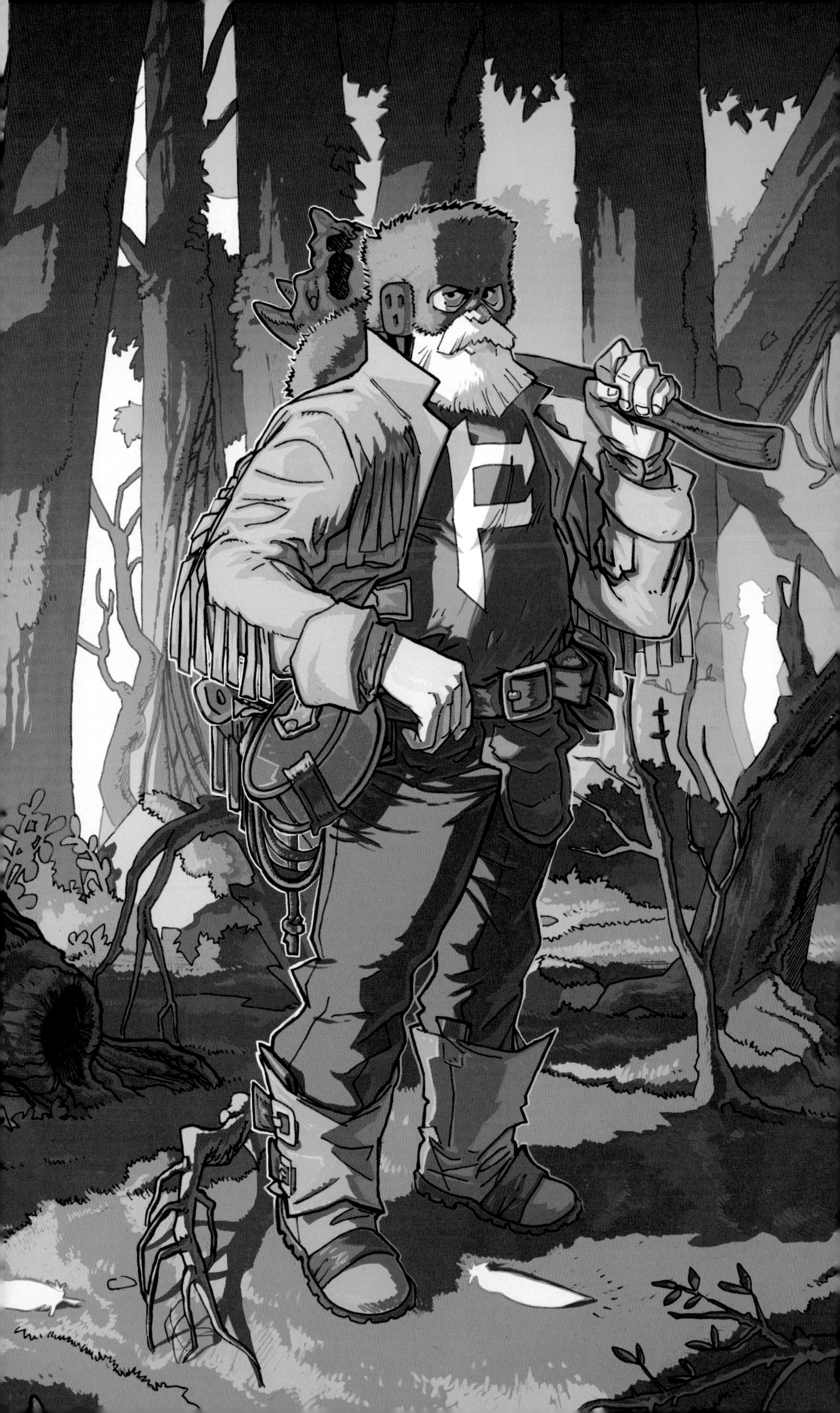

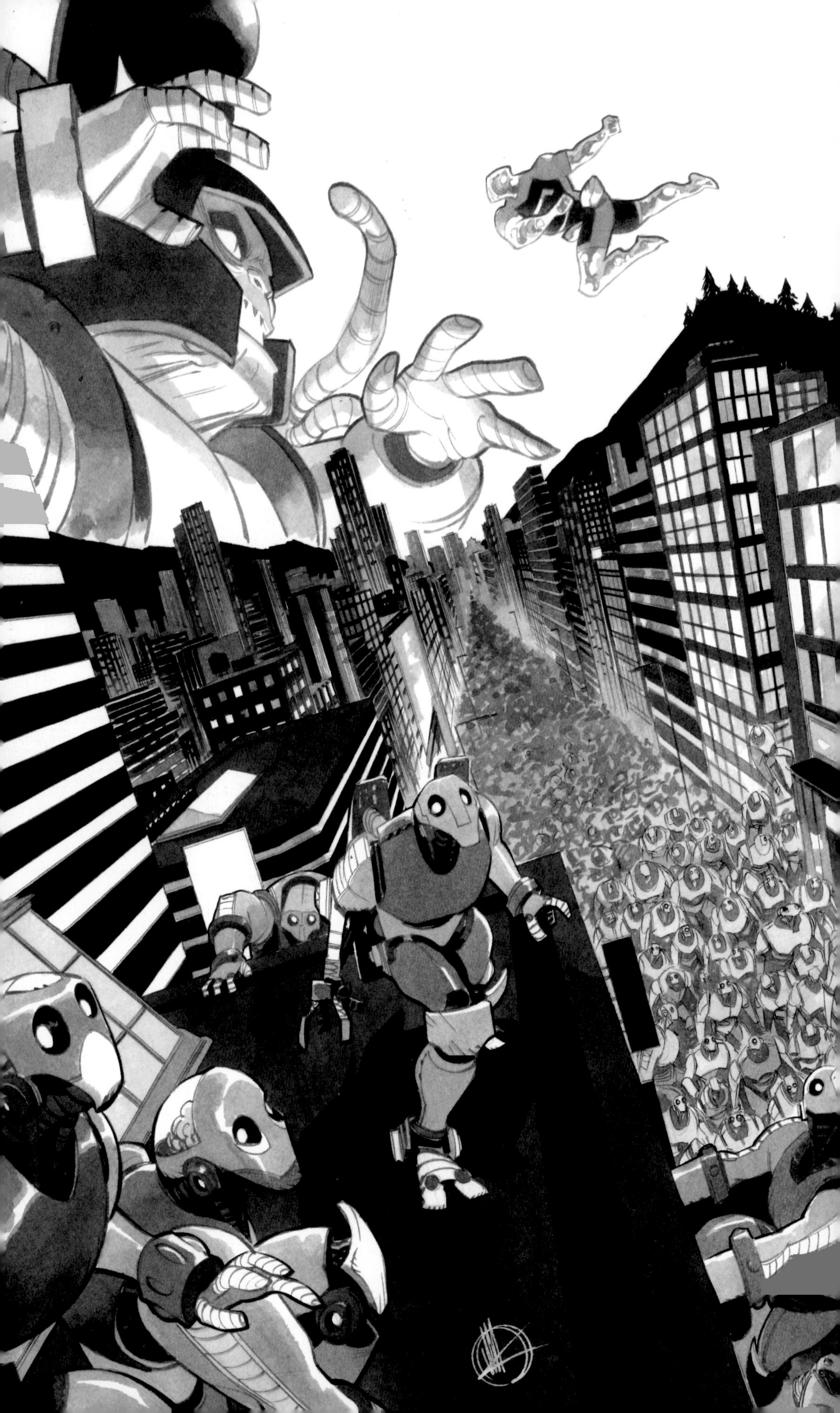

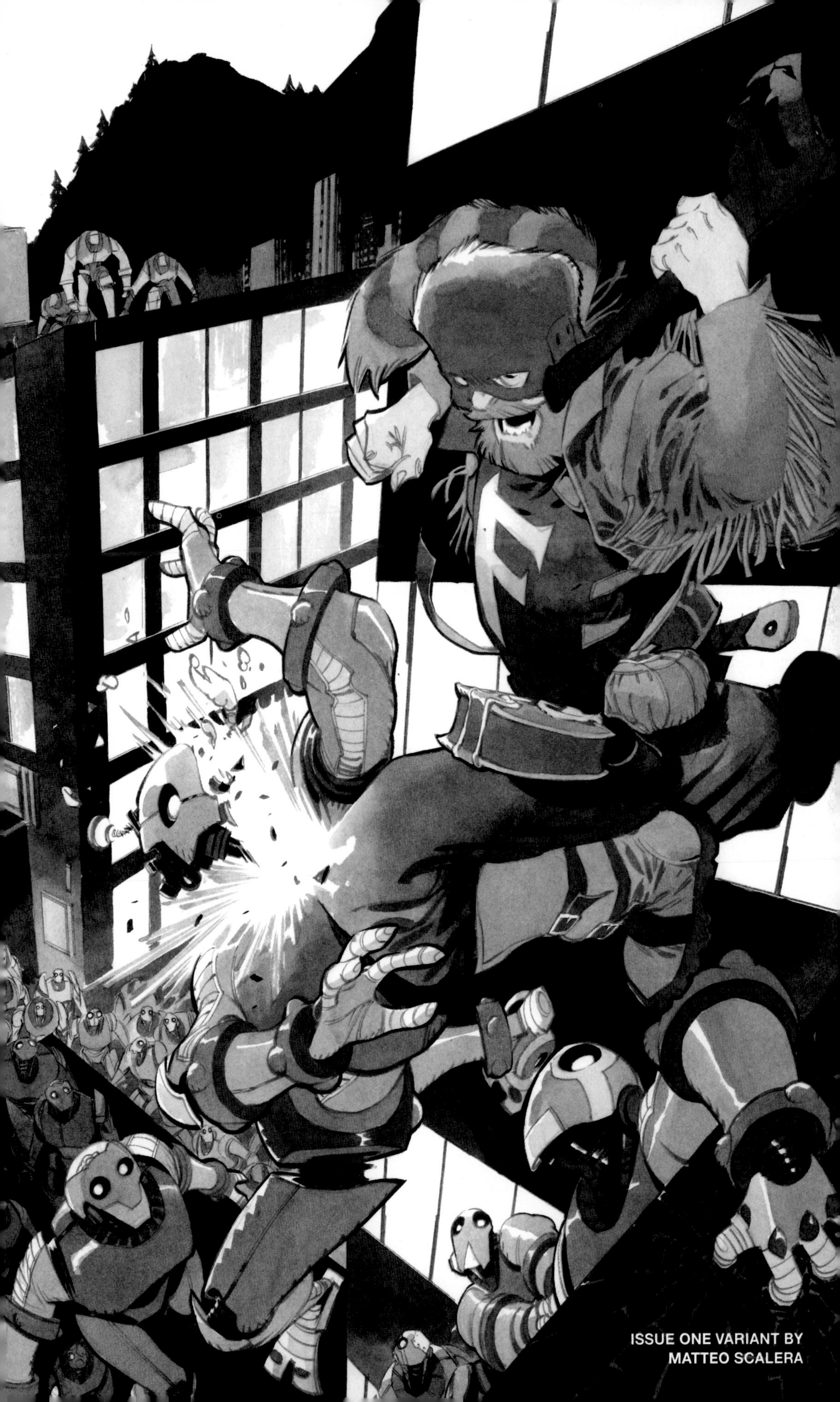

ISSUE ONE VARIANT BY
MATTEO SCALERA

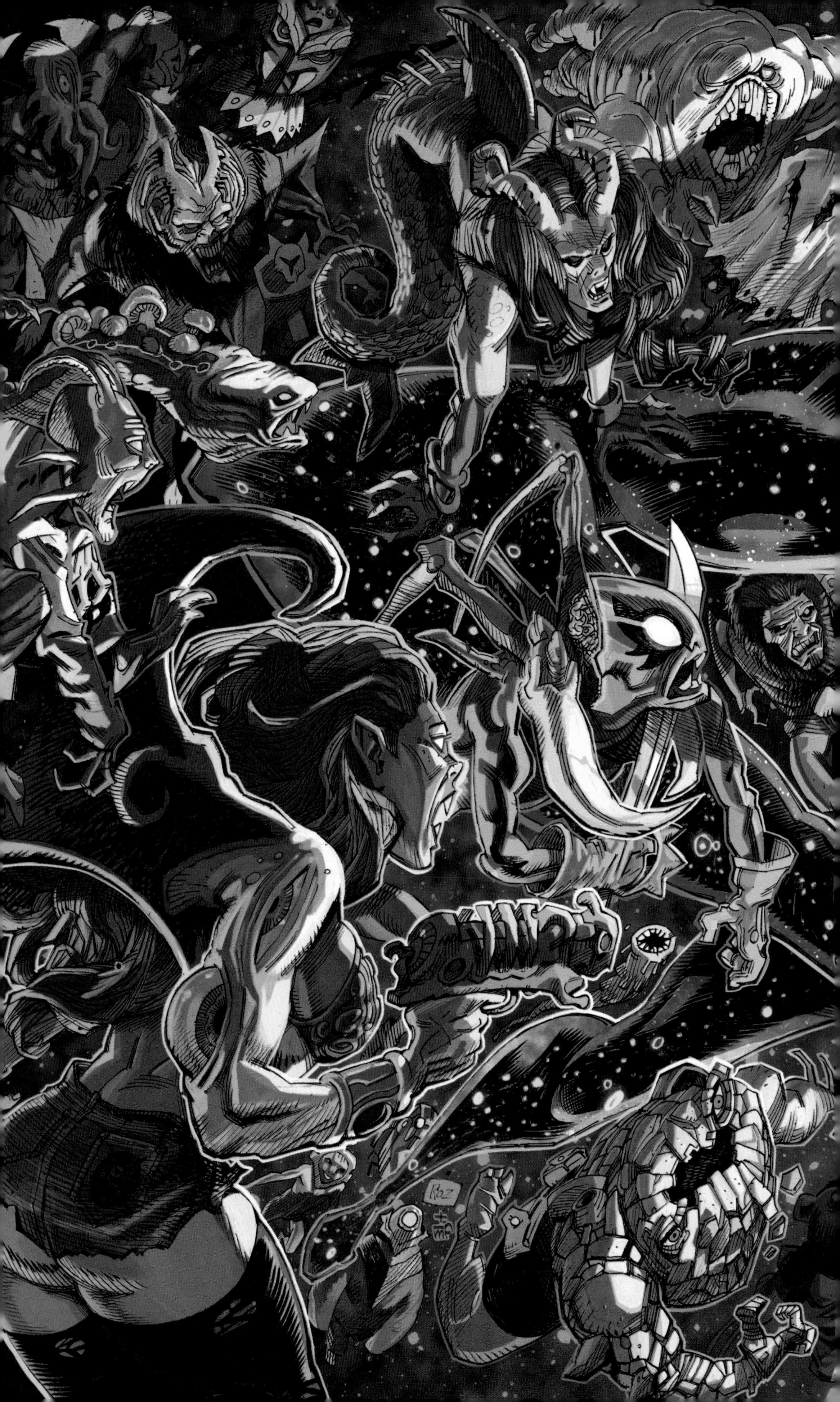

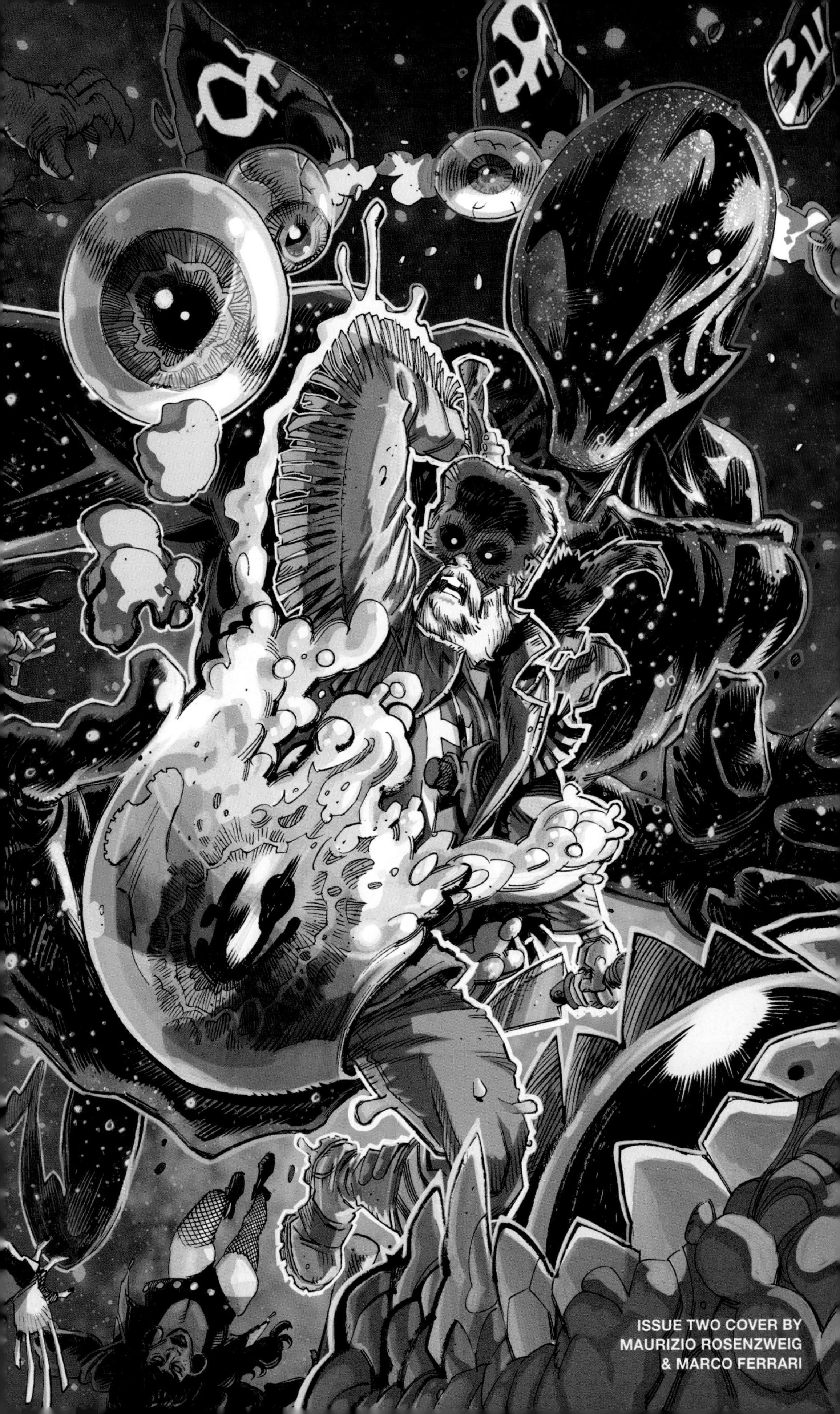

ISSUE TWO COVER BY
MAURIZIO ROSENZWEIG
& MARCO FERRARI

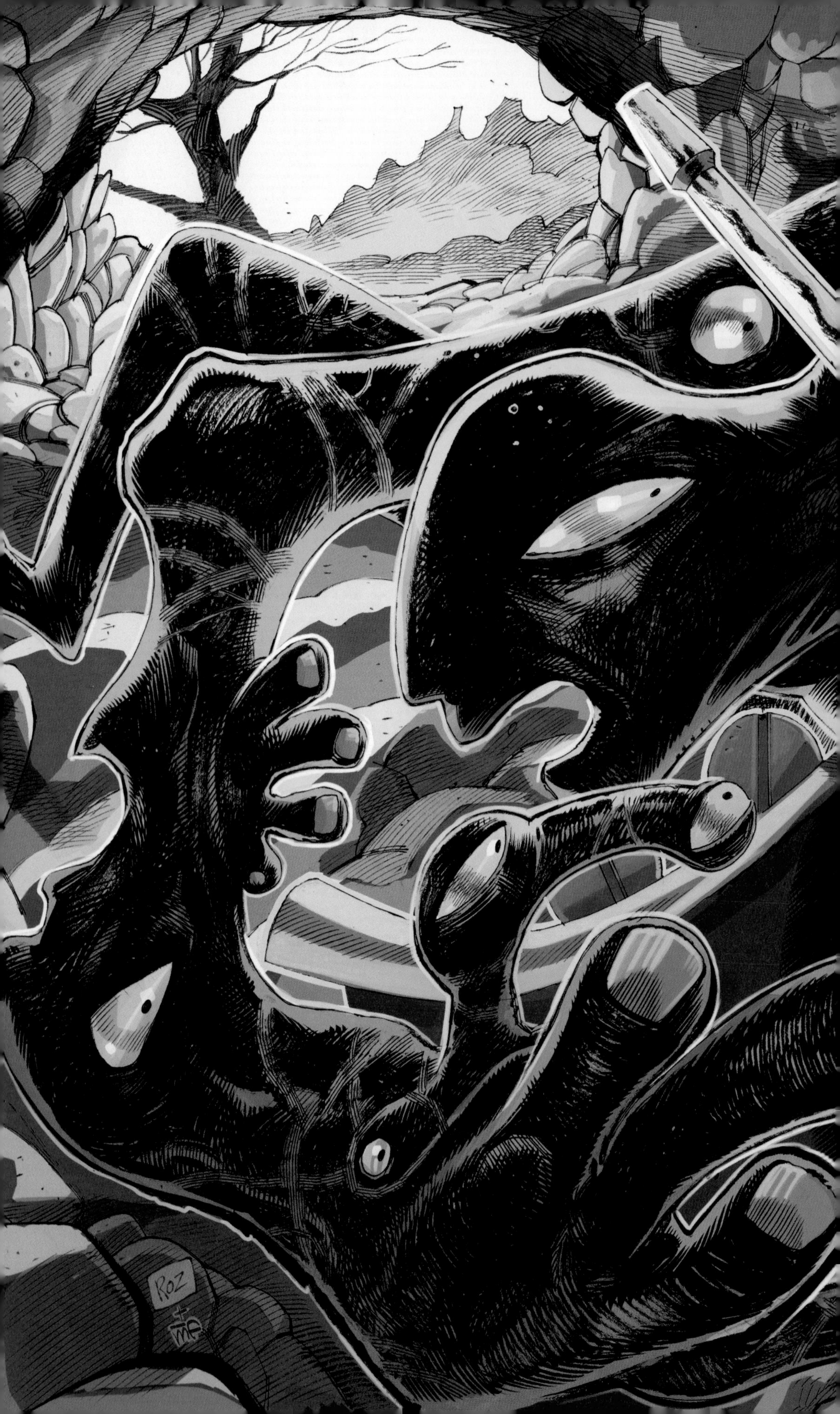
Roz

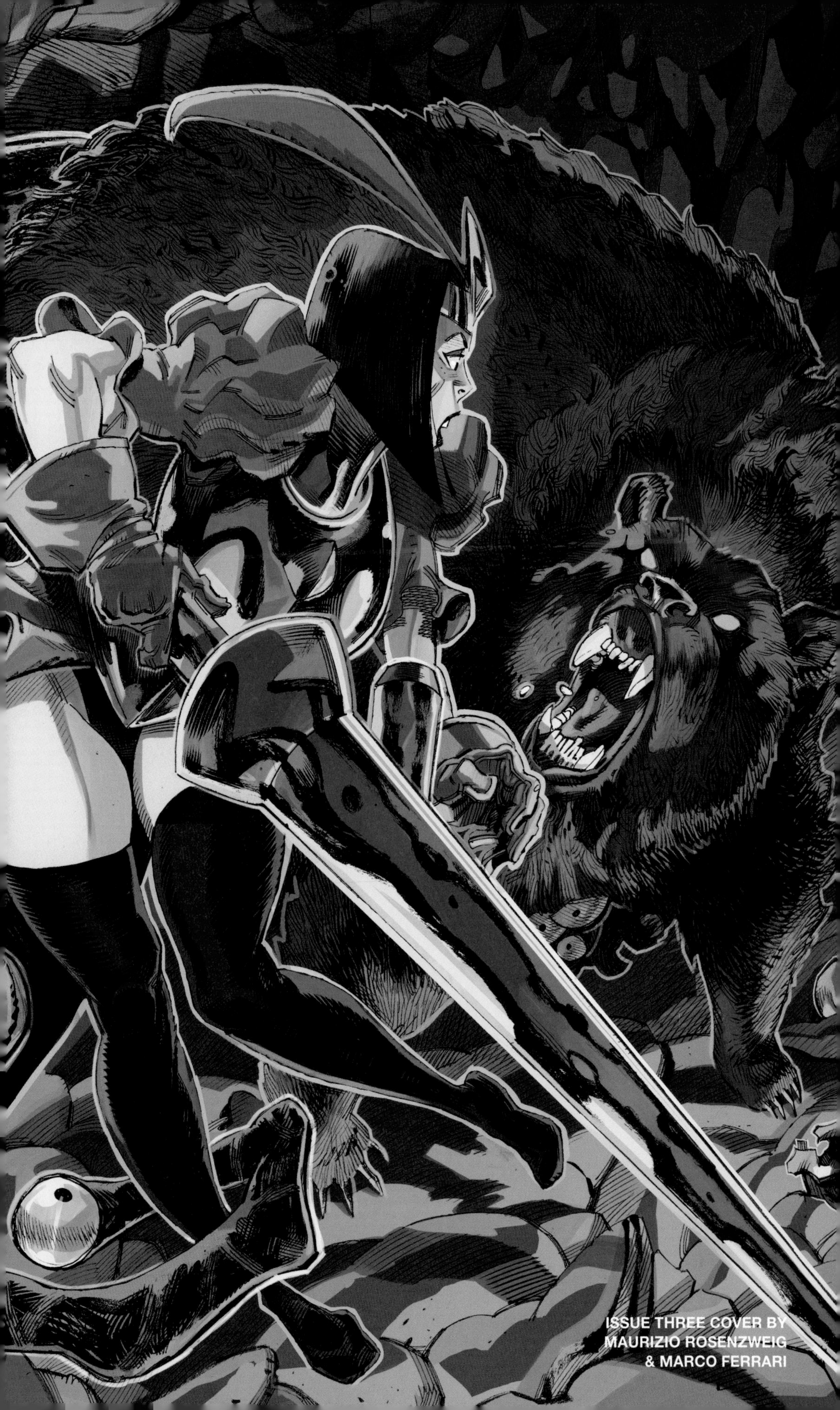

ISSUE THREE COVER BY
MAURIZIO ROSENZWEIG
& MARCO FERRARI

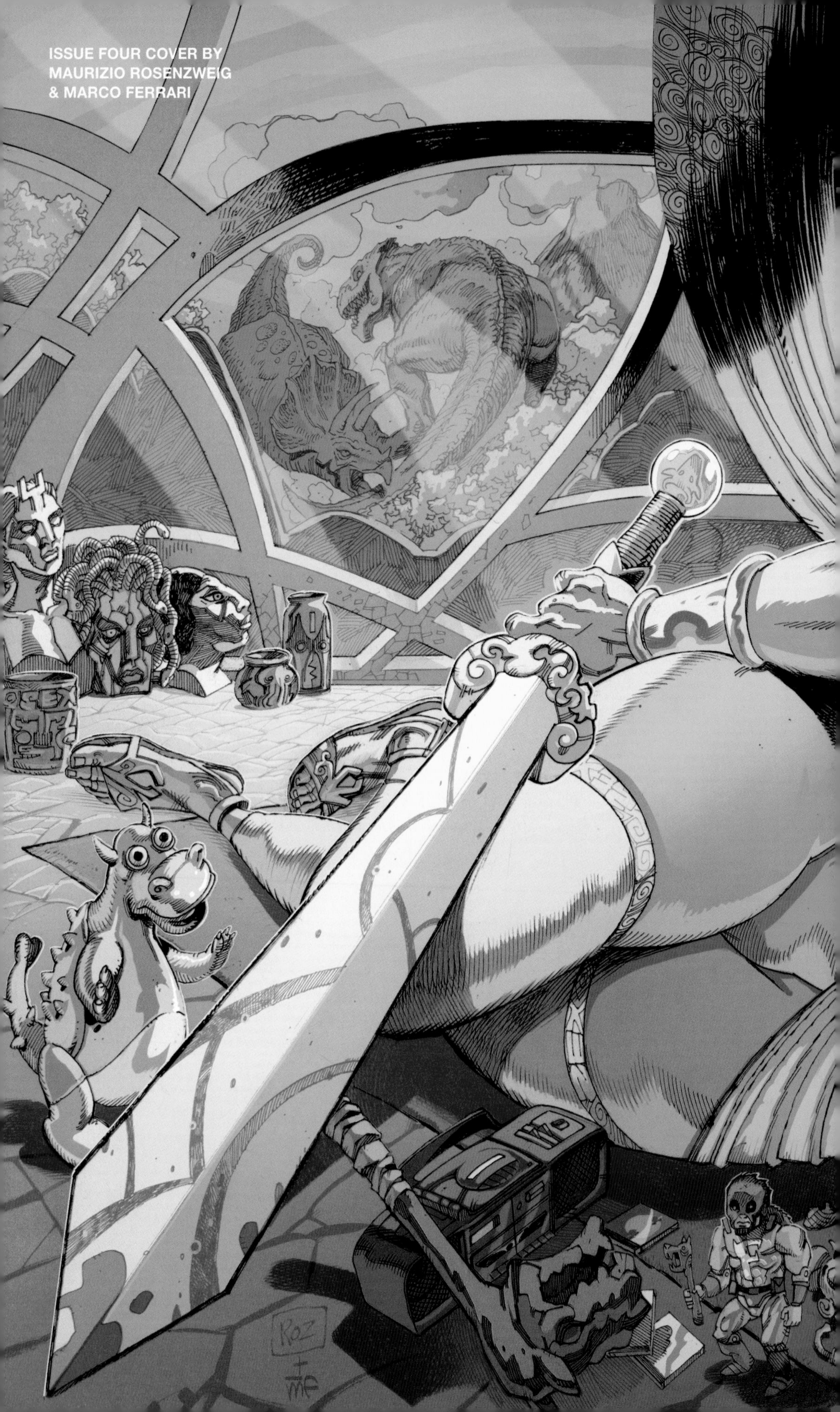

ISSUE FOUR COVER BY
MAURIZIO ROSENZWEIG
& MARCO FERRARI

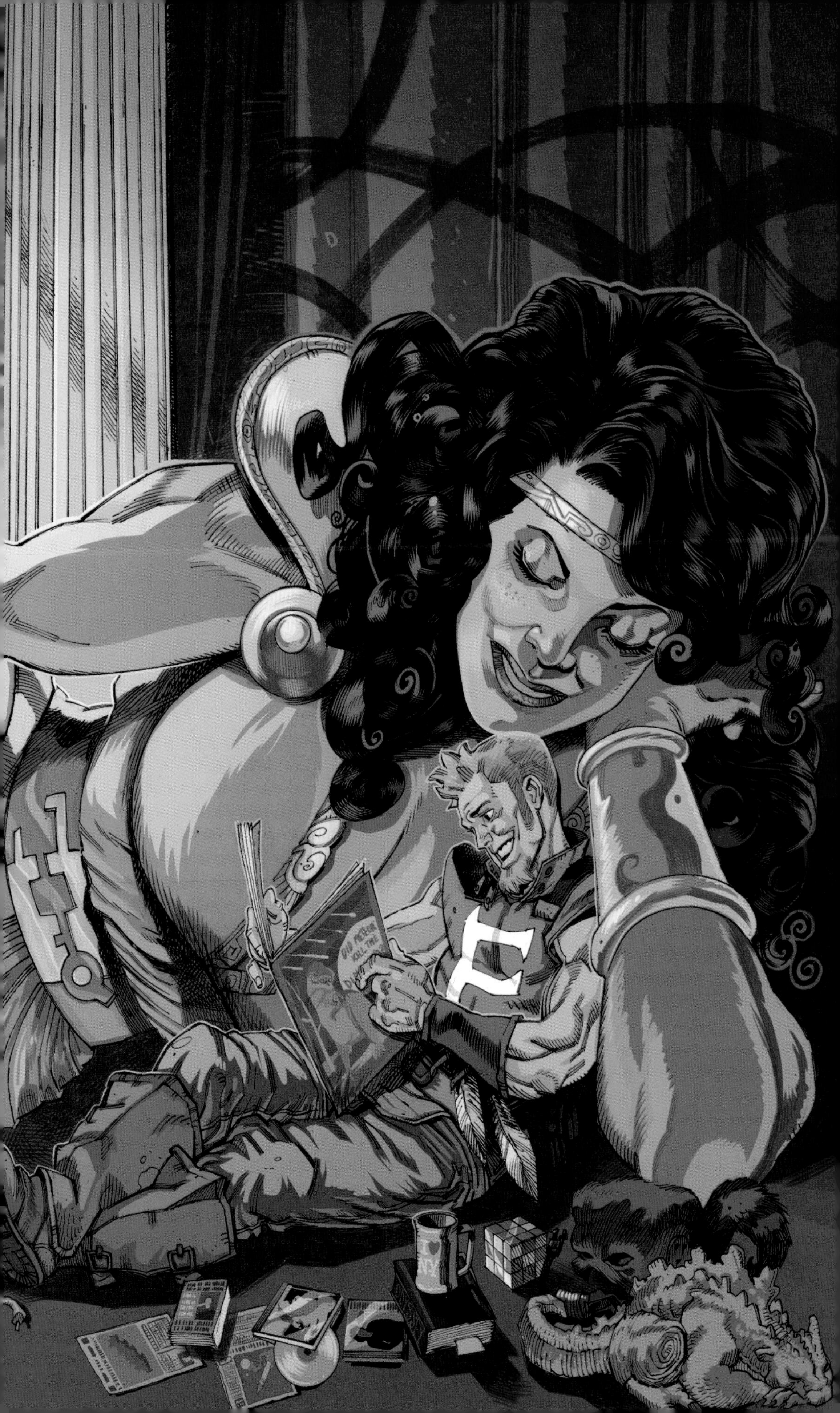
DID METEOR KILL THE
I ♥ NY

ISSUE FIVE COVER BY
MAURIZIO ROSENZWEIG
& MARCO FERRARI

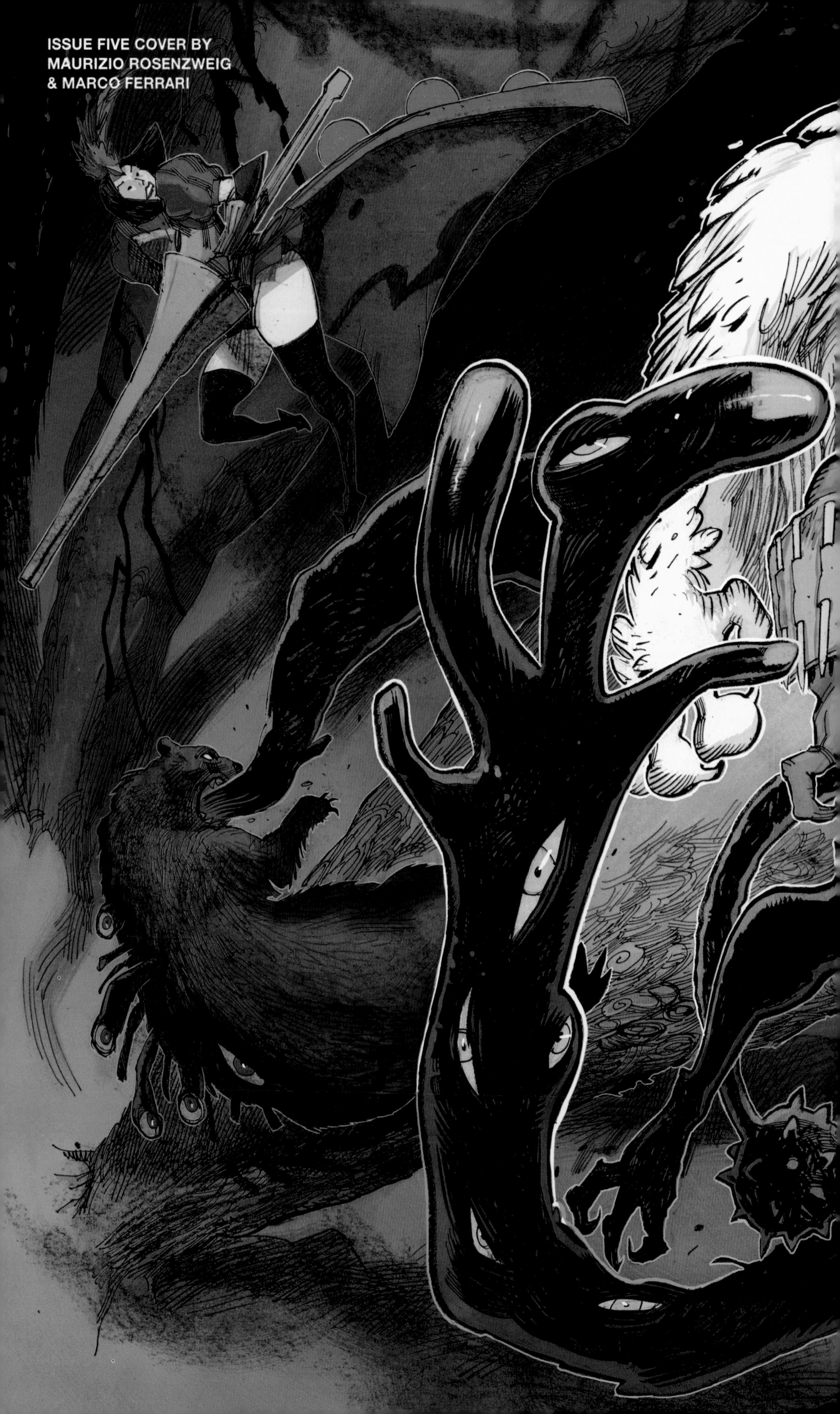

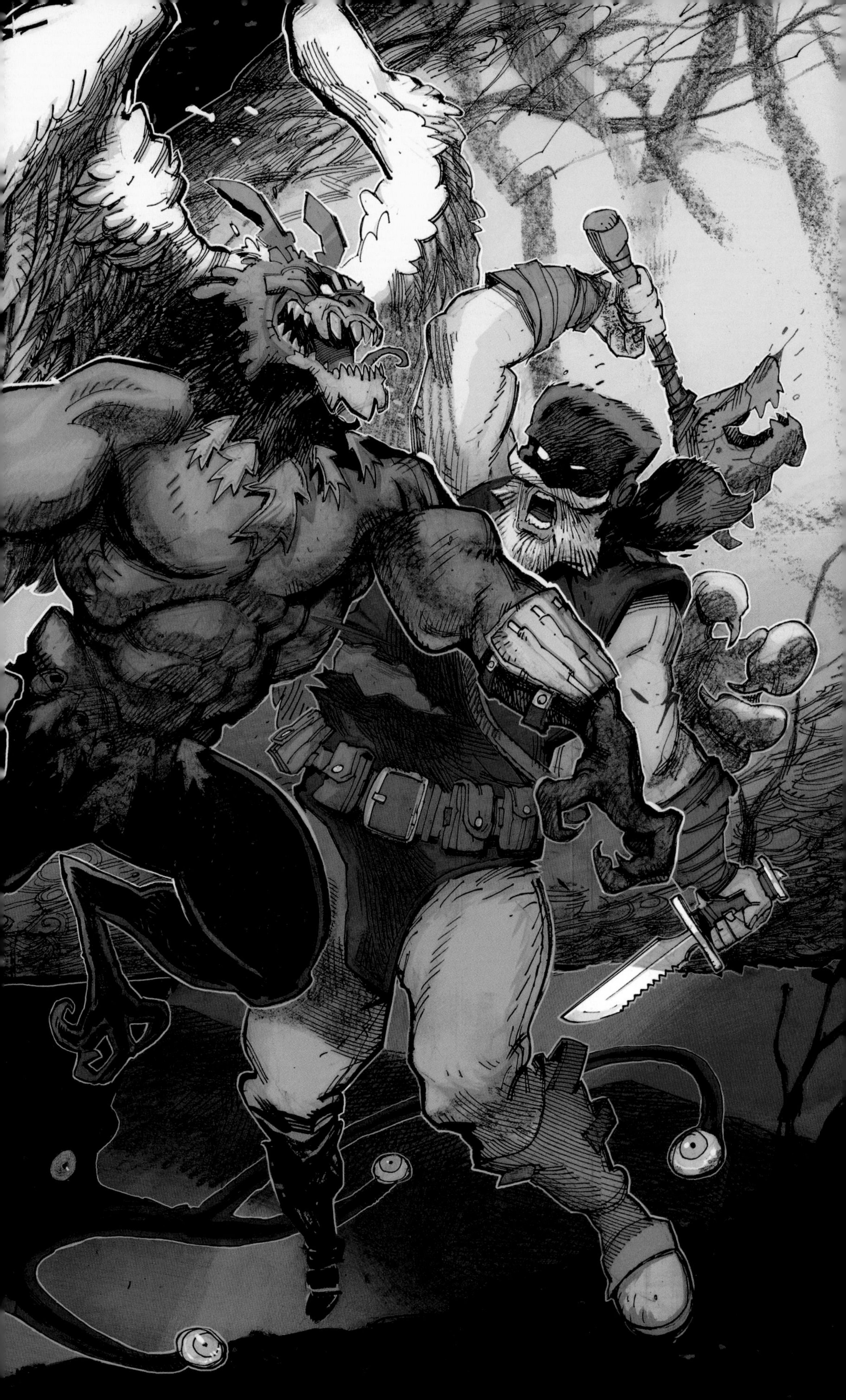

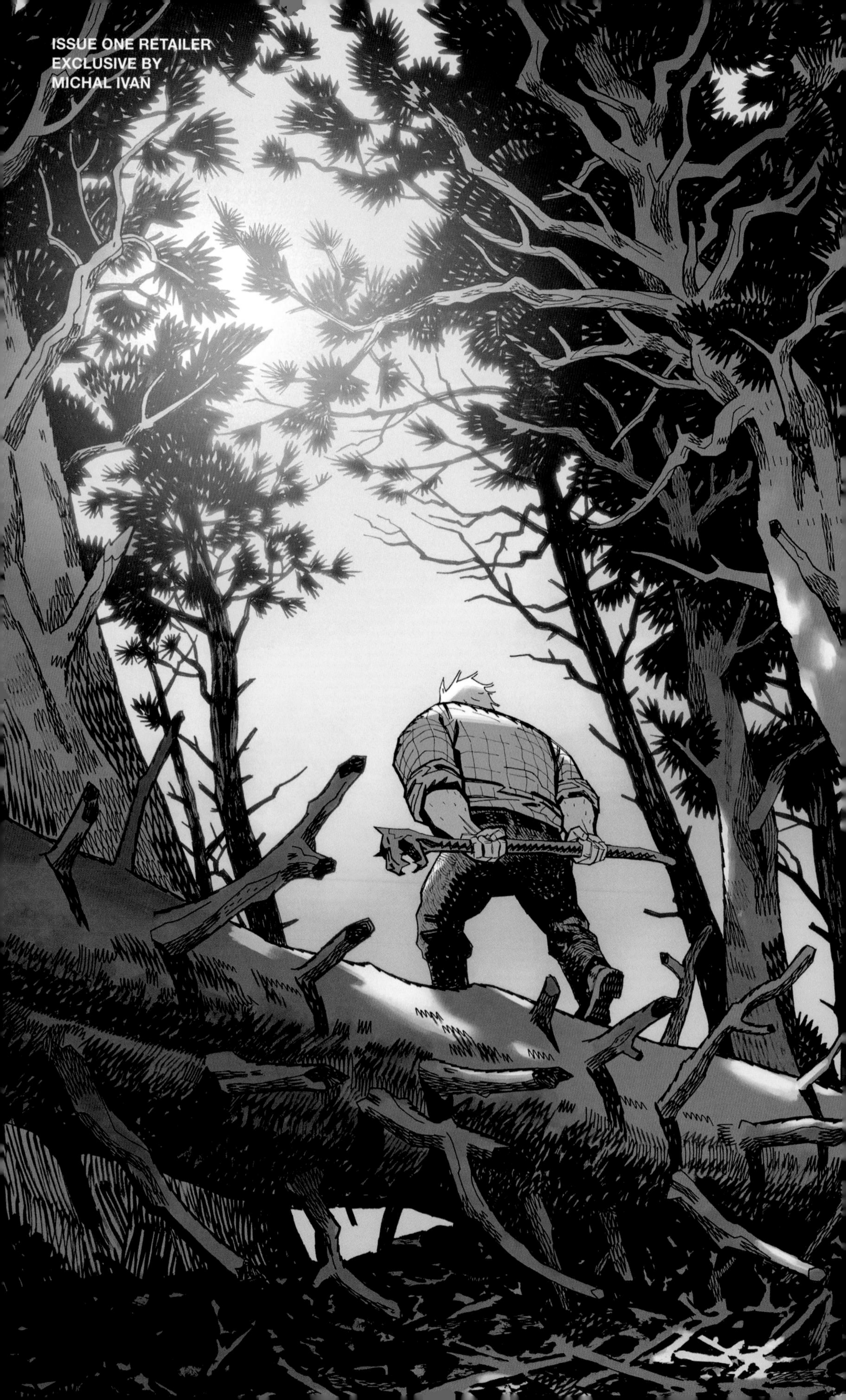

ISSUE ONE RETAILER
EXCLUSIVE BY
MICHAL IVAN

KINDLON/LLOVET
BLACK MASK STUDIOS

THERE'S NOTHING THERE
PATRICK KINDLON & MARIA LLOVET

KINDLON/FUSO
BLACK MASK STUDIOS

KINDLON FUSO
SURVIVAL FETISH
BLACK MASK

KINDLON/TUCKER
BLACK MASK STUDIOS

NOBODY IS IN CONTROL
PATRICK KINDLON PAUL TUCKER WALLACE RYAN
BLACK MASK

# MORE QUALITY WORK FROM THE CREATORS

PATRICK KINDLON • MARCO FERRARI
PATIENCE! CONVICTION! REVENGE!
VOLUME 1
PATRIZIA COMINO
JIM CAMPBELL
MARCH ON VEGAS

KINDLON/FERRARI
AFTERSHOCK COMICS

PATRICK KINDLON • STEFANO SIMEONE
SHOPLIFTERS WILL BE LIQUIDATED
HASSAN OTSMANE-ELHAOU

KINDLON/SIMEONE
AFTERSHOCK COMICS

Patrick Kindlon Goran Gligovic
RUN THE DUNGEON

KINDLON/GLIGOVIC
Z2 COMICS

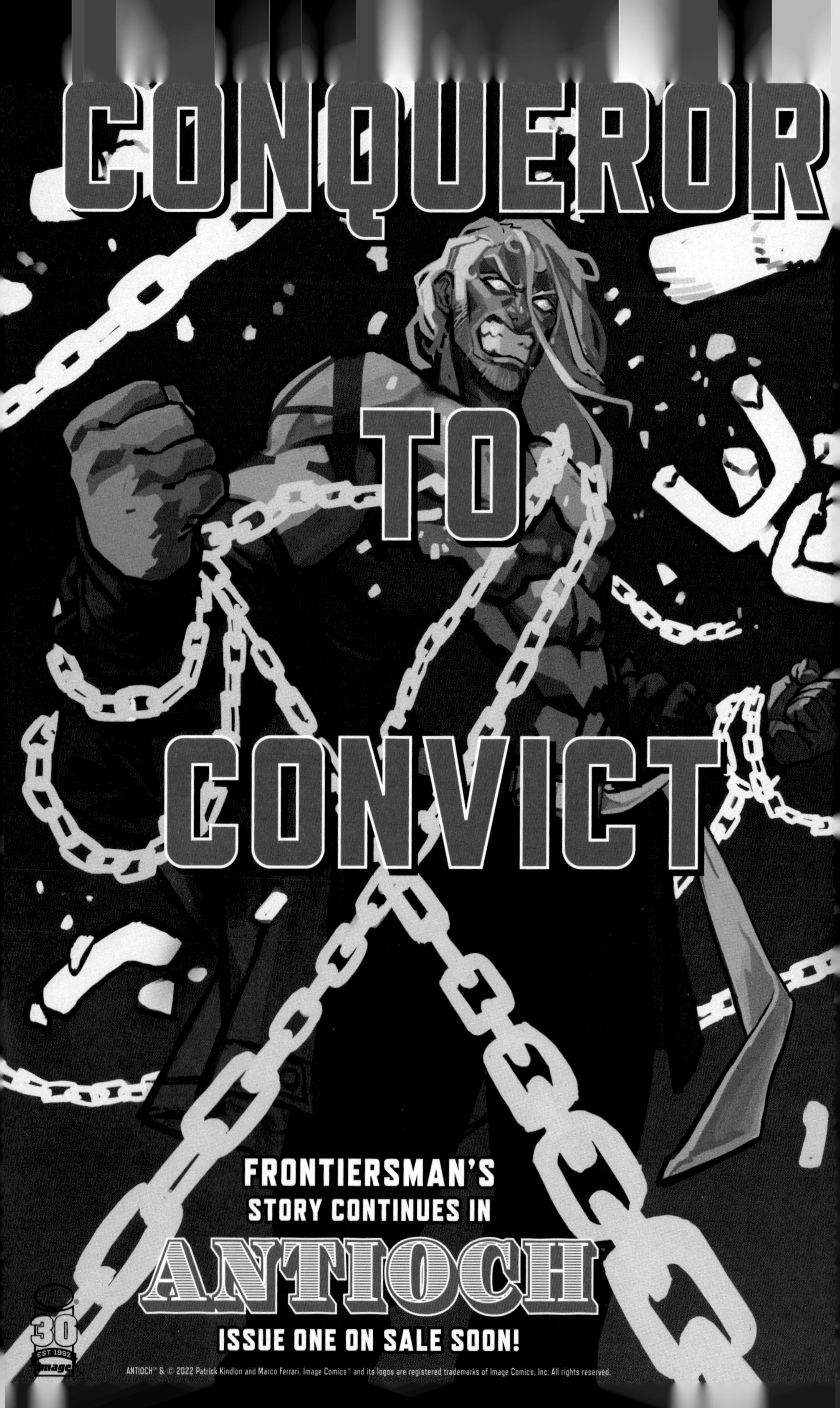

CONQUEROR
TO
CONVICT
FRONTIERSMAN'S
STORY CONTINUES IN
ANTIOCH
ISSUE ONE ON SALE SOON!
30
EST. 1992
image
ANTIOCH™ & © 2022 Patrick Kindlon and Marco Ferrari. Image Comics® and its logos are registered trademarks of Image Comics, Inc. All rights reserved.